DISASTER MANAGEMENT

DISASTER MANAGEMENT

AUTHOR

Dr. Pradeep K. Goyal
Assistant Professor,
Dept. of Civil Engineering
Delhi Technological University Delhi

Prof. Anil Kumar Gupta
Professor (Policy-Planning)
HoD, Director of Projects & COE,
National Institute of Disaster Management (Ministry of Home Affairs)
New Delhi

REVIEWER

Dr. Mahendra Kumar Pal
Assistant Professor,
Dept. of Civil Engineering,
Indian Institute of Technology (BHU),
Varanasi, Uttar Pradesh

KHANNA BOOK PUBLISHING CO. (P) Ltd.
4C/4344, Ansari Road, Darya Ganj,
New Delhi, India

All India Council for Technical Education
Nelson Mandela Marg, Vasant Kunj,
New Delhi, India

Dear Readers,

To prevent the piracy, this book is secured with HIGH SECURITY HOLOGRAM on the front title cover. In case you don't find the hologram on the front cover title, please write us to at contact@khannabooks.com or whatsapp us at +91-99109 09320 and avail special gift voucher for yourself.

Specimen of Hologram on front Cover title:

Moreover, there is a SPECIAL DISCOUNT COUPON for you with EVERY HOLOGRAM.

How to avail this SPECIAL DISCOUNT:

Step 1: Scratch the hologram
Step 2: Under the scratch area, your "coupon code" is available
Step 3: Logon to www.khannabooks.com
Step 4: Use your "coupon code" in the shopping cart and get your copy at a special discount
Step 5: Enjoy your reading!

Thanks,
Khanna Publishing House

ISBN: 978-93-5538-339-6

Book Code: UG428EN

DISASTER MANAGEMENT
by **Dr. Pradeep K. Goyal,**
Prof. Anil Kumar Gupta

First Edition: 2025

To view complete list of books, please scan the QR Code:

Published by:
Khanna Book Publishing Co. (P) Ltd.
CIN: U22110DL1998PTC095547

Visit us at: www.khannabooks.com
Write us at: contact@khannabooks.com

Printed in Bharat

प्रो. टी. जी. सीताराम
अध्यक्ष
Prof. T. G. Sitharam
Chairman

सत्यमेव जयते

आज़ादी का अमृत महोत्सव

अखिल भारतीय तकनीकी शिक्षा परिषद्
(भारत सरकार का एक सांविधिक निकाय)
(शिक्षा मंत्रालय, भारत सरकार)
नेल्सन मंडेला मार्ग, वसंत कुंज, नई दिल्ली–110070
दूरभाष : 011–26131498
ई–मेल : chairman@aicte-india.org

ALL INDIA COUNCIL FOR TECHNICAL EDUCATION
(A STATUTORY BODY OF THE GOVT. OF INDIA)
(Ministry of Education, Govt. of India)
Nelson Mandela Marg, Vasant Kunj, New Delhi-110070
Phone : 011-26131498
E-mail : chairman@aicte-india.org

FOREWORD

Engineers are the backbone of any modern society. They are the ones responsible for the marvels as well as the improved quality of life across the world. Engineers have driven humanity towards greater heights in a more evolved and unprecedented manner.

The All India Council for Technical Education (AICTE), have spared no efforts towards the strengthening of the technical education in the country. AICTE is always committed towards promoting quality Technical Education to make India a modern developed nation emphasizing on the overall welfare of mankind.

An array of initiatives has been taken by AICTE in last decade which have been accelerated now by the National Education Policy (NEP) 2020. The implementation of NEP under the visionary leadership of Hon'ble Prime Minister of India envisages the provision for education in regional languages to all, thereby ensuring that every graduate becomes competent enough and is in a position to contribute towards the national growth and development through innovation & entrepreneurship.

One of the spheres where AICTE had been relentlessly working since past couple of years is providing high quality original technical contents at Under Graduate & Diploma level prepared and translated by eminent educators in various Indian languages to its aspirants. For students pursuing 2nd year of their Engineering education, AICTE has identified 87 books, which shall be translated into 12 Indian languages - Hindi, Tamil, Gujarati, Odia, Bengali, Kannada, Urdu, Punjabi, Telugu, Marathi, Assamese & Malayalam. In addition to the English medium, books in different Indian Languages are going to support the students to understand the concepts in their respective mother tongue.

On behalf of AICTE, I express sincere gratitude to all distinguished authors, reviewers and translators from the renowned institutions of high repute for their admirable contribution in a record span of time.

AICTE is confident that these outcomes based original contents shall help aspirants to master the subject with comprehension and greater ease.

(Prof. T. G. Sitharam)

Preface

This book titled "Disaster Management" is an outcome of the rich experience of our teaching of Disaster Management courses. The initiation of writing this book is to expose the engineering students with the fundamentals of Disaster Management as well to enable them to get an insight of the subject. Keeping in mind the purpose of wide coverage as well as to provide essential supplementary information, we have included the topics recommended by AICTE, in a very systematic and orderly manner throughout the book. Efforts have been made to explain the fundamental concepts of the subject in the simplest possible way.

During the process of preparation of the manuscript, we have considered the various standard text books, training manuals, reports. While preparing the different sections, emphasis has also been laid to provide not only an overview of the basic concepts of disaster management, but also to enable the reader to delve deep into their applications in real world. We have made extensive use of illustrations and examples to enrich this book for proper understanding of the related topics. The book covers five units dealing with the various aspects of Disaster Management. For further reading, QR codes have been inserted into every chapter to point towards resources that students might want to explore beyond the textbook.

We sincerely hope that the book will inspire the students to learn and discuss the ideas behind basic concepts of disaster management and will surely contribute to the development of solid foundation of the subject. We would be thankful to all beneficial comments and suggestions which will contribute to the improvement of the future editions of the book. It was indeed a big pleasure to work on different aspects covering in the book. It gives us an immense pleasure to place this book in the hands of the teachers and students.

Dr. Pradeep K. Goyal

Prof. Anil K. Gupta

Acknowledgement

The authors are grateful to the authorities of AICTE, particularly Prof. T.G. Sitharam, Chairman, Dr. Abhay Jere, Vice-Chairman; Prof. Rajive Kumar, Member-Secretary, Dr. Ramesh Unnikrishnan, Advisor-II and Dr. Sunil Luthra, Director, Training and Learning Bureau and Dr Amit Kumar Srivastava, Ex. Director, Faculty Development Cell for their planning to publish the books on Disaster Management. We sincerely acknowledge the valuable contributions of the reviewer of the book Dr Mahendra Kumar Pal, Assistant Professor, Dept. of Civil Engineering, IIT (BHU) Varanasi for making it students' friendly and giving a better shape in an artistic manner.

I, Pradeep K. Goyal, would like to express my gratitude to Prof. T.K. Datta, Ex. Professor, IIT Delhi for his motivation and blessings. I am extremely grateful to my mother Smt. Sushila Devi whose blessings have brought out the best in me for writing this book. I am thankful to my wife Ms. Anju Goyal and son Mr. Bhavya Goyal for their continuous support without which this work would not have been possible. I would also like to thank faculty members of the department for their sincere encouragement and continuous support.

I, Prof. Anil K. Gupta acknowledge the encouragement and motivation received from members of NDMA and Senior Officials of the Ministry of Home Affairs, viz. Shri Kamal Kishore, Dr. Krishna Vatsa, Shri Rajendra Singh, Shri H.K. Makwana, Sanjeev Jindal, and the Executive Director NIDM Shri Rajendra Ratnoo.

We would like to thank Dr. Shailesh Agrawal, Executive Director, BMTPC, Delhi for his motivation and kind support. We would like to acknowledge the sincere efforts of Ms. Sakshi Bhutani for her continuous support and hard work in writing the book. Above all, we offer respectful obeisance to Almighty God for illuminating our path and inspiring us to accomplish this book.

This book is an outcome of various suggestions of AICTE members, experts and authors who shared their opinions and thoughts to further develop the engineering education in our country. Acknowledgements are due to the experts in this field whose published books, reviewed articles, papers, photographs, footnotes, references and other valuable information enriched us at the time of writing the book.

Dr. Pradeep K. Goyal
Prof. Anil K. Gupta

Outcome Based Education

For the implementation of an outcome-based education the first requirement is to develop an outcome-based curriculum and incorporate an outcome-based assessment in the education system. By going through outcome-based assessments evaluators will be able to evaluate whether the students have achieved the outlined standard, specific and measurable outcomes. With the proper incorporation of outcome-based education there will be a definite commitment to achieve a minimum standard for all learners without giving up at any level. At the end of the programme running with the aid of outcome-based education, a student will be able to arrive at the following outcomes:

PO1. **Engineering knowledge**: Apply the knowledge of mathematics, science, engineering fundamentals, and an engineering specialization to the solution of complex engineering problems.

PO2. **Problem analysis**: Identify, formulate, review research literature, and analyze complex engineering problems reaching substantiated conclusions using first principles of mathematics, natural sciences, and engineering sciences.

PO3. **Design / development of solutions**: Design solutions for complex engineering problems and design system components or processes that meet the specified needs with appropriate consideration for the public health and safety, and the cultural, societal, and environmental considerations.

PO4. **Conduct investigations of complex problems**: Use research-based knowledge and research methods including design of experiments, analysis and interpretation of data, and synthesis of the information to provide valid conclusions.

PO5. **Modern tool usage**: Create, select, and apply appropriate techniques, resources, and modern engineering and IT tools including prediction and modeling to complex engineering activities with an understanding of the limitations.

PO6. **The engineer and society**: Apply reasoning informed by the contextual knowledge to assess societal, health, safety, legal and cultural issues and the consequent responsibilities relevant to the professional engineering practice.

PO7. **Environment and sustainability**: Understand the impact of the professional engineering solutions in societal and environmental contexts, and demonstrate the knowledge of, and need for sustainable development.

PO8. **Ethics**: Apply ethical principles and commit to professional ethics and responsibilities and norms of the engineering practice.

PO9. **Individual and team work**: Function effectively as an individual, and as a member or leader in diverse teams, and in multidisciplinary settings.

PO10. **Communication**: Communicate effectively on complex engineering activities with the engineering community and with society at large, such as, being able to comprehend and write effective reports and design documentation, make effective presentations, and give and receive clear instructions.

PO11. Project management and finance: Demonstrate knowledge and understanding of the engineering and management principles and apply these to one's own work, as a member and leader in a team, to manage projects and in multidisciplinary environments.

PO12. Life-long learning: Recognize the need for, and have the preparation and ability to engage in independent and life-long learning in the broadest context of technological change.

Course Outcomes

After completion of the course the students will be able to:

CO-1: Apply the concepts of Disaster Management

CO-2: Analyse the Relationship between Development and Disasters

CO-3: Understand the various Categories of Disasters

CO-4: Realize the responsibilities towards society

CO-5: Understand Disaster Risk Reduction and Mitigation

CO-6: Conceptualize Disaster Risk Reduction and Mitigation measures towards sustainable recovery.

Course Outcomes	Expected Mapping with Programme Outcomes (1- Weak Correlation; 2- Medium correlation; 3- Strong Correlation)											
	PO-1	PO-2	PO-3	PO-4	PO-5	PO-6	PO-7	PO-8	PO-9	PO-10	PO-11	PO-12
CO-1	3	2	3	1	1	1	1	1	2	2	3	3
CO-2	2	3	2	1	2	2	1	1	2	3	1	2
CO-3	2	1	2	2	2	2	1	1	2	2	1	3
CO-4	1	3	3	2	2	3	2	2	3	1	1	2
CO-5	1	1	2	3	3	2	2	2	2	2	1	2
CO-6	2	2	3	2	3	2	3	2	2	3	1	3

Guidelines for Teachers

To implement Outcome Based Education (OBE) knowledge level and skill set of the students should be enhanced. Teachers should take a major responsibility for the proper implementation of OBE. Some of the responsibilities (not limited to) for the teachers in OBE system may be as follows:

- Within reasonable constraint, they should manoeuvre time to the best advantage of all students.
- They should assess the students only upon certain defined criterion without considering any other potential ineligibility to discriminate them.
- They should try to grow the learning abilities of the students to a certain level before they leave the institute.
- They should try to ensure that all the students are equipped with the quality knowledge as well as competence after they finish their education.
- They should always encourage the students to develop their ultimate performance capabilities.
- They should facilitate and encourage group work and team work to consolidate newer approach.
- They should follow Blooms taxonomy in every part of the assessment.

Bloom's Taxonomy

Level	Teacher should Check	Student should be able to	Possible Mode of Assessment
Create	Students ability to create	Design or Create	Mini project
Evaluate	Students ability to justify	Argue or Defend	Assignment
Analyse	Students ability to distinguish	Differentiate or Distinguish	Project/Lab Methodology
Apply	Students ability to use information	Operate or Demonstrate	Technical Presentation/ Demonstration
Understand	Students ability to explain the ideas	Explain or Classify	Presentation/Seminar
Remember	Students ability to recall (or remember)	Define or Recall	Quiz

Guidelines for Students

Students should take equal responsibility for implementing the OBE. Some of the responsibilities (not limited to) for the students in OBE system are as follows:

- Students should be well aware of each UO before the start of a unit in each and every course.
- Students should be well aware of each CO before the start of the course.
- Students should be well aware of each PO before the start of the programme.
- Students should think critically and reasonably with proper reflection and action.
- Learning of the students should be connected and integrated with practical and real-life consequences.
- Students should be well aware of their competency at every level of OBE.

Symbols and Abbreviations

LIST OF ABBREVIATIONS

General Terms			
Abbreviations	**Full form**	**Abbreviations**	**Full form**
BBB	Build Back Better	**GOI**	Govt. of India
BMTPC	Building Materials and Technology Promotion Council	**HADR**	Humanitarian Assistance Disaster Relief
CBDM	Community Based Disaster Management	**HIS**	Healthcare Information System
CBRN	Chemical, Biological, Radiological, and Nuclear	**HPC**	High-Powered Committee
CCA	Climate Change Adaptations	**IND**	Improvised Nuclear Device
CRZ	Coastal Regulations Zone	**LPA**	Long Period Average
CWC	Central Water Commission	**LRMS**	Landslide Risk Mitigation Scheme
DDMA	District Disaster Management Authority	**MDG**	Millenium Development Goal
DFID	Department for International Development	**MSK**	Medvedev, Sponheuer and Karnik
DM	Disaster Management	**MMI**	Modified Mercalli Intensity
DRM	Disaster Risk Management	**NCRMP**	National Cyclone Risk Mitigation Project
DRR	Disaster Risk Reduction	**NDMF**	National Disaster Mitigation Fund
EWDS	Early Warning Dissemination Systems	**NDMP**	National Disaster Management Plan
EWS	Early warning systems	**NDRF**	National Disaster Response Force
FGD	Focus Group Discussion	**NERMP**	National Earthquake Risk Mitigation Project
GHG	Green House Gasses	**NGO**	Non-Government Organizations
GLOF	Glacial Lake Outburst Floods	**NPDM**	National Policy on Disaster Management
NRE	Nuclear and Radiological Emergencies	**SH**	Shear strength

General Terms			
Abbreviations	**Full form**	**Abbreviations**	**Full form**
ODR	Owner Driven Reconstruction	**SS**	Shear Stress
PSMHS	Psycho-Social Support and Mental Health Services	**UNGA**	UN General Assembly
PTSD	Post-Traumatic Stress Disorder	**UNDRR**	United Nations Office for Disaster Risk Reduction
PwD	Persons with Disability	**UNISDR**	United Nations International Strategy for Disaster Reduction
RDD	Radiological Dispersal Device	**VCA**	Vulnerability and Capacity Assessment
SDG	Sustainable Development Goal	**WCDRR**	World Conference on Disaster Risk Reduction
SDMA	State Disaster Management Authority	**WHO**	World Health Organization
SFDRR	Sendai Framework for Disaster Risk Reduction	**WMO**	World Meteorological Organization
SHG's	Self Help Groups		

List of Figures

Unit 1: Introduction

Unit 2: Disasters

Unit 3: Disaster Impacts

Unit 4: Disaster Risk Reduction

Unit 5: Disasters, Environment and Development

List of Tables

Unit 1: Introduction

Unit 2: Disasters

Unit 3: Disaster Impacts

Unit 4: Disaster Risk Reduction

Unit 5: Disasters, Environment and Development

Contents

01 INTRODUCTION

UNIT SPECIFICS

The salient objectives of this unit are to familiarize the students with the following:

- *The key concepts of Disaster, Hazard, Vulnerability and Capacity with respect to disaster management.*
- *Explain the relationship between hazard, risk, vulnerability and capacity.*
- *To understand the challenges posed by disasters.*
- *Ability to understand the concept of disaster risk.*

The basic concepts of disaster management are discussed for getting an overview of the key terminologies that are used, to be able to get insights into the subject of disaster management, and delve into it for further curiosity.

A number of multiple-choice questions are given as well as questions of short and long answer types are marked in two categories following lower and higher order of Bloom's taxonomy. A list of references and suggested readings are given in the unit so that one can go through them for practice. It is important to note that for getting more information on various topics of interest some QR codes have been provided in different sections which can be scanned for relevant supportive knowledge.

RATIONALE

This fundamental unit is an attempt to introduce the reader to the basic aspects of Disaster Management. It defines and explains the key terminologies that are used in the subject in order to be able to comprehend it. There is a growing realization that disaster management is a multi-layered process which involves working at various levels to be able to manage them. Thus, understanding these concepts becomes significant. It then explains the unique relationship that binds them together and differentiates them. Furthermore, it elucidates these concepts through discussing various examples from our real life. Additionally, it tries to give an analytical view point on the causes of these issues and the likely response strategy. These terms are discussed at length to give an in-depth understanding. Some of the concepts will also be discussed in detail in the next few chapters as we begin understanding the basics.

Disaster management is thus crucial in overcoming the barriers to development. The study and inquiry into the subject of Disaster Management is increasingly revealing Human contributions behind disaster phenomenon. This guides us to the topic of Sustainable Development to stress on the development aspect while focusing on the conservation of environment and protecting people from adverse situations. The Sendai Framework for Disaster Risk Reduction (SFDRR) (2015-2030) is the guiding principle for

Sustainable development adopted at the United Nations Third World Conference on Disaster Risk Reduction (WCDRR) after the Hyogo Framework for Action. These emphasize on not just disaster response but on all the stages of Disaster Management cycle through prioritizing on four key areas: a) Understanding Disaster Risk b) Strengthening disaster risk governance to manage disaster risk c) Investing in disaster risk reduction for resilience, and (d) Enhancing disaster preparedness for effective response and to Build Back Better in recovery, rehabilitation and reconstruction.

This unit, thus, is an attempt to prompt the reader into looking at all dimensions that surrounds us to become an aware and responsible manager during, before and after a disaster. It tries at inculcating a holistic understanding about getting introduced to managing disaster risks.

PRE-REQUISITES

NIL

UNIT OUTCOMES

List of outcomes of this unit is as follows:

U1-O1: Realize the need to study Disaster Management

U1-O2: Explain the concepts of vulnerability and disaster management

U1-O3: Ability to learn the relationship between hazard, vulnerability, exposure, risk and capacity

U1-O4: Correlate disaster severity and its frequency

U1-O5: Explain the significance of disaster prevention and mitigation

Unit-1 Outcomes	EXPECTED MAPPING WITH COURSE OUTCOMES (1- Weak Correlation; 2- Medium correlation; 3- Strong Correlation)					
	CO-1	CO-2	CO-3	CO-4	CO-5	CO-6
U1-01	3	3	3	2	3	2
U1-02	3	2	1	1	2	3
U1-03	2	3	1	-	-	1
U1-04	1	-	1	1	2	1
U1-05	1	1	-	1	3	2

1.1 BACKGROUND

Disasters have been a companion of humans for as long as history. However, the frequency and magnitude with which the damage and destruction is being caused by them in recent years have become a cause of global concern. Additionally, climate change has raised alarms not only for environmentalists, climatologists, but for everyone as it is threatening to disrupt almost all aspects of life and aggravating extreme events while decreasing capacities of the society. This has led to inexorable increase in disastrous events. According to the Emergency Event Database (EM-DAT), there were 432 disastrous events in 2021 which emerged from natural hazards globally. These events caused 10,492 deaths, affecting 101.8 million people and causing economic losses of worth US $252.1 billion. The comparison of the annual average occurrence of various disasters from 2001-2020

EM-DAT DISASTER DATA

to 2021 is shown in Fig.1.1. This shows that annual average disasters that occurred in 2021 including earthquakes, floods, storm etc. were large in number i.e.,432 disaster events as compared to 347 disaster events that occurred during 2001-2020 (CRED,2021). This reflects an overall rise in the frequency of disasters worldwide.

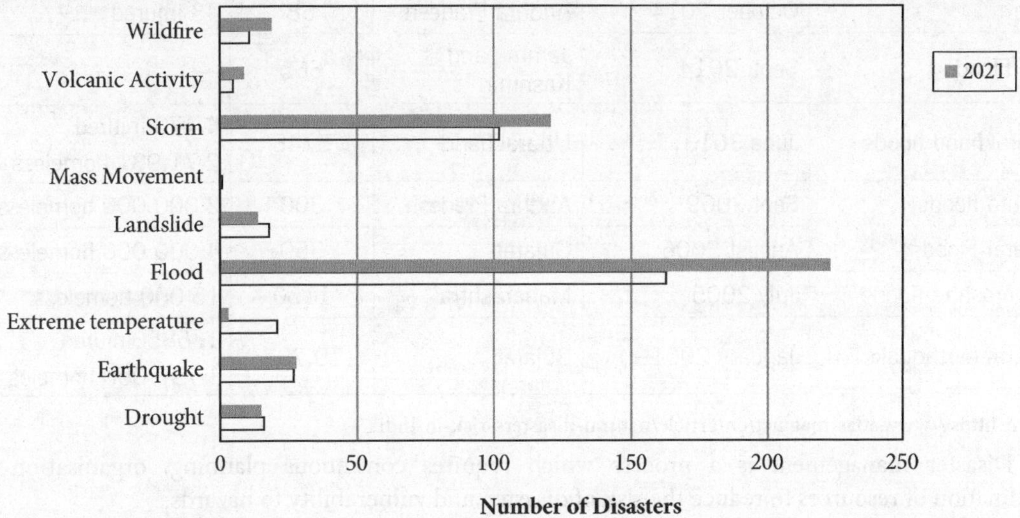

Fig.1.1: Comparison of annual average occurrence of various disasters from 2001- 2020 to 2021

The rise in frequency of disasters and related damages and deaths are mainly due to climate change, ecological degradation, industrialization, urbanisation, infrastructure development in high risk zones and population explosion among others.

India with its unique geo-climatic conditions, geographical diversity and natural features, coupled with poor economic and social conditions is one of the most vulnerable countries in the world for disasters. It is highly vulnerable to floods, earthquakes, droughts, cyclones, volcanoes, landslides as well as other natural and human-made hazards. This causes considerable damages to life, livelihood and properties. Some of the major disasters that struck India in the last 20 years which have caused considerable damage to life and properties are given in Table 1.1. Therefore, there is a need to reduce the risk of disaster through disaster management.

Table 1.1: List of some of the major disaster events in last two decades

Disaster	Date	Place	Deaths	No. of people affected
Cyclone Tauktae	May 2021	Gujarat	174	200000 homeless
Locust attack	2020	More than 23 countries	-	-
Hurricane Amphan	May 2020	West Bengal	103	5,00,000 homeless
Bihar floods	May 2019	Bihar	130	88.4 lakh people affected
Kerala Floods	August 2018	Kerala	504	2,23,139 homeless

Disaster	Date	Place	Deaths	No. of people affected
Chennai Floods	Nov. 2015	Tamil Nadu	289	-
Storm	April 2015	Himachal	78	20,000 injured
Storm	October 2014	Andhra Pradesh	68	43 injured
J&K Floods	Sept. 2014	Jammu and Kashmir	665	—
Uttarakhand floods	June 3013	Uttarakhand	5748	4,473 injured 2,71,931 homeless
Andhra floods	Sept.2009	Andhra Pradesh	300	2 000 000 homeless
Gujarat Floods	August 2006	Gujarat	350	4 000 000 homeless
Maharashtra floods	July 2005	Maharashtra	1150	15 000 homeless
Gujarat earthquake	January 2001	Gujarat	19 737	166850injured 1 790 000 homeless

Source: https://www.atlas-mag.net/en/article/natural-disasters-risk-in-india

Disaster management is a process which requires continuous planning, organisation and coordination of resources to reduce the risk of disaster, and vulnerability to hazards.

To understand the holistic meaning of Disaster Management, it is necessary to understand the basic concepts of disaster, vulnerability, risk, hazard, capacity, mitigation and prevention. These have been discussed in the subsequent sections.

1.2 DISASTER

A disaster is an extraordinary event which can be natural or human-made, rapid or slow, sudden or accruing, endogenic or exogenic, capable of creating great damage to property, environment and loss of lives among the affected community. Thus, in a simple way, if a hazard causes heavy loss to life, properties and environment, it is termed as a disaster.

Disasters disturb the equilibrium over years and can alter the benefits of development. For example, during the Bhuj earthquake (2002) many buildings collapsed and people died, which brought shock waves among the entire country and brought everything to a standstill. It took many years to redevelop what was already developed, but the losses, especially in terms of lives lost could never recovered. A disaster is thus an undesirable event which can occur with little or no warning and requires extensive efforts on part of the society and the government to deal with them.

Disaster can be defined as "A serious disruption of the functioning of a community or a society at any scale due to hazardous events interacting with conditions of exposure, vulnerability and capacity, leading to one or more of the following: human, material, economic and environmental losses and impacts." (UNISDR 2016). Furthermore, the Disaster Management Act which was enacted in India in 2005 defines a disaster as "a catastrophe, mishap, calamity or grave occurrence in any area, arising from natural or manmade causes, or by accident or negligence which results in substantial loss of life or human suffering or damage to and destruction of, property, or damage to, or degradation of environment and is of such a nature or magnitude as to be beyond the coping the coping capacity of the community of the affected area".

Disasters happen as a result of exposure to hazards coupled with vulnerabilities which might include communities, cities or villages. Therefore, there are mainly two components of disaster i.e., Hazard and vulnerability as shown in Fig. 1.2.

Fig.1.2: Disaster occurs when Hazard meet Vulnerability

Therefore, mere hazard is not sufficient, vulnerability and inadequate capacity of the affected community are required to turn a hazard into a disaster. Have you ever seen people crying after a disastrous event? This happens because maybe they were never prepared for it and suffered losses in terms of their loved ones or property. So, not being prepared made them vulnerable and their vulnerability impacted what could have been controlled.

Disasters are thus, a result of unchecked vulnerabilities over time which combine to form an event which can assume high magnitude. Hazards may not be prevented but losses due to hazards can be minimized by proper disaster preparedness. Our aim is not to allow hazards to turn into a disaster, thus, we have to break the link between hazards and disasters.

1.2.1 Causes of Occurrence of Disasters

Disasters occur because of the underlying vulnerability during a hazard. Some of the main reasons are given below:

- **Environmental degradation**- Processes including removal of tree cover, soil erosion, clogging of the drainage, groundwater depletion, solid waste disposal among others, damages the environment, leading to loss of biodiversity, ecosystem services, etc. This increases the vulnerability and lowers the capacities of people, increasing the risk of exposure to disasters.
- **Unsustainable Development**- Rapid urbanisation, unplanned use of the land, failure of major infrastructure, development of infrastructure without keeping in mind the resilience of the structures to the disasters causes increase in the vulnerability of people turning the hazard into disasters.
- **Political issues**- Conflicts between countries or political parties for power becomes a reason of war. The disasters like Hiroshima nuclear explosion, Syrian civil war, growing militarisation of oceans, etc. occur in such situations.
- **Industrialization**- This has led to global warming and has increased the rate of Climate Change making it unsustainable to adopt. The frequency of extremities in the weather has therefore, increased.
- **Biological activities**- these include pandemics, epidemics or other public health crisis. For example, Covid-19 caused disasters and death at a large scale.

1.3 HAZARD

Disasters do not occur randomly just by an accident. They are the consequences of convergence among hazards and vulnerability. Hazard is an event or phenomenon that has the potential to cause loss of life, damage to properties and disruption of social and economic activities and degradation of the environment. Hazards may be classified on the basis of their origin into two categories.

- Natural Hazards
- Human-Induced Hazards or Anthropogenic Hazards

Natural hazards occur due to natural processes and phenomenon i.e., physical forces working on the surface of the earth(exogenic)or within the surface of the earth(endogenic). They can be geological, hydrometeorological, or biological which includes earthquake, tsunami, cyclones, landslides, floods, storm, drought etc. As these processes are due to physical forces of the earth, they become inevitable but the impact of natural hazards can be minimized by taking effective steps for efficient disaster management.

Human-Induced hazards occur due to human negligence or human activities. They can be environmental degradation, infrastructural failure and technological hazards which includes pollution, dam failure, explosions etc.

Hazards can be determined by their intensity or magnitude, frequency and time of occurrence, sudden or slow onset, its geographical location and extent, damage potential and risk potential. It can be single, combined or can have cascading effects.

The words hazard and disaster are often confused and used interchangeably. However, this is a mistake that should be avoided to be able to understand and implement disaster management. Hazard is not a disaster but it becomes a disaster, only if it causes damage and destruction in terms of life, property or economic losses and social disruption and environmental degradation. Thus, a hazard in itself does not poses a threat but when it combines with vulnerable situations, it becomes a disaster. For example, if an earthquake of magnitude 8.6 occurs in a no man's land, it will not lead to death, damage or destruction, but it still has the potential to cause destruction. Thus, it is because of no human presence that there would be no vulnerability and so it would not be a disaster and will remain a hazard. This is a major difference between a hazard and a disaster. How each hazard interacts with vulnerability is important in determining the extent and magnitude of a disaster.

Therefore, it is important to classify any location by identifying which type of hazards can occur at that place. This helps us analyse the risks, and the risk potential according to the existing capacities. For example, if we are aware of which hazards can affect a given area, we can make plans regarding prevention, mitigation and response.

1.3.1 Types of Hazards

According to the Sendai Framework for Disaster Risk Reduction 2015-2030 (SFDRR), hazards are classified as geological, biological, hydrometeorological, environmental, and technological processes and phenomenon. They are described below:

- **Geological Hazards**- these originate from inside the earth. For example, earthquakes, volcanic activity, mass movements, landslides, debris, mud flows.
- **Hydrometeorological Hazards**- these are of hydrological, atmospheric, or oceanographic origin. For example, floods, flash folds, droughts, heatwaves, cold spells, coastal storm surges.

- **Biological Hazards**- these are of organic origin and communicated by biological vectors including bioactive substances, toxins, microorganisms. For example. bacteria, viruses, disease carrying agents such coronavirus.
- **Environmental Hazards**- these include chemical, biological or natural which are created by chemical pollution of water, air and soil or environmental degradation. However, these may not be hazardeous in themselves but are rather drivers of hazards.
- **Technological Hazards**- these originate from industrial or technological conditions, dangerous procedures, infrastructure failures, or specific human activities. For example, factory explosions, hospital fires, chemical spills, transport accidents, dam failures, industrial pollution etc.

1.3.2 Measuring Hazards

Hazards need to be assessed to be able to plan concretely. The essential steps include:

- Collection of hazard related data.
- Obtaining other underlying information such as geographical area it covers, intensity of past events, etc.
- Preparing a hazard catalogue involving spatial characteristics, temporal characteristics, and intensity to be used in a deterministic or probabilistic manner with risk models.

Thus, improving information and knowledge regarding hazards and conducting regular assessments of hazards can help anticipate and locate over different temporal situations over when and where these might occur, thus reducing their impacts.

1.4 VULNERABILITY

The coming to light of the concept of vulnerability is one of the most significant tasks achieved during the last decade in the field of studies in Disaster Management. Vulnerability refers to the physical, economic, social, and environmental conditions which increase the susceptibility of the affected community to cope with the impact of hazards. However, it is pertinent to ask here an important question about susceptibility of whom? The answer to which is that it could be flora, fauna, life, property, human community, spatial unit or a physiographic unit. It involves various factors such as capacity to cope, resist, recover which determine their intensity of impact. According to UNISDR (2016), vulnerability is defined as "The conditions determined by physical, social, economic and environmental factors or processes which increase the susceptibility of an individual, a community, assets or systems to the impacts of hazards".

It has two main components: extent of exposure to hazards and inability to cope. Vulnerability in this sense is a relative concept. It varies from individuals, groups, communities and can be different for different locations having varying levels of exposure. For example, studies show that during a disaster, the poor, women, children and the old are ones most affected by a disaster. This shows that disasters affect different groups differently.

Vulnerability can be categorised as under: -

- **Economic Vulnerability**- This highlight towards having lack or no resources to build a disaster resilient house. For example, People who find it expensive to stay in safer places in cities stay in high-risk areas which are inexpensive.
- **Physical Vulnerability** – It is based on the physical conditions of the individual, society and elements at risk. For example, poor designing or construction of buildings etc.

- **Social Vulnerability**- It means lack of ability in the social structure to withstand the adverse impacts of a hazard. It indicates a lack of social capital to help each other. It also includes other aspects such as literacy, security, human rights, good governance, values, customs, and beliefs etc. For example, having such cultures like wearing saree might interfere in mobility during disaster evacuation.
- **Environmental Vulnerability**- It implies poor environmental management like overconsumption of natural resources, climate change, resource depletion and degradation.

1.4.1 Approaches to reducing vulnerability

Some of the ways to reduce vulnerabilities and increase capacity are given below. These are: -

- Implementing building codes
- Knowledge and awareness generation
- Preparedness measures
- Insurance and social protection
- Resilient livelihoods
- Emphasizing economic diversity

UNDRR Terminology

1.5 CAPACITY

Capacity is defined as "The combination of all the strengths, attributes and resources available within an organization, community or society to manage and reduce disaster risks and strengthen resilience". (UNISDR Terminology, 2016)

It means to reduce the level of risk or the effects of a disaster by being able to cope with, resist, recover, and anticipate disasters. It may be noted that vulnerability is inversely proportional to capacity. Capacity is about "having" coping strategies to deal with a hazard, while vulnerability is about "not having" capacity to resist. Capacity depends on various factors such as social, economic, political, environmental, psychological etc. Capacity may include human knowledge, infrastructure, institutions, collective attributes such as social relationships, leadership and management or even capability.

The effect of disasters can be felt at the level of society, families or even individuals and can impact the city, state or even the entire country. The ability to absorb the impact of a disaster depends much upon the magnitude of the disaster or preparedness and resilience of the affected community. The level of magnitude cannot be controlled but the ability to absorb and withstand can be strengthen by increasing the capacity.

Coping capacity- It is the ability to use available skills and resources to manage risks and disasters. It depends on the availability of adequate assets. In general, this involves managing resources, both in normal times as well as during crisis or adverse conditions so as to build resilience to withstand the effects of natural and human-induced hazards. For example, if a building or structure which is built in wind-zone 6 is not according to the relevant building standards and codes, then the structure or building becomes vulnerable to wind or storm and hence coping capacity to deal with a storm decrease. However, if the same structure or building is built in wind-zone 5 according to the standards and codes of wind-zone 6, then the structural vulnerability is very less and it can be said that the building has the capacity to cope with the certain intensity of wind or storm.

Capacity development: It relates to all the aspects of strengthening and sustaining capacity of mechanisms, institutions, and capacities of all stakeholders. It is the process through which all aspects of society are driven to acquire a strategic approach to improvement in knowledge, skills, institutions etc. It involves continuous efforts to develop. It seeks to bring about transformation: not only in physical assets such as technological systems, financial resources, but also through change in mindsets such as political awareness and building an institutional framework, effective allocation of resources, and developing strategies for managing disasters. These measures ensure translation of capacity into performance.

Capacity is crucial in reducing disaster risk and henceforth significant for development. Disaster Risk Reduction demands all-inclusive participation. Any natural hazard can turn into a disaster due to structural and managerial errors and underlying vulnerabilities. However, a Disaster Resilient City/ Society/Community has the capacity to cope with such disasters.

1.5.1 Measuring capacity

Capacity is assessed as per the requirements of the existing risks. This helps identify the capacity gaps for further action. Capacity operates at three levels, in individuals, in organizations, and in overall working environment where individuals and organizations interact, this is known as an enabling environment. These are explained below: -

- **Individual level**- it has to be understood within the domain of enabling environment and organisational level. This level relates to knowledge, experience and skills of people that enable them to perform.
- **Organisational level**- it helps to develop the organisation's mandate such as internal policies, procedures and frameworks, arrangements. It focuses on the policies, systems and procedures, internal structure that determines an organisation's ability and effectiveness to provide individuals to work together.
- **Enabling environment**- it is a system where organizations and individuals function. Capacities at this level relate to laws and legislations, policies, rules, power relations, social norms. Here the government, civil society and private sector have a platform to work together for a better future.

1.6 EXPOSURE

Exposure refers to anything tangible which is at risk of the impact of a hazard. It can be people, property, infrastructure etc. It is one of the most significant parameters for determining the risk of disasters. For example, if a hospital building is exposed to a certain type of hazard, say fire, it would be more difficult to evacuate people, instead of an office building, because the mobility of the people in a hospital is limited. Therefore, exposure depends on the particular type of situation in disaster prone areas. Thus, exposure to a hazard will impact the community depending on the level of vulnerability. For example, if the people, or assets exposed are more vulnerable, the impact of a hazard will be severe and moderate or mild if they are less vulnerable.

This means that different demographics such as age groups, sex, number of people, profession and type of assets would have different levels of vulnerability and the exposure would be much more for vulnerable groups for the same hazard. So, when specific vulnerability gets combined with the capacity of the affected community, the level of exposure can be estimated. Thus, an in-depth assessment and estimation of the exposure becomes the foundation for implementing risk reduction measures in a particular area.

1.7 RISK

Risk of disasters have always been a part of life. However, the risk perception and acceptance vary from person to person and region to region. It encompasses different types of possible losses. The social and economic milieu in which the risks take place along with the potential hazards determines to a large extent the probability of the risk.

Risk is defined as "probability of expected damages, loss of life, or destruction due to the occurrence of a hazard in a given area over a specific period of time".

A locality or community is considered at "risk" if they are incapable to cope with the hazards they are exposed to and thus are expected to suffer adversely in terms of losses, if a hazard strike. Thus, a disaster risk is widely recognized as a result of the interaction between hazards, vulnerability, exposure and capacity. It can be written mathematically as: -

$$\text{Risk} = \frac{\text{Hazard} \times \text{Vulnerability} \times \text{Exposure}}{\text{Capacity}}$$

The degree of risk depends upon: -

- Magnitude of a hazard.
- Exposure of human activities to hazards.
- Vulnerability of the elements at risk.
- Capacity of the community/locality exposed.

It is seen that the vulnerabilities and exposures are high in underdeveloped and developing countries as compared to the developed countries. The greater exposure to a hazard and higher probability of vulnerability aggravates the impact of disaster. It is clear that hazards cannot be avoided, but the vulnerability can be reduced by increasing the capacities of the community thus reducing the overall level or risk. The reduction in vulnerability can be achieved through mitigation and preparedness measures.

1.8 IMPACT

Disaster impact refers to the effects that materialize at the time of the occurrence of a disaster. It happens upon the elements at risk such as people, society, locality, or even upon nations. The impact or the repercussions of disasters can be felt physically through loss of life, injury, health and disability, damage to property and environment as well as psychologically through mental health. Furthermore, they result in not only huge economic losses but also damages to the environment through habitat destruction, ecological stress and loss of biodiversity, water scarcity, food scarcity and many more. This leads to migration of people, who have to relocate and start a new life without adequate resources all over again which pushes them into poverty. Disaster impact thus depends on various factors such as types and duration of hazard. For example, some hazards are annual while some are seasonal, some hazards are predictable in advance like cyclones, and floods while some are sudden and unpredictable which makes it more difficult and challenging to respond. For example, earthquakes may occur within a few seconds making it difficult to respond immediately.

1.9 PREVENTION

Disaster Prevention denotes the need to avoid potential adverse impacts of hazardous events completely. If it is determined that the risk could be completely eliminated then such steps could be taken so as to prevent the occurrence of a disaster. For example, if an area, village or community is prone to fire hazard, then measures such as placing fire alarms, conducting mock drills, using materials that are fire safe, continuous monitoring of points of failure can be done to avoid the occurrence of fire and the locality could be safe-guarded from fire hazard. Appropriate prevention measures can play a vital role for reducing the vulnerabilities and increasing the capacities thus, not letting the hazard to turn into disaster. Thus, prevention aims at reducing the exposure and vulnerability in such a manner so that the risk of disaster is removed completely, avoiding the potential risks of adverse consequences. For example, flood risk can be prevented or reduced by constructing dams or embankments in the flood prone region.

1.10 MITIGATION

Disaster mitigation refers to measures aimed at reducing the vulnerabilities and adverse consequences of a hazard. It simply means that if it is not possible to prevent the risk of a hazard like an earthquake completely then we can adopt such measures so as to reduce the risk or impact of the hazard.

Mitigation may include measures such as hazard resistant construction and engineering techniques as well as public policy and awareness. As already discussed, hazards are not avoidable but adopting measures such as using water harvesting techniques in a drought prone area will reduce the impacts of a drought. Earthquake resistant buildings in high seismic risk areas will reduce the severity. Thus, it can be said that mitigation involves adopting such strategies and actions which can reduce the damages accruing from a disaster.

UNIT SUMMARY

- Disaster management is a process of how we organize and manage our resources and share responsibilities for dealing with human, economic, environmental and material impacts of a disaster in order to reduce its severity.
- A Hazard is an event or phenomenon that has the potential for causing loss of life, damage to property and disruption of social and economic activities and degradation of the environment. Hazards can be natural or human-induced.
- Vulnerability refers to the physical, economic, social, and environmental conditions which increase the susceptibility of the affected community to cope with the impact of hazards.
- Capacity means the combination of all the resources available to manage and reduce disaster risks and strengthen resilience to cope with the effects of a disaster. While coping capacity utilizes the available resources, coping capacity focuses on building and strengthening resource availability.
- Exposure refers to anything tangible which is at risk of the impact of a hazard. Exposure depends on the particular type of situations in disaster prone areas. When specific vulnerability gets combined with the capacity of the affected community, the level of exposure can be estimated
- Risk is the probability of occurrence of a hazard and the likely damages it may cause. A disaster risk is widely recognized as a result of the interaction between hazards, vulnerability, exposure and capacity.

- Disaster impact refers to the effects that materialize at the time of the occurrence of a disaster. This means that the elements at risk can be affected by loss of life, injury, health and disability, damage to properties and environment, mental health, etc.
- Disaster Prevention refers to the need to avoid potential adverse impacts of hazardous events completely.
- Mitigation refers to measures aimed at reducing the vulnerabilities and adverse consequences of a hazard. This means it involves adopting such strategies and actions which can reduce the damages accruing from a disaster.

EXERCISES

Multiple Choice Questions

Q.1 Which of the following is the guiding principle for Sustainable development presently adopted by the world?

a. Sendai Framework b. Hyogo Framework
c. Paris agreement d. World disaster summit

Q.2 Which of the following is not a natural disaster?

a. Tsunami b. Earthquake
c. Civil war d. Volcanic eruption

Q.3 The disaster management act was enacted in?

a. 2004 b. 2015
c. 2003 d. 2005

Q.4 Which of the following will reduce the vulnerability of the people?

A. Capacity
B. Capability
C. Mitigation measures
D. Exposure

a. A and Band C b. All the above,
c. A and C only d. C only

Q.5 The risk of a disaster can be completely eliminated in which of the following?

a. Preparedness b. Mitigation
c. Prevention d. Awareness

Q.6 Disaster Risk decreases with

a. increase in vulnerability b. increase in capacity
c. increase in intensity of Hazard d. None of these

Q.7 The degree of risk depends upon

a. Magnitude of a hazard
b. Exposure of human activities to hazards,
c. Capacity of the community/locality exposed
d. All of these

Q.8 Which of the following is not an example of Geological Hazards?

a. Mass movements b. Chemical spills,
c. Earthquake d. Tsunami

Q.9 Technological hazards emerge from?

A. Technological conditions,
B. Industrial Conditions,
C. Environmental degradation

a. A and B only b. All the above,
c. A only d. A and C only

Q.10 Volcanic eruption in an area which is not habitable is known as

a. disaster b. hazard,
c. both d. none

Q.11 Which of the following can be said to be true regarding hazard and disaster?

a. a hazard is always is disaster but a disaster may or may not be a hazard.
b. a disaster is always is hazard but a hazard may or may not be a disaster.
c. a hazard can never be a disaster.
d. a disaster can never be a hazard.

Answers of Multiple-Choice Questions

Answers of Multiple-choice questions				
1.1 **a**	1.2 **c**	1.3 d	1.4 **a**	1.5 **c**
1.6 **b**	1.7 **d**	1.8 b	1.9 **a**	1.10 **b**
1.11 **b**				

SHORT AND LONG ANSWER TYPE QUESTIONS

Category I

1. Elucidate the relationship between hazard and vulnerability. How does capacity determine vulnerability?
2. Explain risk. On what parameters does the magnitude of risk depend?
3. What is the difference between disaster and vulnerability?
4. Discuss the significance of planning for ensuring disaster prevention.
5. What is capacity? What is the difference between coping capacity and capacity development?

Category II

1. What is the importance of risk assessment and vulnerability for pre-disaster management? As a disaster manager, what are key areas that you would focus on in a Disaster Management System?
2. Disasters are just an "act of God" but also determined by human activities. Comment?
3. Discuss the importance of people in being the first responders in disaster management?

4. Write a note on interlinkages between prevention and mitigation. How does risk determine their role in managing adverse effects?
5. Vulnerability is a crucial aspect for defining the impact of disasters and its threat to people. How and in what ways can vulnerability to disasters be characterized? Explain various types of vulnerabilities with reference to disasters.

REFERENCES AND SUGGESTED READINGS

1. UNISDR (2016): Report of The Open-Ended Intergovernmental Expert Working Group On Indicators And Terminology Relating To Disaster Risk Reduction https://www.undrr.org/terminology/disaster (accessed on Aug. 1,2022)
2. Sendai Framework for Disaster Risk Reduction (2015-2030)
3. Determinants of Risk, Exposure and Vulnerability. In: Managing the Risks of Extreme Events and Disasters to Advance Climate Change Adaptation. A Special Report of Working Groups I and II of the Intergovernmental Panel on Climate Change (IPCC). Cambridge University Press, Cambridge, UK, and New York, NY, USA, pp. 65-108.
4. https://www.ipcc.ch/site/assets/uploads/2018/03/SREX-Chap2_FINAL-1.pdf
5. Disaster resilient cities: Lessons from Srinagar and Guwahati on how to protect our cities from natural disasters. (https://irade.org/Disaster%20Resilient%20Cities.pdf)
6. Training of Trainer's programme on Basics of Disaster Management: Basic Reading Material of the National Training Programme, NIDM,
7. https://nidm.gov.in/PDF/trgreports/2017/December/11-15_NIDM_south.pdf
8. UNIT1: Meaning and Classification of Disasters: IGNOU
9. https://www.egyankosh.ac.in/bitstream/123456789/25912/1/Unit-1.pdf
10. CRED 2021: 2021 Disasters in numbers: Centre for Research on the Epidemiology of Disasters. https://cred.be/sites/default/files/2021_EMDAT_report.pdf
11. GOI (2005): Disaster Management Act 2005

02 DISASTERS

UNIT SPECIFICS

The salient objectives of this unit are to familiarize the students with the following:

- *To understand the classification of Disasters.*
- *To explain the different types of Natural and Man-made Disasters*
- *To describe various disasters and its causes.*
- *To understand the Vulnerability profile of India.*
- *To understand the various hazard maps of India.*
- *To describe the mountain and coastal land-forms.*

In this unit, the classification of disasters is discussed into natural and manmade disasters. Natural disasters such as droughts, floods, earthquakes, cyclones, tsunamis, avalanches, volcanic eruptions, landslides, etc., and their causes are described in detail. Man-made disasters such as chemical, biological, radiological, nuclear, accidents, terrorist strikes, etc., are also explained. An overview of the vulnerability profile of India is presented along with maps, which gives an idea about India's vulnerability to various disasters. Furthermore, the concept of ecological fragility is explained with emphasis on mountain and coastal landforms.

A number of multiple-choice questions are given as well as questions of short and long answer types are marked in two categories following lower and higher order of Bloom's taxonomy. A list of references and suggested readings are given in the unit so that one can go through them for practice. It is important to note that for getting more information on various topics of interest some QR codes have been provided in different sections which can be scanned for relevant supportive knowledge.

RATIONALE

This unit helps students to gain insights on classifications of disasters. It explains different kinds of natural and man-made disasters, which are discussed at length to develop an understanding of various disasters. This understanding of disasters helps the students gain insights into the different ways in which the society is at risk from these disasters. An introduction into the causes of these disasters lets the reader analyse the different disasters so as to arrive at disaster management solutions. Moreover, the chapter further discusses the vulnerability profile of India which lets the students understand the actual situation and makes them capable to go deeper into the subject matter. Thereafter, the concept of ecologically fragile zones is discussed with particular focus on India. Overall, the chapter elucidates the various types of disasters known to us and brings out its reasons, thereby acknowledging that by reducing the causes, the disaster risks can be reduced. This will help in furthering the objective of mainstreaming disasters into the development agenda.

PRE-REQUISITES

NIL

UNIT OUTCOMES

List of outcomes of this unit is as follows:

U2-O1: Understand the classification of disasters into various types.

U2-O2: Describe the various types of disasters and its causes.

U2-O3: Understand the Vulnerability profile of India.

U2-O4: Comprehend the hazard maps of India with respect to various disasters.

U2-O5: Explain the concept of ecological fragility, with particular focus on mountain and coastal landforms.

Unit-2 Outcomes	EXPECTEDMAPPINGWITHCOURSEOUTCOMES (1-Weak Correlation; 2-Medium correlation; 3-Strong Correlation)					
	CO-1	CO-2	CO-3	CO-4	CO-5	CO-6
U2-01	1	1	3	-	-	1
U2-02	-	1	3	1	1	1
U2-03	1	1	1	-	1	3
U2-04	-	1	2	1	1	-
U2-05	1	2	1	2	2	2

2.1 INTRODUCTION

A disaster is a natural or anthropogenic phenomenon or a combination of both, which can lead to a disruption in the normal life, damage to the environment and property, thus requiring external assistance to cope. The term 'Disaster' originates from the French word 'desastre' which means 'evil star' which depicts that disasters are destructive. In earlier times, it was understood that disasters are caused by natural forces of nature and humans are mere victims to it. However, lately due to industrialization, it has been recognized that human activities are also responsible for disasters such as Bhopal gas tragedy, Chernobyl nuclear accident etc., Moreover, humans not only directly cause these anthropogenic disasters but also indirectly contribute to natural disasters by increasing vulnerability, aggravating risk and contributing to climate change. Disasters are increasingly occurring with greater magnitude and severity due to factors such as climate change, urbanization, overpopulation, etc., and leading to greater losses thus aggravating further disasters. So, it is important to understand the typology of disasters, their causative factors and the vulnerability profile of these disasters in various regions of India. This will help us to understand the risks posed by each hazard to better understand them, to be able to manage them efficiently.

2.2 Classification of Disasters

Disasters may be classified on the basis of their source of origin into natural and human- induced/ anthropogenic disasters. Natural disasters are a consequence of the natural hazards which occur due to natural processes and phenomenon i.e., physical forces working on the surface of the earth(exogenic)or within the surface of the earth(endogenic). They can be geological, hydrometeorological, or biological which includes earthquake, tsunami, cyclones, landslides, floods, storm, drought etc. Man-made disasters are a consequence of human-induced hazards which happen due to human negligence. The examples of human induced disasters are terrorism, civil war, accidents, fire, etc.

In India, the first significant effort to classify disasters was made in August, of the year 1999 just before the occurrence of super-cyclone in Odisha in Nov. 1999, by formulating a High-Powered Committee (HPC) for managing disasters in India. The committee followed an intensive systematic and participatory approach at the district, state and national levels. The committee recognized 31 disasters for Indian context after several rounds of discussions and categorized these disasters into five sub-groups depending upon their origin as given below: -

- Water and Climate related disasters
- Geologically related disasters
- Chemical, Industrial & Nuclear related disasters
- Accident related disasters.
- *Biologically related disasters*

Classification

These disasters in each sub-category are shown in Table 2.1.

Table 2.1: Classification of Disasters as per High power committee

Category	Hazard	
Water and Climate related disasters	– Floods and Drainage Management – Cyclones – Tornadoes and Hurricanes – Hailstorm – Cloud Burst	– Heat Wave and Cold Wave – Snow Avalanches – Droughts – Sea Erosion – Thunder and Lightning
Geologically related disasters	– Landslides and Mud flows – Earthquakes	– Dam Failures/ Dam Bursts – Mine Fires
Chemical, Industrial and Nuclear related disasters	– Chemical and Industrial Disasters	– Nuclear Disasters
Accident related disasters	– Forest Fires – Urban Fires – Mine Flooding – Oil Spill – Major Building Collapse – Serial Bomb Blasts	– Festival related disasters – Electrical Disasters and Fires – Air, Road and Rail Accidents – Boat Capsizing – Village Fire
Biologically related disasters	– Biological Disasters and Epidemics – Pest Attacks	– Cattle Epidemics – Food Poisoning

In December 2004, a powerful Tsunami hit the Indian coast and caused widespread death and destruction affecting millions. Thereafter, in 2005, Tsunami was added to the list of disasters

The Sendai Framework for Disaster Risk Reduction (2015-2030) was embraced by the world community at the third World Conference on Disaster Risk Reduction (WCDRR). The conference was held in Sendai, Japan. It was one of the first major agreements to be adopted by the UN General Assembly (UNGA) including the Paris agreement and Sustainable Development Goals.

The National Disaster Management Plan (NDMP) has been revised in 2019 to synchronize these three international agreements, keeping in view the need to curb climate change, reduce disaster risk and hence move towards sustainable development. The classification of disasters which are used globally for Sendai Targets Monitoring is given in NDMP (2019) is discussed below.

2.2.1 Disasters caused due to natural hazards

- **Geophysical: These** are events which originate from inside the earth. For example, earthquakes, volcanic activity, mass movements, landslides, debris, etc.
- **Hydrological**: These processes are events which are caused by overflow of water in the water bodies or by the disruption in the water cycle. For example, floods, flash folds, avalanches.
- **Meteorological**: These Events are caused by the action of atmospheric processes. For example, storm surges, cyclones, etc.
- **Climatological**: These events are caused by shifts in the climate patterns and lead to climate variability. For example, cold waves, heat waves, droughts etc.,
- **Biological:** These are organic in origin and are communicated by biological vectors which includes bio-active substances, toxins, microorganisms. For example, bacteria, viruses, disease carrying agents such as corona-virus.

Natural/Man-Made

Disasters emerging from natural factors from these five sub-categories are given in Table 2.2.

Table 2.2: Classification of Natural Hazards

Categories of Hazards	Hazards
Geophysical	Earthquake; Tsunami; Landslide; Volcano; Mass Movement (Dry)
Hydrological	Flood; Mass Movement (Wet); Avalanche
Meteorological	Cyclone; Thunderstorm; Dust Storm; Squall; Hailstorm; Cloudburst; Blizzard; Lightning
Climatological	Drought; Wildfire; Heat Wave; Cold Wave; GLOF
Biological	Epidemic; Food Poisoning; Pest attack; Cattle Epidemics; Infections

2.2.2 Human-Induced Disasters

Human society is vulnerable to not only natural hazards but also human- induced hazards which occur due to various factors such as poor planning and construction, overpopulation, environmentally insensitive practices, industrialization and urbanization, climate change and so on. These human activities can cause potential damage and threat to life, property, and environment. Human society is thus prone to Chemical, Biological, Radiological, and Nuclear (CBRN) disasters and events that might trigger disasters. Other human- induced disasters emerging from human activities include terrorist activities, violence, conflict, civil war, various types of accidents such as road, rail, air, sea, river, industrial, fires, building collapse, oil spills, urban flooding, mine flooding, etc.

2.3 NATURAL DISASTERS

2.3.1 Earthquakes

Earthquakes are one of the most destructive hazards among all the natural hazards. They can be highly traumatic as it shocks the entire society due to their characteristic of being uncertain and unpredictable, affecting large areas. They are a sudden onset disaster which occurs within a few seconds, but can cause widespread damage and destruction to life and property and can erode gains achieved from years of development, sometimes disrupting the social structure or even the economy.

Earthquake

Earthquakes means shaking of the earth. Earthquakes originate from various sources such as volcanic eruption, land subsidence, landslides, rock fall and most severely by tectonic activity of the earth. Earthquake is a sudden motion of the earth due to release of strain energy by the collision or movement of tectonic plates underneath the surface of the earth. A building damaged due to the Gujarat, 2001 earthquake is shown in Fig. 2.1.

Fig. 2.1: Building damaged due to Gujarat 2001 earthquake

source: http://sdmassam.nic.in/pdf/publication/undp/disaster_management_in_india.pdf

The point inside the earth from which the seismic waves originate or from where the fault movement initiates is known as focus or hypocentre of an earthquake as shown in Fig. 2.2. The point on the surface of the earth vertically above the focus is called the epicentre. It can be represented by the latitude and longitude of the location. Focal depth is the depth of the point of focus from the epicentre. The distance between the point of epicentre and the place of interest is known as epicentral distance. The earthquakes having a focal depth less than 70 km, i.e., having shallow focus causes the most damaging earthquakes.

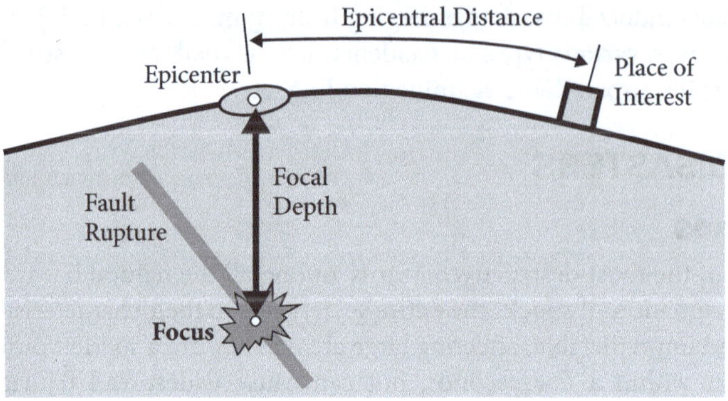

Fig. 2.2: Terminology of Earthquake

Source: https://www.nicee.org/EQTips.php

2.3.1.1 Seismic waves

When earthquakes occur, large strain energy is released which travels as seismic waves of different types in all directions through the layers of the Earth as shown in Fig.2.3. The ground shaking is caused due to seismic waves. These waves can be categorized into two types:

- Body waves
- Surface waves

It is seen from the figure that the body waves are the ones that travel through the inner layers of Earth, whereas surface waves can move only near the surface of earth. These waves are responsible for ground shaking.

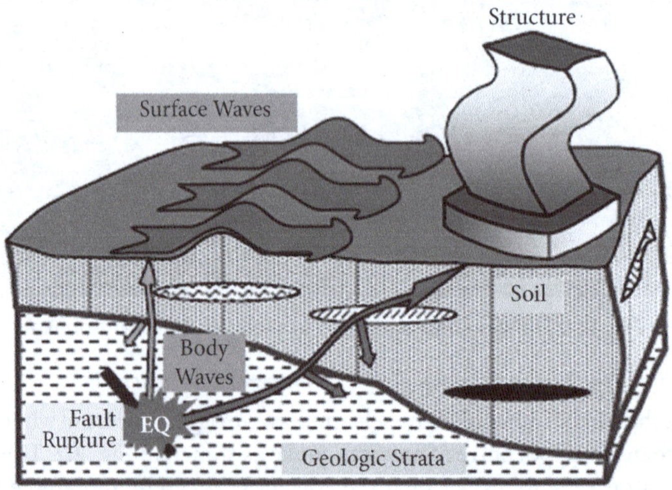

Fig. 2.3: Seismic Waves at a Site

Source: https://www.nicee.org/EQTips.php

Body Waves: Body waves are further divided into two types i.e., P-waves (Primary Waves), S-waves (Secondary Waves).

Primary Waves (P-waves): P waves also known as primary, compressional, or longitudinal waves. P waves involve successive extension and compression of the material along the direction of energy transmission as shown in Fig.2.4. Primary waves are faster than all other types of seismic waves. These can move through solids and fluids like sound waves.

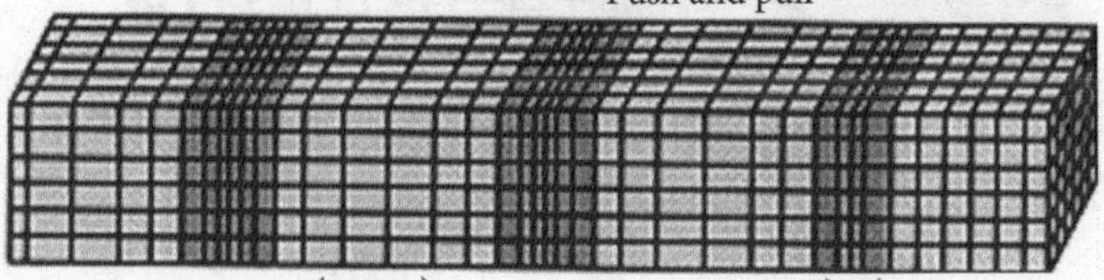

Fig. 2.4: P- Waves

Source: https://www.nicee.org/EQTips.php

S-waves (Secondary Waves)

S Waves are also called secondary, transverse waves which are slower than P Waves. S- waves involve material particles which oscillate at right angles to the direction of energy transmission as shown in Fig. 2.5. These cause shear deformations when they travel through a material. These waves cannot pass through fluids.

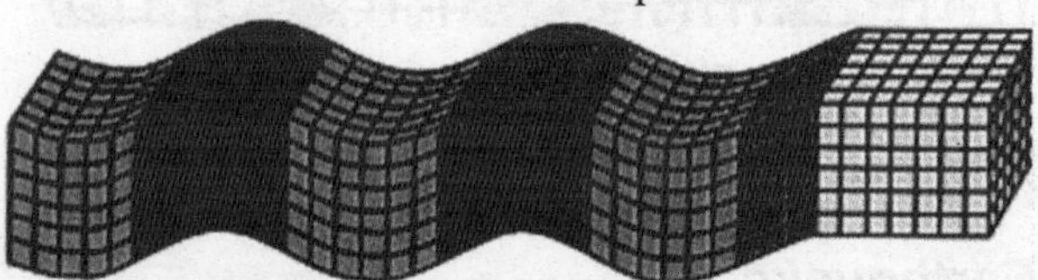

Fig. 2.5: S-Waves

Source: https://www.nicee.org/EQTips.php

Surface waves

Surface waves travel along the earth's surface with amplitudes that decrease roughly exponentially with depth. Surface waves are the most damaging waves. For the engineering point of view, Surface waves are classified into two categories:

- Love waves
- Rayleigh wave

Love waves

The Love wave is named after a British mathematician, A.E.H. Love. The waves move the ground side by side with no vertical or longitudinal component as shown in Fig. 2.6. These waves are a little slower than S waves and therefore it arrives after P and S waves. Love waves have similar surface motions as generated by S- waves but do not have a vertical component. These waves cannot travel through liquids.

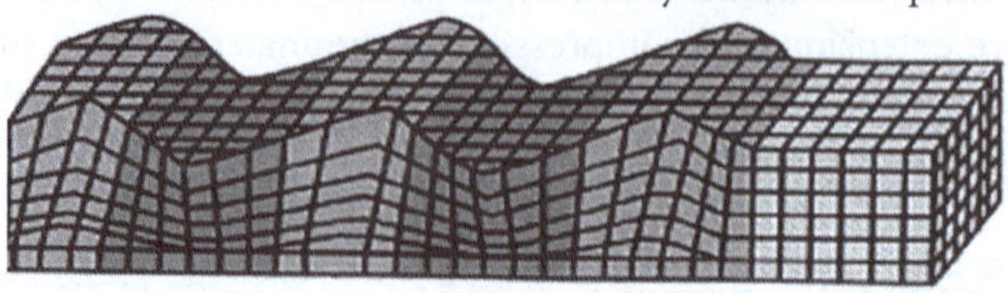

Fig. 2.6: Love Waves

Source: https://www.nicee.org/EQTips.php

Rayleigh wave

The Rayleigh wave is named after a mathematician, Lord Rayleigh. Rayleigh waves as shown in Fig. 2.7 make a material particle oscillate in an elliptic path in the vertical plane with horizontal motion along the direction of energy transmission. These waves move the ground up and down and side-to-side in the same direction as that of the wave propagation. These can be the largest waves. Most of the ground shaking that happens during an earthquake is due to these waves.

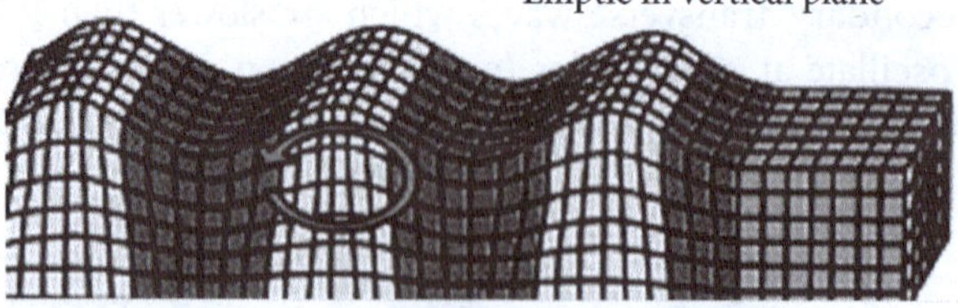

Fig. 2.7: Rayleigh wave

Source: https://www.nicee.org/EQTips.php

2.3.1.2 Causes of Earthquake

The earthquake waves travel through the Earth's layers. The radius of the earth is about 6371 km which encompasses mainly four layers namely crust, mantle, the inner core and outer core as depicted in Fig. 2.8.

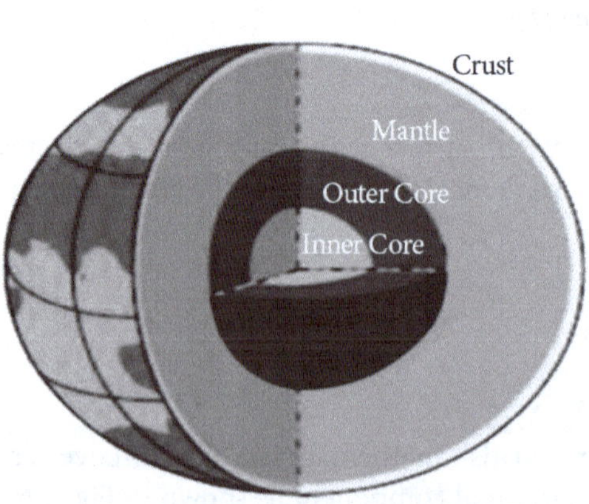

Fig. 2.8: Inside the earth

Source: http://nicee.org/EQTips.php

Crust is the outermost layer of the earth having thickness of about 5-40 km. The mantle layer lies just below the crust having a thickness of about 2900 km. The mantle can further be classified into two layers, i.e., upper mantle and lower mantle. The core is sub- divided into outer core and inner core constituted by heavy metals like iron and nickel. The crust and the uppermost layer of the mantle constituting the hard and rigid outer layer of the Earth is known as the Lithosphere. The upper portion of the mantle is called the asthenosphere as shown in Figure 2.9.

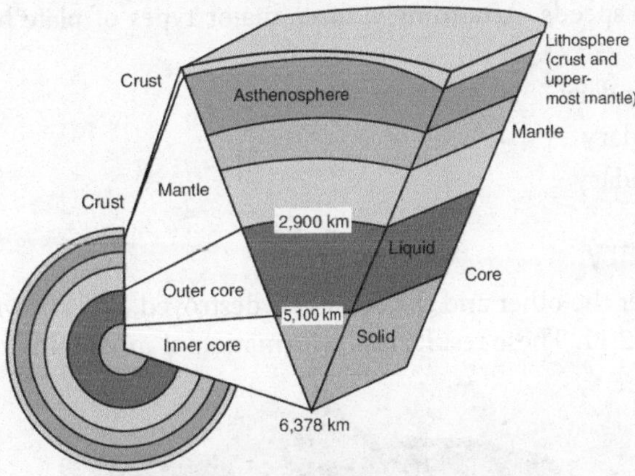

Fig. 2.9: Internal structure of the Earth

Source: https://pubs.usgs.gov/gip/dynamic/inside.html

The crust of the earth and upper mantle (lithosphere) move on the hot molten outer core because of convective flow of mantle material. This movement of earth mass occurs in pieces known as tectonic plates. The Earth's surface is divided into seven major and many smaller pieces (plates) which are in constant motion with respect to each other as shown in Fig.2.10.

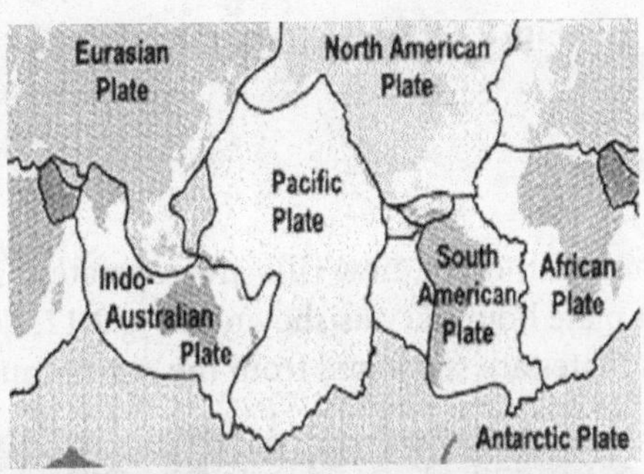

Fig. 2.10: Major Tectonic plates on earth's surface

Source: http://nicee.org/EQTips.php

The edges (where the plate boundaries meet) of the plates are known as plate boundaries. The major plates are:

- Antarctic plate
- Pacific plate
- North American plate
- South American plate

- Eurasian plate
- India-Australia, plate
- African plate

The plate boundaries consist of various faults. Maximum number of earthquakes in the world occur on these faults. The movement of these plates occurs due to convective currents in the lower mantle because of temperature gradient. The movement of these plates may take place in different directions and at different speeds. Accordingly, three major types of plate boundaries are identified. These boundaries are:

- Convergent boundary
- Divergent boundary
- Transform boundary

Convergent boundary

When one plate sinks under the other and the crust gets destroyed, it is known as the Convergent plate boundary as shown in Fig. 2.11. These results in the formation of mountains.

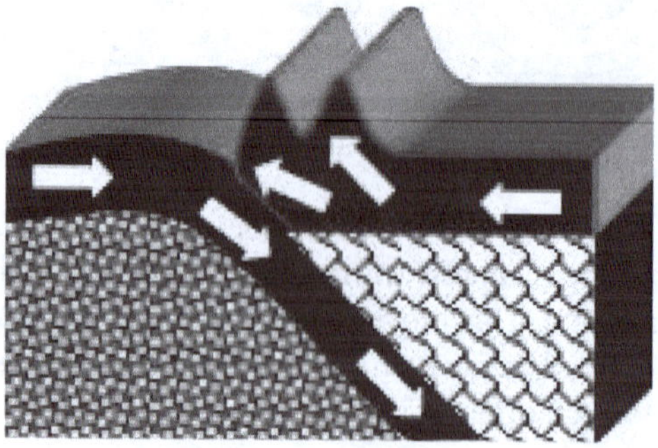

Fig. 2.11: Convergent Boundary

Source: http://nicee.org/EQTips.php

Divergent boundary

When the plates move away from each other, new rifts are generated. This form of interaction among the plates is known as divergent plate boundary as shown in Fig.2.12. For example, Mid-Atlantic Ridge where the Eurasian and African Plates are separated from the American Plate(s).

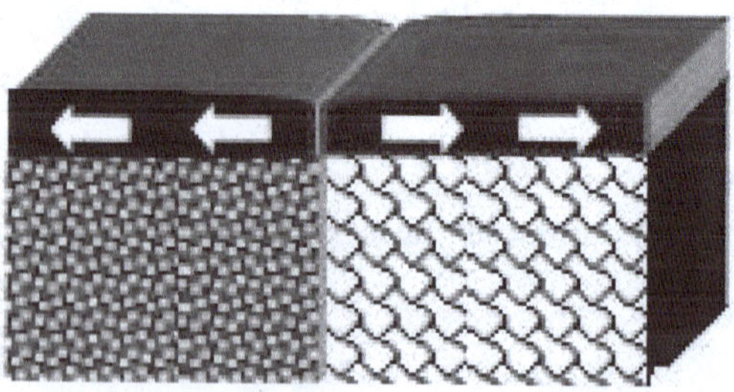

Fig. 2.12: Divergent boundary

Source: http://nicee.org/EQTips.php)

Transform boundary

When the plates slide horizontally past each other, the crust neither gets created nor destroyed, but the slowing motion frequently causes big earthquakes. This form of interaction among the plates is known as divergent plate boundary, as shown in Fig.2.13. When they touch each other, it creates stress, forcing the rocks to slip or crack, lurching the plates forward, and creating earthquakes.

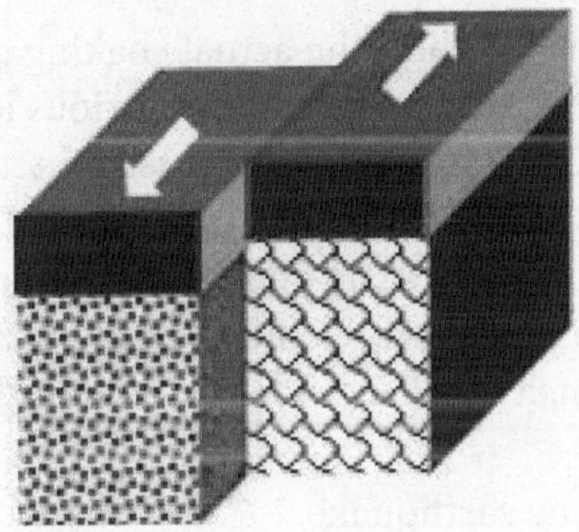

Fig. 2.13: Transform Boundary

Source: http://nicee.org/EQTips.php

The movement of the plate varies considerably across the globe. On an average, it is observed to be moving at a rate of a few cm per year. India lies at the north-western end of the Indo Australian Plate, which is colliding against the Eurasian Plate and is moving beneath this plate.

Earthquakes usually occur when a subsurface rock breaks suddenly along a plane which is known as a fault plane. The release of such a sudden energy generates seismic waves producing vibrations, thus causing the ground to shake. When two plates or blocks rub against each, they do not slide smoothly but create friction. However, at a certain point, the friction breaks and the rocks break thereby causing earthquakes. This theory was explained by the seismologist H.F. Reid, and is known as the elastic rebound theory.

2.3.1.3 Types of Earthquake

There are two types of earthquake:

- **Inter-plate Earthquakes** which take place along the boundaries of tectonic plates.
- **Intra-plate Earthquakes** which take place within the plate itself but are away from the plate boundaries.

2.3.1.4 Measurement of an earthquake

The seismic waves which are produced during the occurrence of an earthquake, are recorded by an instrument which is known as Seismograph. There are two ways to describe the size of an earthquake:

- Magnitude
- Intensity

Magnitude

Magnitude is the quantitative measure of the earthquake, which expresses the actual size of the earthquake. Therefore, it is represented by a fixed value for a given earthquake. The magnitude of the earthquake is measured by the Richter Scale. This scale is also known as the Local Magnitude scale.

If the magnitude of the earthquake increases by 1.0, the energy released increases about 31times. For example, an earthquake of magnitude 8.0 releases energy about 31 times higher the energy released by an earthquake of magnitude 7.0, and is approximately 1000 ($\approx 31 \times 31$) times higher the energy released by an earthquake of magnitude 6.0.

Intensity

Intensity is a qualitative measure that indicates the actual shaking at a given site during an earthquake. It gives the damage effect due to a particular earthquake at various locations. Therefore, it is represented by Roman capital numerals (I,II,...,XII). Most commonly used intensity scales are the MSK (Medvedev, Sponheuer and Karnik) scale and Modified Mercalli Intensity (MMI) scale. The MSK intensity scale which is quite similar to the MMI intensity scale and the scale ranges from I, i.e., least perceptive) to XII, i.e. most severe. The MSK scale is more convenient for application in the field as compared to the MMI scale. Therefore, the MSK intensity scale is widely used in India. The intensity scales are based on following impacts of shaking:

- The way people perceive the earthquake,
- The way the buildings performed, and
- The changes that took place in the natural surroundings.

2.3.2 Floods

The term "Flood" originates from the English word "Flod" which means "Flow of water/tide". India gets heavily flooded every year, marking to be the second worst affected country in the world.

Flood means a rise in the level of water that results in the inundation of land which is usually dry along the coast or a river channel. The time taken for flooding to take place can range from a few hours to a few minutes with little or no warning due to heavy rains, spill over or even a breach in the embankment. This occurs as the rivers have inadequate capacity to hold water. This forces the people to move to relatively safer locations, and may damage property and other vital resources.

2.3.2.1 Types of floods

There are various types of Floods some of which are mentioned below: -

- Flash Floods;
- Riverine Floods;
- Coastal Floods, and
- Urban Floods

Flood

Flash Floods

These floods take place in the low-lying areas such as dry lakes, depressions, and washes very quickly (usually within six hours). These are often associated with heavy rains, thunderstorms, tropical storms and cloud bursts. Moreover, it can also occur due to the collapse of a man-made dam. These are more destructive than regular floods as the people have less time to evacuate. Example of flash flood is shown in Fig. 2.14.

Fig. 2.14: Uttarakhand Flash Floods, June 2013

Source: https://www.adrc.asia/countryreport/IND/2018/India_CR2018A.pdf

River Flood

These floods take place when the river exceeds its usual capacity to hold water. The water flows out due to precipitation, melting of snow or a combination of both. These floods are different from the flash floods as they occur over an extended period of time.

Coastal Floods

These floods are catastrophic which usually occur due to cyclonic activities such as storms, high tides caused by severe weather, and heavy rainfall. However, Climate Change contributes as one of the biggest factors for sea level rise and the resultant coastal flooding. This has become a matter of major concern worldwide especially for low lying Island countries.

Urban Flood

Urban flooding refers to the inundation of densely populated areas in a built environment, breaching the capacity of the drainage system. Unlike rural floods, the primary reason for urban flooding is the unplanned urbanization that increases the flood peaks from 1.8 to 8 times and flood volumes by up to 6 times. Urban floods usually occur mainly due to two factors which are:

- Natural factors
- Land use changes due to human activities

These floods are usually associated with a combination of hydrological, meteorological, and human factors. The land use changes can exacerbate the intensity of floods in a rapid manner.

When floods occur in urban areas, streets can become flowing rivers as they get filled with water and concretisation makes it difficult to absorb water, considering that the drainage system has reached their capacity.

Thus, Urban floods occur due to faster flow of water on paved surfaces, improper drainage facilities, lack of maintenance of drainage systems, unauthorized construction, improper waste management system, precipitation, climate change and the resultant melting of snow.

These factors have continued to damage the urban infrastructure which are the centres of economic growth, leading to immense economic losses apart from the suffering and misery that it brings. Fig. 2.15 shows an example of urban flooding in Mumbai which took place in 2006.

Fig. 2.15: Urban Flood, Mumbai in 2006

Source: Disaster Management in India, MHA, 2011

2.3.2.2 Causes of Flood

Floods can happen for a variety of reasons some of these are mentioned below:

- Physical factors
- Meteorological factors
- Anthropogenic factors

Physical Factors

The Physical factors include:

- **Overwhelmed catchment area:** Catchment area is an area where the rainwater gets collected (forming a river, reservoir or a lake). When this area gets excess water, the water flows out and floods the nearby areas, usually during the monsoons.
- **Improper maintenance of the Drainage system:** Irregular and unplanned maintenance of the drainage system can lead to congestion and clogging in the drainage due to waste, thus generating floods.

Meteorological Factors

The Meteorological Factors include:

- Heavy rains: Heavy precipitation is one of the primary cause of flooding in India. The rainfall of about 15 cm or more in a day usually exceeds the capacity of the river to carry this much water leading to flood. In India, this can be commonly seen in Assam, Sub Himalayan West Bengal and Western ghats.
- Change in the River course: The meandering nature of rivers usually leads to a change in the path of the river over a period of time. Additionally, Natural calamities such as earthquakes, landslides also lead to the change in the river course. This disturbs the habitat of humans as well as other species as the river floods their areas.
- Sediment Deposition: when river beds experience sedimentation, they usually become shallow. This reduces their water carrying capacity usually resulting in overflow of water.

- Cloud Burst: When thunderstorms cause heavy rainfall in a very short span of time, water may exceed the carrying capacity of the rivers. This spills the water to nearby areas sometimes causing extensive damage and destruction.
- Climate Change: A rise in the global temperature causes the glacial ice to melt.

Anthropogenic factors

Floods may also take place due to human activities, some of which are mentioned below: -

- Unplanned Urbanization: Unplanned and haphazard construction leads to obstruction in the flow of rivers and clogging of the drainage systems. This produces floods.
- Obstruction in River Paths: The construction of railway lines, embankments, roads in the path of river flows creates obstructions thereby generating floods.
- Population expansion: the rapid rise in the population of urban regions causes faulty land use practices. This increases the surface runoff causing the water to flow in large proportions flooding the nearby regions.
- Failure of Dams: Dams are usually built to contain water that can be used by the people for their needs. However, it is natural for any such structure to worn out or collapse. Moreover, if there is heavy precipitation, the government may need to open the dam gates, thereby generating destructive floods.
- Deforestation: Trees act as a natural buffer for the water to get absorbed and prevent surface runoff. Felling of trees results in more water runoff towards rivers, generating floods.
- Improper Solid waste management: Improper practices of solid waste management can block the drains reversing the flow of water and collecting in concentrated areas. This leads to flooding in the nearby areas.

2.3.2.3 Categorization of Flood Situations

For monitoring the flood situation in the country, the Central Water Commission (CWC) has categorized the flood situation as under:

- Normal Flood
- Above Normal Flood
- Severe Flood
- Extreme Flood

Normal Flood: When the water level of the river (L) is below the Warning level (WL), then the flood situation is categorized as a "NORMAL FLOOD" situation i.e., L < WL.

Above Normal Flood: When the water level of the river (L) reaches or crosses its Warning level (WL), but is lower than the Danger Level (DL), then it is categorized as "ABOVE NORMAL" situation i.e., DL > L > WL. It is indicated by the color yellow.

Severe Flood: When the water level of the river (L) reaches or crosses its danger level (DL), but is lower than the Highest Flood Level (HFL), then it is categorized as "SEVERE FLOOD" situation i.e., FL > L > DL. It is indicated by the color Orange.

Extreme Flood: When the water level of the river (L) reaches or crosses the "HIGHEST FLOOD LEVEL" (HFL) recorded at any forecasting site so far, then it is categorized as an "EXTREME FLOOD" situation i.e., L > HFL. It is indicated by the color Red. The Flood categorization is shown in the Fig. 2.16.

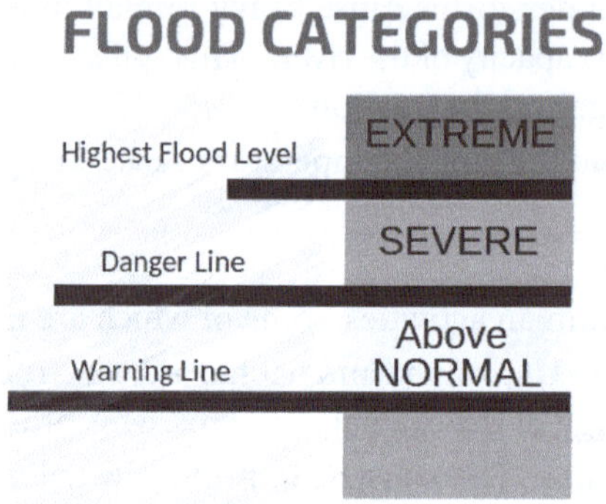

Fig. 2.16: Flood Categories

Source: https://cwc.gov.in/ffm_dashboard

2.3.3 Droughts

Due to its varying characteristics, drought is generally characterized in terms of its duration, spatial extent and intensity. Drought is an insidious hazard which is primarily caused due to either deficiency or absence of precipitation/rainfall from the expected, multi-year average for a region for an extended period of time/season. This usually leads to an insufficient supply of water for human, animal or plant activities.

According to IMD, "the country is said to be drought affected when the overall rainfall deficiency is more than 10 percent of the long period average (LPA) and more than 20 percent of the country area is affected by such drought conditions". A photograph of Drought is shown in Fig. 2.17.

Fig. 2.17: Photograph of Drought

Source: Disaster Management in India, MHA, 2011

Droughts are unique and differ from other natural hazards as given below:

- No universal definition exists.
- It is difficult to distinguish between the beginning and end of its occurrence due to its slow onset nature.
- Its duration may change from months to years.

- Its core area may change over a period of time.
- Multiple indicators are required to determine its onset and severity.
- It extends over a large geographical area which makes it difficult to analyze and respond efficiently.
- Its impacts are difficult to quantify.
- Its effects magnify if they continue from one season/year to another.

2.3.3.1 Classification of drought

As per the National Commission on Agriculture, droughts are classified mainly into three categories as: -

- Hydrological drought
- Meteorological Drought
- Agricultural drought

Hydrological drought

Hydrological Drought is defined as the shortfall of the precipitation levels on the surface and subsurface water supplies such as groundwater, lake, reservoir, or streamflow levels. Although precipitation levels are generally low, it may also be due to increased water usage. Thus, it takes longer for the hydrological system to show the water deficiency in its components such as groundwater levels, soil moisture, streamflow because it is not replenished.

Meteorological Drought

It is defined as the condition in which the precipitation is deficient from the normal levels. It occurs when the precipitation is less than 25% in an area of its long-term average value. Furthermore, it is said to be at moderate level if the rainfall deficiency is 26-50% and at severe level if the rainfall deficiency exceeds 50% of its normal value.

Agricultural drought

Agricultural Drought can be described as a condition in which rainfall and soil moisture are inadequate to support growth and health of crops. The demand of water for plants may depend upon the temperature, prevailing weather conditions, plant's growth stage, its characteristics, and properties. Thus, it depends upon the susceptibility of crops.

2.3.3.2 Drought Situations

According to IMD, following drought situations are recognized: -

- Drought Week: it occurs if the weekly rainfall level is less than 50% of the normal level.
- Agricultural Drought: It occurs if four drought weeks take place continuously during mid-June to month of September.
- Seasonal Drought: It occurs if the seasonal rainfall is deficient by more than the standard deviation.
- Drought Year: It occurs if the annual rainfall level is less than 20% of the normal level.
- Severe Drought Year: It occurs if the annual rainfall level is less than 25-50% of the normal level or even more.

2.3.4 Cyclones

Cyclones are observed to be one of the most destructive natural hazards in context of their frequency of occurrence, areas of destruction and severity. The word cyclone originates from the Greek word 'cyclos' which means 'coiling of a snake'.

Tropical cyclones are like massive engines that use moist air, warm ocean waters as fuel. This is the reason they form near the equator as the equator receives sun rays directly which increases the heat received, unlike the polar regions which receive the slanting sun rays. As a result, the air near the equator becomes warm and rises upward from the surface. However, the warm air near the surface decreases because of the rise, causing a low air pressure area below (which is a gap). This causes the higher air pressure to move from the surrounding areas towards the low-pressure zone, because the air always moves from high pressure to low pressure. Thereafter the process continues, where the new air becomes warm and rises. As the air gets warm, it continues to rise making a swirl and cool off making a cloud, the whole system of wind spins and clouds grow making it huge.

Tropical cyclones are generally known as "cyclones" used globally, that originate in the tropical region over the ocean. It is an intense vortex or a whirl with a swiftly rotating storm system in which wind speeds exceed or are equal to a minimum of 34 knots (62 kmph). A picture of a tropical cyclone is shown in Fig.2.18

Fig. 2.18: Picture of a tropical cyclone

Source: https://rsmcnewdelhi.imd.gov.in/uploads/report/61/61_af65e6_sop.pdf

Following are the favourable conditions for the formation of cyclones:

- A warm sea surface temperature which is higher than 26°C- 27 °C and having a depth of minimum 60 mts.
- A high relative humidity in the atmosphere i.e., degree at which the air gets saturated by water vapor, up to the height of about 5000 mts.
- Instability in the vertical wind speed of the atmosphere which supports/aids the formation of huge vertical cumulus clouds.
- Existence of vorticity i.e., the rate at which the air rotates, that enables the rotation of air cyclonically.
- Presence of Coriolis force.

Due to the effect of the earth's rotation i.e. Coriolis force, these winds circulate in clockwise and anti-clockwise direction. In the Northern Hemisphere winds circulate in clockwise direction which is known as cyclonic flow whereas in the Southern Hemisphere it circulates in anti-clockwise direction which is known as anticyclonic flow.

They develop within the belt of the tropic of cancer and tropic Capricorn. The cyclogenesis takes place over the warm sea water away from the equator. Cyclones do not form at or near the equator due to the absence of Coriolis force. Coriolis force increases with the latitude. At 5° latitude, Coriolis force is significant enough to create a storm. Hence, most of the tropical cyclones develop between 5° to 30° north and south as shown in Fig.2.19.

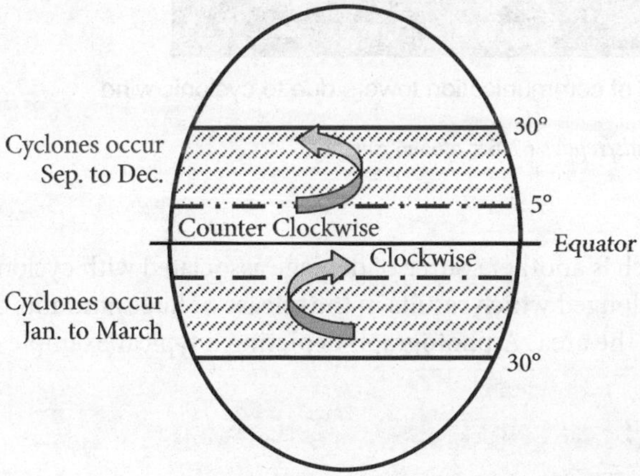

Cyclone

Fig. 2.19: Formation of Cyclones

Source: https://www.iitk.ac.in/nicee/IITK-GSDMA/W03.pdf

People call these tropical storms by various names in different regions, such as hurricanes, typhoons, cyclones, willy-willies. However, all tropical cyclones form in a similar way. Cyclones are known by hurricanes in the Atlantic Ocean, typhoons in the pacific, and willy-willies in the Australia seas, and Tropical cyclones in the north and south Indian Ocean.

2.3.4.1 Hazards due to Cyclone

Following are the hazards which are associated with a cyclone that leads to damage to property and loss of life.

- Strong Winds
- Heavy rainfall
- Storm surge

Strong winds

It can cause extensive damage to the structures including houses and other infrastructures like power and communication towers, bridges, dams, culverts, roads, etc., due to high wind speed. The damages thus caused cover a larger area as compared to heavy rains and storm surges. A typical example of damage to the communication tower due to cyclonic wind is shown in Fig.2.20.

Fig. 2.20: Damage of communication towers due to cyclonic wind

Source: https://rsmcnewdelhi.imd.gov.in/uploads/report/61/61_af65e6_sop.pdf)

Heavy rainfall

Heavy Rainfall can cause flooding which is another source of damage associated with cyclones. Cyclonic rainfall is generally very heavy and prolonged which results in the release of huge amounts of water over a larger area. This leads to flooding in the area. A photograph depicting a typical example of flood due to cyclone is shown in Fig. 2.21.

Fig. 2.21: Flood caused due to Cyclones

Source: https://rsmcnewdelhi.imd.gov.in/uploads/report/61/61_af65e6_sop.pdf

Storm Surge

It is defined as an enormous rise of sea water caused by a storm. The storm surge develops through the interaction of air, sea and land. As the cyclone reaches near the coast, a very high horizontal atmospheric pressure gradient develops due to additional force provided by it. This leads to strong surface wind causing rise in the sea level. Storm surge thus increases with the decrease in depth of sea water. Storm surge leads to sudden inundation of low-lying areas which causes flooding in the coastal regions. This leads to damage of property and loss of life. Moreover, it also results in erosion of beaches and embankments thereby reducing the soil fertility. A typical example of damage due to storm surge is shown in Fig.2.22.

Fig. 2.22: Impact of storm surge caused by Cyclones

Source: https://rsmcnewdelhi.imd.gov.in/uploads/report/61/61_af65e6_sop.pdf

2.3.4.2 *Structure of a cyclone*

A tropical cyclone is a large storm which has a funnel-shape. It has a wide top which can reach up to 1000 km in diameter and narrow bottom ranging from 300 to 500 km in diameter. The height of the storm is usually 10 to 15 km. The diameter of a cyclone encompassing the region of relatively strong wind in order of 500 km. Following are the three major different parts of a fully developed tropical storm as shown in Fig.2.23.

- Eye
- Eye wall
- Spiral rain bands

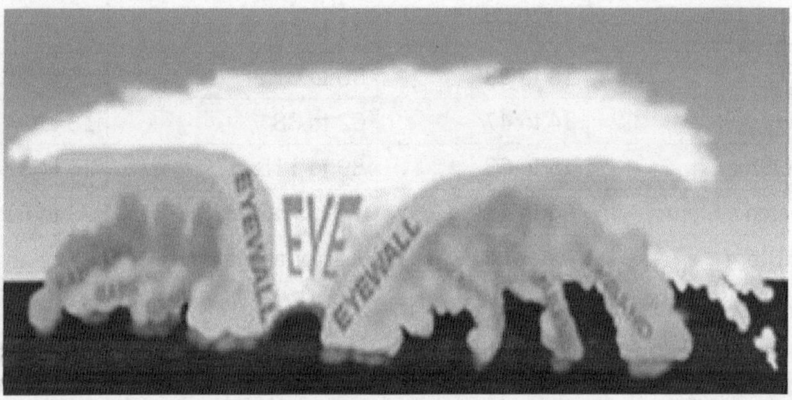

Fig. 2.23: Different part of a cyclone

Source:https://mausam.imd.gov.in/imd_latest/contents/faq.php#

The centre part of a cyclone is known as its eye. The average radius of the eye usually ranges from about 20 to 30 km. The pressure in the eye is the lowest while the temperature is highest. A ring of extremely strong winds surrounds the eye which extends from 30 to 50 km beyond the centre. This area is known as the eye wall. Deep convection and often the most powerful winds can be found in the eyewall. Outer part of a cyclone is known as rain bands. These bands may be hundreds of kilometres long and a few kilometres wide. The general structure of cyclones is shown in Fig. 2.24.

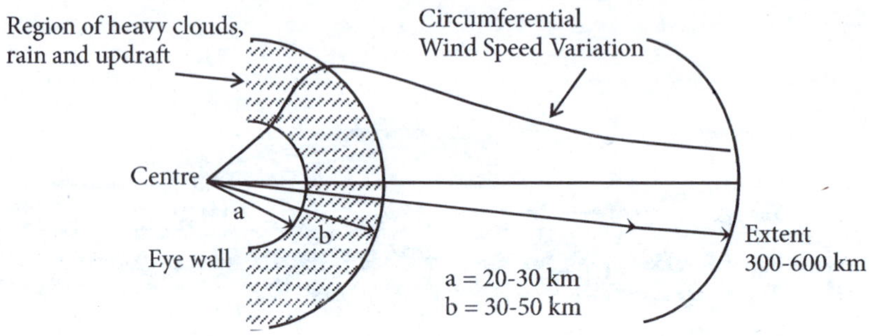

Fig. 2.24: General Structure of a cyclone

Source: https://www.iitk.ac.in/nicee/IITK-GSDMA/W03.pdf

2.3.4.3 Classification of Cyclones

As per IMD, these low-pressure systems have been classified in the Bay of Bengal and in the Arabian Sea on the basis of wind speeds during their circulation. However, the classification is based on the World Meteorological (WMO)'s classification on the basis of maximum sustained winds associated at the surface level. Indian Classification of Cyclone Disturbances is given in Table 2.3.

Table 2.3: Indian Classification of Cyclonic disturbances

Type	Associated Maximum sustained wind		
	in Knots	in Km/h	in m/s
Low pressure area	Less than 17	Less than 31	Less than 9
Depression	17 to 27	31 to 49	9 to 14
Deep Depression	28 to 33	50 to 61	15 to 17
Cyclonic Storm	34 to 47	62 to 88	18 to 24
Severe Cyclonic Storm	48 to 63	89 to 118	25 to 32
Very Severe Cyclonic Storm	64 to 119	119 to 121	33 to 61
Super Cyclonic Storm	120 or above	222 or above	62 or above

Note: one knot = 1.852 kmph=0.t5144 m/s ƒSource: IMD, 2013

However, categorization of cyclones differs from region to region. In the United States, Hurricanes are categorized on the basis of their wind speeds into five different categories represented on the Saffir–Simpson Hurricane Wind Scale (SS Scale). The classification is shown in Table 2.4.

Table 2.4: Saffir-Simpson Hurricane Scale

Category	Wind Speed			Damage
	In m/h	In Knot	In Km/h	
1	74 to 95	64 to 82	118 to 152	Minimal
2	96 to 110	83 to 95	153-176	Moderate

3	111 to 130	96 to 113	177-208	Extensive
4	131 to 155	114 to 135	209 to 250	Extreme
5	156 or above	135 or above	250 or above	Catastrophic

Source: NWS, NOAA

The expected damage caused by tropical cyclones in the coastal region of India with the cyclonic disturbances of different intensities is shown in Table 2.5. This Table also shows the suggested action according to the intensities of cyclones. This information is derived from Standard Operation Manual of Cyclone Warning in India published by, IMD, Delhi in 2013.

Table 2.5: Storm Intensity, associated damage and suggested actions

Categories	Storm Intensity in Knots	Damage expected	Action Suggested
Deep Depression	28-33	Minor damage to loose and unsecured structures	Fishermen advised not to venture into the open seas.
Cyclonic Storm	34-47	Damage to thatched huts. Breaking of tree branches causing minor damage to power and communication lines	Total suspension of fishing operations
Severe Cyclonic Storm	48-63	Extensive damage to thatched roofs and huts. Minor damage to power and communication lines due to uprooting of large avenue trees. Flooding of escape routes.	Total suspension of fishing operations. Coastal hutment dwellers to be moved to safer places. People in affected areas to remain indoors.
Very Severe Cyclonic Storm	64-90	Extensive damage to kutcha houses. Partial disruption of power and communication line. Minor disruption of rail and road traffic. Potential threat from flying debris. Flooding of escape routes.	Total suspension of fishing operations. Mobilize evacuation from coastal areas. Judicious regulation of rail and road traffic. People in affected areas to remain indoors.
Very Severe Cyclonic Storm	91-119	Extensive damage to kutcha houses. Some damage to old buildings. Large-scale disruption of power and communication lines. Disruption of rail and road traffic due to extensive flooding. Potential threat from flying debris.	Total suspension of fishing operations. Extensive evacuation from coastal areas. Diversion or suspension of rail and road traffic. People in affected areas to remain indoors.

Categories	Storm Intensity in Knots	Damage expected	Action Suggested
Super Cyclone	120 knots or more	Extensive structural damage to residential and industrial buildings. Total disruption of communication and power supply. Extensive damage to bridges causing large- scale disruption of rail and road traffic. Large- scale flooding and inundation of sea water.	Total suspension of fishing operations. Large-scale evacuation of coastal population. Total suspension of rail and road traffic in vulnerable areas. People in affected areas to remain indoors.

Source: IMD, 2013

2.3.5 Volcanoes

A volcano refers to an opening on the Earth's surface which allows warmer material to escape from its interior. During the escape, an eruption occurs which contains materials such as liquid rocks, cinders, ash or gasses. The eruption is of various types ranging from explosive which sends material against the gravity to calm which sends material gently like flows. The eruption results in the formation of mountains that are built from many layers of rocks, ash or other material that collect around them. Volcanic eruptions can be threatening for life around its vicinity and even dangerous for aircrafts. A photograph of a volcanic eruption is shown in Fig. 2.25.

Fig. 2.25: Volcanic Eruption

Source: https://nidm.gov.in/PDF/Disaster_geo.pdf

2.3.5.1 Causes of Volcano formation

The earth is so hot from inside, that it can cause rocks to melt (molten rocks) and flow as magma. This magma is less dense or lighter than the solid rock around it collects in magma chambers. This magma erupts as lava. The Magma is made of molten rocks, dissolved gasses and crystals. Molten rocks are made of manganese, titanium, potassium, silicon, aluminium, iron, calcium, oxygen.

There are various types of mountains that develop by the process of erosion, uplift, folding, faulting etc., of the earth's crust. The magma which becomes lava emerges from deep beneath the ground. The vent can be of a small bowl-shaped depression or shield shaped mountain. There are a series of cracks which lie beneath or within the volcano; this vent connects to one or more of the magma chambers and continuously supplies fresh magma. This way, it keeps on becoming larger and larger until it becomes stable.

Magma can rise to cause eruptions due to the following reasons: -

- When tectonic plates move apart from each other. The magma rises up to fill the space. This leads to underwater volcanoes.
- When tectonic plates move towards each other. The crust of the earth can move deep inside which can melt due to high heat and cause magma to rise.
- When hot spots inside the earth heat up the magma, it can make magma to become less dense and thus cause it to rise.

2.3.5.2 Types of Volcanoes

There are mainly three types of volcanoes: -

- Shield Volcano- These comprise of very hot magma which makes them gentle to flow over great distances. After which it cools down. They have a broad flattened dome shape. The temperature of these range between 800°C to 1200°C
- Composite Volcano- These are also known as strato-volcano. These have slightly cooler magma which makes them viscous, thick and sticky. This leads to faster cooling, making it difficult for gasses to escape. This results in pressure build up leading to violent explosions and formation of steep sided cones. The temperature of these ranges between 800°C-1000°C.
- Caldera Volcano- These are the coolest and thus very viscous. These are so violent that they fall upon themselves emptying the magma chamber. This results in a basin-shaped depression. These have a temperature of 650°C-800°C.
- Cinder Cone- They are the most common type of volcanoes. Cinders are small pieces of solid lava that erupt from vents. These are formed when the lava is gas-charged and is blown into the air with great force. This breaks it into small fragments, which then solidifies.

2.3.5.3 Classification of Volcanoes

The volcanoes can be classified into different stages depending upon their frequency of eruption. These are classified into three categories: -

- Active Volcanoes- Volcanoes are classified as active if at a particular time they might erupt or erupt regularly or they are already erupting.
- Dormant volcanoes-Volcanoes are referred to as dormant when they have been quiet for a long time and are not likely to erupt in near future. These are also known as inactive volcanoes.
- Extinct volcanoes- Volcanoes which did not erupt since ages and might never erupt again.

Barren Island Volcano in India located in Andaman Sea in the union territory of the Andaman and Nicobar Islands is the only active volcano extending between Sumatra and Myanmar. However, this was dormant for 150 years until it recurred in 1991. The emissions include thermal anomalies and ash emissions.

2.3.6 Tsunami

The term Tsunami originates from the two Japanese words 'tsu' means 'harbor' and 'nami' means 'waves'. These are also known as seismic waves.

A Tsunami is a series of ocean waves having extremely long wavelengths, generated by sudden displacement in the sea floor, caused due to earthquakes, landslides, or volcanic activity. These waves have high energy and high magnitude. These waves move with very high speeds but with low crests. However, they move silently but assume a devastating shape as they approach the shallow coastal waters. They, thus cause widespread destruction along the gentle slope and low height of coastlines. This is the reason they are also known as killer waves.

Generally, most of the tsunamis generate from shallow and large earthquakes usually along the fault lines/plate boundaries. Due to such an earthquake in the ocean, the seafloor may get deformed. This leads to the sudden vertical displacement of a large volume of water or disturbance in the sea/ocean. This transfers energy to the water at a rate faster than the water can absorb, generating Tsunami waves.

In case the movement of the seafloor is horizontal, no tsunami is generated. Critical value of an earthquake is a magnitude of more than 6.5 for Tsunami generation. Tsunami's can also be triggered due to landslides into or under the water surface. It can be generated due to meteorite impacts, volcanic activity.

Many times, people get confused between Tsunami waves and Tidal waves. However, both are very different. While the Tsunami waves are almost always caused due to earthquakes under water, the Tidal waves are caused due to the ocean tides. Wave Train of Tsunami shown in Fig. 2.26.

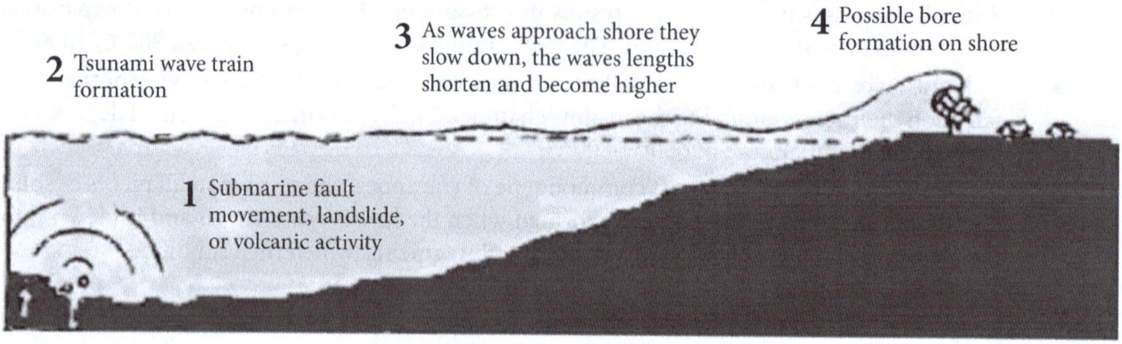

Fig. 2.26: Wave train of Tsunami

Source: International Tsunami Information Centre – Geologic Hazard

2.3.6.1 Tsunami Velocity

The velocity of a Tsunami depends on the depth of water from which it passes. It is equal to the square root of water depth (h)times the gravitational acceleration (g), i.e., $V = \sqrt{gh}$. The speed of Tsunami slows down in shallow water whereas wave height increases rapidly as shown in Fig. 2.27.

It is seen from the figure that the Tsunami travels at a velocity of 700 kmph(approx.) in 4000 m depth of sea water whereas the tsunami travels at velocity of 40 kmph at 10 m of water depth. Even on the shore, a tsunami can assume a speed of approx. 35-40 kmph which is much faster than the speed at which a person can run.

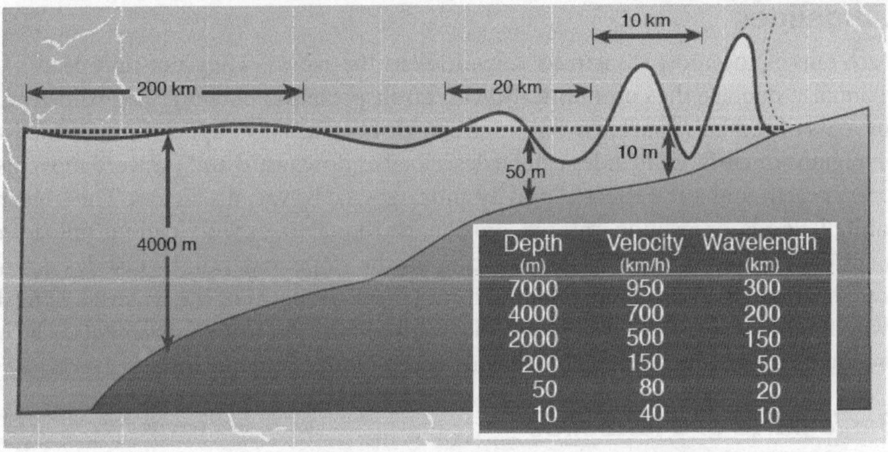

Fig. 2.27: Tsunami Velocities

Source: http://itic.iocunesco.org/images/stories/awareness_and_education/great_waves/great_waves_en_low_v14.pdf

As the Tsunami waves hit the coastline, the energy of the waves gets compressed into a much shallower depth and shorter distance thus becoming life threatening killer waves.

2.3.6.2 Size of Tsunami

Size of Tsunamis varies from a few centimetre's to over 30 m. However, most of the Tsunamis have a height of less than 3m. The tsunamis are rarely over 1m in height in deep water (greater than 200 m) and will not be noticed by ships because of their long period (time period between two crests). The wave height can increase by over ten times when it propagates into shallow waters. Thus, the height of the Tsunami varies greatly along the coast. It can flood land up to 1.5 km from the coast. Some Tsunami's can assume an enormous force.

2.3.6.3 Causes of Tsunami

Tsunamis are caused due to three major reasons.

- Earthquake
- Landslide
- Volcano

Earthquake: This is the most common reason for the occurrence of Tsunami. It causes fault movements on the seafloor which releases huge amounts of energy. This has the capacity to cross oceans and cause widespread destruction. However, all earthquakes may not cause Tsunamis as only those earthquakes which occur on the floor of the ocean can cause Tsunami.

Landslide: Landslides are the second most important reason responsible for causing Tsunami. When a landslide originates above the sea or occurs under the ocean, it disturbs the water thus causing a Tsunami to occur.

Volcano: Volcanoes are the third major cause of Tsunami. Volcanoes are violent and can cause impulsive disturbances. This happens when a volcano occurs underwater, it displaces great volumes of water, resulting in the formation of Tsunami.

2.3.7 Landslides

Landslides are one of the most disastrous calamities in the world. They not only lead to death and destruction but also damage the communication and transportation network. Landslides occur when a large rock or mass of soil falls apart at a very high speed. They usually happen in steepened slopes such as mountain regions or cliffs. Landslides can be described as downward and outward movement of mass of rock, debris or earth under the effect of gravity and triggered by various factors. The triggering factors are heavy rainfall, floods, excavation, mining, erosion, earthquakes, or with loading/unloading of slopes etc. Movement depends on balance of forces acting on the slope material. Landslides occur when the driving force (shear stress) exceeds the resisting force (shear strength) of the material. Landslides occur in areas having fragile slopes. The term 'Landslides' is used for most slope movements. The other terms mass movement, mass wasting, slope failure are also used in place of landslides.

2.3.7.1 Basic parts of a landslide

Landslides have several features that can be commonly seen among various types of mass wasting. It is not necessary that every mass movement/landslide has the same parts/ features. Fig.2.28 shows the most common parts/features of landslides.

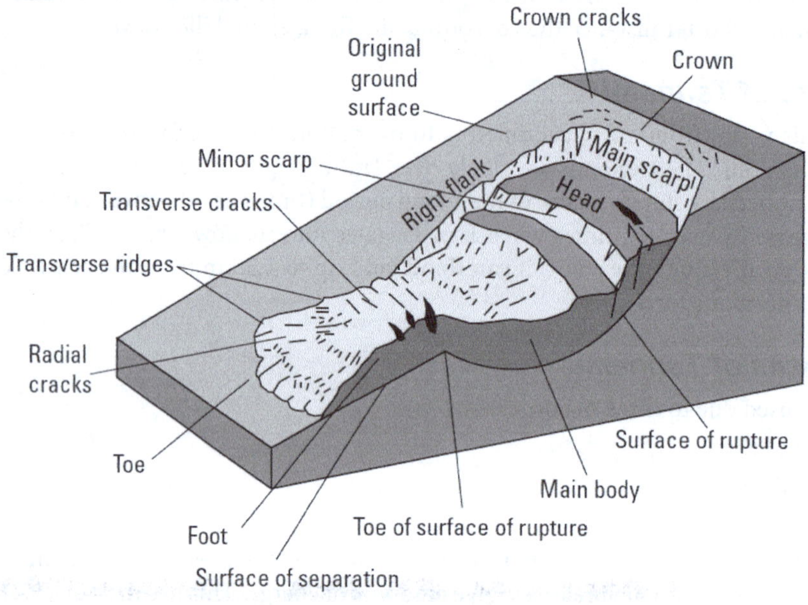

Fig. 2.28: Basic parts of a Landslide

Source: http://pubs.usgs.gov/circ/1325/pdf/C1325_508.pdf

The basic parts / features of a landslide are described given below:

- **Crown**: The undisturbed material which lies above the top of the main scarp is known as crown.
- **Main scarp:** It is a steep surface on the undisturbed ground lying just above the head. This is the visible part of the slide surface.
- **Flank:** The undisplaced materials adjoining the sides of the landslide are termed as flank. Flanks are generally described as left and right.

- **Head:** The upper portion of the landslide material which has contact between the displaced material and the main scarp is termed as head.
- **Toe:** The lower end of the slide, which is at the maximum distance from the main scarp is termed as the toe of a landslide.
- **Foot:** The portion of the landslide that overlies the original ground surface (i.e. right below the surface of rupture) is known as a Foot of the landslide.
- **Original ground surface:** The surface of the slope that existed before the landslide took place is termed as the original ground surface.
- **Surface of rupture:** The surface which forms (or has formed) the lower boundary of the displaced material below the original ground surface is known as surface of rupture.

2.3.7.2 Classification of Landslide

Landslides can be classified on the basis of failure process and materials involved, as under: -

- Falls
- Slide
- Topples
- Spread Flow
- Creep
- Complex

Land Slide

Falls

A Landslide is classified as "fall" if rock/earth gets detached from a steep slope or cliffs and move down rapidly. The material subsequently drops mainly through the air by processes like free falling, bouncing, or rolling. This collects the fall, rock or debris near the base of a slope. A typical sketch of failure in fall and example of a rock fall are shown in Figs. 2.29-2.30. respectively.

Fig. 2.29: Failure in Fall

Fig. 2.30: Example of Failure in Fall

Source: https://nidm.gov.in/PDF/pubs/LandslidesModule_2020.pdf

Slides

A "slide" refers to downslope movement of material i.e., rock/earth mass that occurs along a shear surface. These are further classified into two categories:

- Rotational slide
- Translational/ /planar slides

Rotational slide: Slide is referred to as rotational if the slip surface is curved upwards, i.e., spoon-shaped. A typical sketch of rotational landslide and example of a rotational landslide are shown in Figs. 2.31-2.32 respectively.

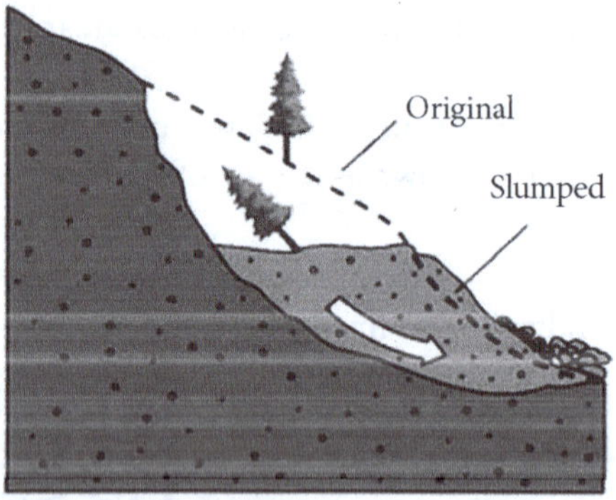

Fig. 2.31: Rotational Landslide

Source: https://nidm.gov.in/PDF/pubs/Landslide_Preparedness_Guide_.pdf)

Fig. 2.32: Example of Rotational Landslide

Source: https://nidm.gov.in/PDF/pubs/LandslidesModule_2020.pdf

Translational/ Planer slide: A slide is said to be Translation when the material, i.e., rock/earth mass slides down along a relatively planar surface of weakness. A typical sketch of planer landslide and example of a planer landslide are shown in Figs. 2.33-2.34 respectively.

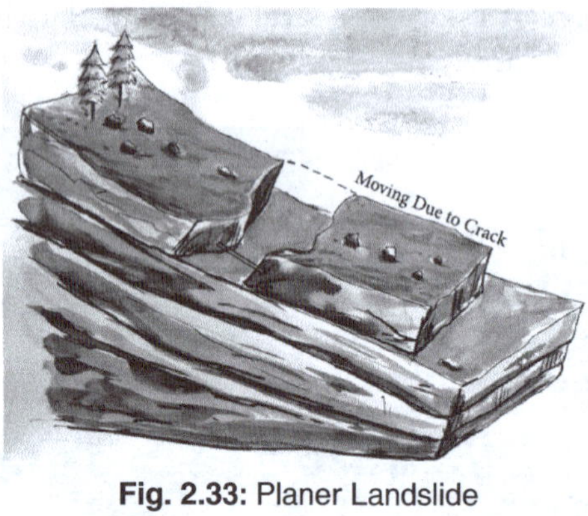

Fig. 2.33: Planer Landslide

Fig. 2.34: Example of planer rockslide

Source: https://nidm.gov.in/PDF/pubs/LandslidesModule_2020.pdf

Topples

"Topple failure" is the forward spinning and movement of the material about a point or axis. The movement can be extremely slow or extremely rapid. A typical sketch of toppling failure of rock and example of a toppling failure of rock are shown in Figs. 2.35-2.36 respectively.

Fig. 2.35: Toppling of rocks

Fig. 2.36: Example of Toppling failure in rocks

Source: https://nidm.gov.in/PDF/pubs/LandslidesModule_2020.pdf

Spreads

Spreads may occur due to flow of the softer underlying material. Spreads may be further subdivided into three types of spreads which includes Block spreads, Liquefaction spreads and Lateral spreads. When such rocks which are cohesive spreads laterally over a deforming mass of softer underlying material due to shear or tensile failure, it is referred to as Lateral spreads as shown in Fig.2.37. An example of lateral spreading is shown in Fig. 2.38.

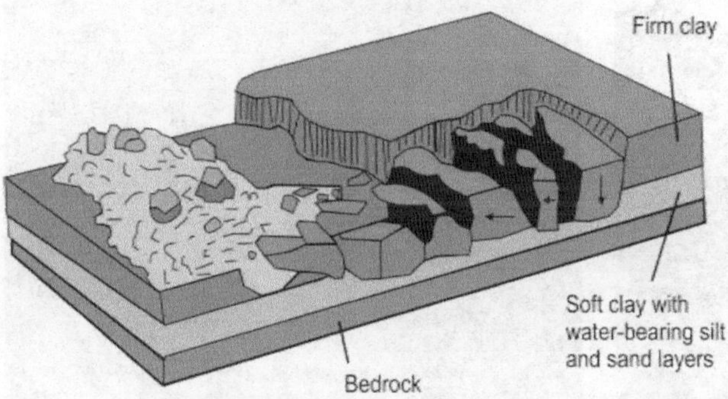

Fig. 2.37: Lateral Spreading

Source: https://nidm.gov.in/PDF/pubs/LandslidesModule_2020.pdf

Fig. 2.38: Example of lateral spreading

Source: https://nidm.gov.in/PDF/pubs/LandslidesModule_2020.pdf

Flow

"Flow" refers to a spatially continuous movement in which the individual particles which are closely spaced travel separately within a moving mass. This is a general term which may include many types of mass movements such as debris flow, lahar, debris avalanche, earthflow or mudflow. A typical sketch of flow failure and example of a flow failure are shown in Figs. 2.39-2.40 respectively.

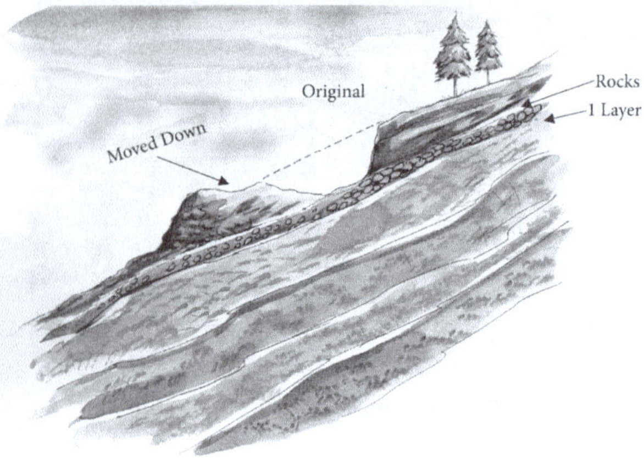

Fig. 2.39: Flow

Fig. 2.40: Example of Flow

Source: https://nidm.gov.in/PDF/pubs/LandslidesModule_2020.pdf

Creep

"Creep" is extremely slow, steady downslope movements of rock or soil, usually a few millimeters per year. It can be indicated by curved tree trunks, tilted poles or fence and tilted retaining wall. A typical sketch of creep and example of creep are depicted in Figs. 2.41-2.42 respectively.

Fig. 2.41: Creep

Source: https://nidm.gov.in/PDF/pubs/LandslidesModule_2020.pdf

Fig. 2.42: Example of Creep

Source: https://nidm.gov.in/PDF/pubs/LandslidesModule_2020.pdf

Complex Landslides

Complex landslides are said to be complex when a combination of one or more mechanisms of landslides as discussed above are involved. In such a type of landslide, the failure process is not consistent and changes with time. The example of a complex landslide is shown in Fig. 2.43.

Fig. 2.43: Complex Landslide

Source: https://nidm.gov.in/PDF/pubs/LandslidesModule_2020.pdf

2.3.7.3 Causes of Landslides

Landslides occur because of several reasons. Slope movements occur when gravity, which is the main driving force (shear stress), is greater than the resisting force, i.e., shear strength of the material. The main forces acting on the slope material are driving force and resisting force. The slope movement depends on these forces. Driving force i.e., shear stress tends to move the material downwards. Resisting force, i.e. shear strength resists the downward movement of slope material. Shear strength (Resisting force) is a function of normal stress, cohesion, and internal friction. Driving force, which is responsible for mass movements, depends on the weight of the material and slope angle. The sliding material rests on a plain surface with the angle of slope at 0° as shown in Fig.2.44. In this case, the gravity force (W) acts downwards. So, no mass movement will take place.

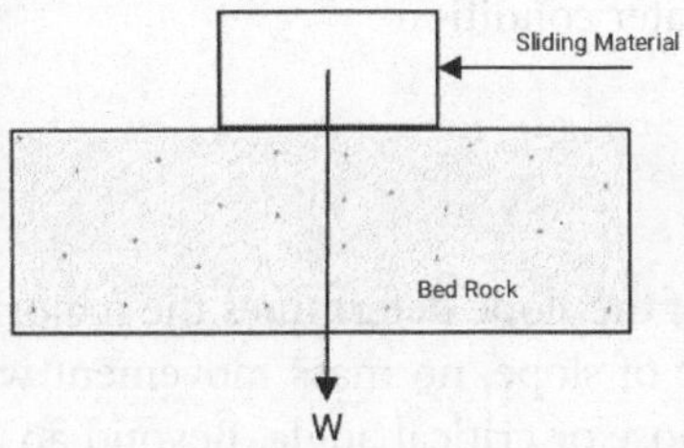

Fig. 2.44: Sliding material on Horizontal Bedrock

If the sliding material rests on the inclined bedrock as shown in Fig.2.45.

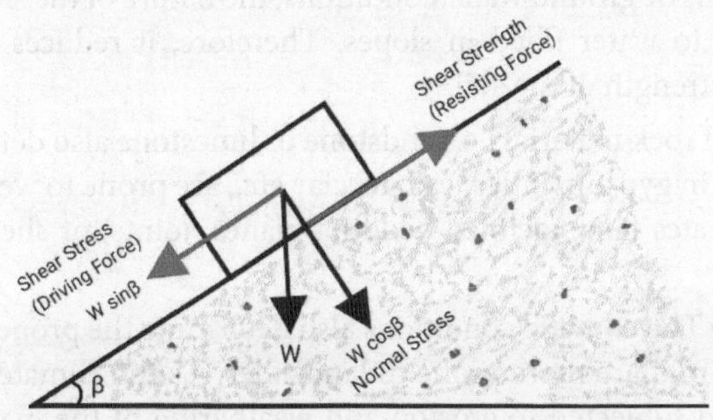

Fig. 2.45: Sliding material on inclined bedrock

In this case, force of gravity can be resolved into horizontal and perpendicular to the slope. Force perpendicular to slope (W cos β) is termed as normal stress. Whereas force tangential to the slope (W sin β) is termed as shear stress. It is also known as Driving Force. Shear strength (SH) of the slope material is calculated by using the Coulomb-Terzaghi equation given as

$$SH = C + \sigma (\tan\emptyset)$$

Where SH is the total shear strength, C is the cohesion and sigma σ is the normal stress and tan∅ is the coefficient of internal friction.

The normal stress depends on the slope of the bedrock. Normal stress decreases with the increase in slope. Therefore, the shear strength (SH) of the slope material decreases with the increase in slope. The factor of safety (FOS) is the ratio of shear strength to shear stress. If the FOS is greater than 1.3, then the slope is said to be stable.

When the shear strength is less than or equal to the shear stress, then no mass movement will take place. If the shear strength is greater the shear stress (driving force), then mass movement is likely to take place.

Landslides may be triggered due to internal or external causes such as earthquake, snow-melt, heavy rainfall, groundwater changes, earthquakes, volcanic activity, and human activities, or a combination of any of these causes.

However, gravity force is the primary factor responsible for causing landslides, regardless of the triggering factors.

2.3.7.3.1 Internal Causes

Internal and external factors affect the slope process. The internal factors are:

- Nature of slope
- Heavy rain or Ground water condition
- Lithology
- Climatic Conditions
- Types of Vegetation

Nature of slope: The nature of the slope determines the majority of mass movements. It has been observed that up to a certain angle of slope, no mass movement will take place in most of the cases. This angle is termed as angle of repose or critical angle. Beyond an angle, where the slope gets steeper, landslides may occur.

Heavy rain or Ground water condition: Heavy rains are the main important factor in causing landslides. Due to heavy rains or ground water conditions, the nature of the slope may change. Porewater pressure may develop due to water filled in slopes. Therefore, it reduces the normal stress thereby resulting in reduced shear strength of the soil.

Lithology: The type of rock material i.e. sandstone or limestone also determines the strength of the slope. Rocks which are rich in gypsum, mica, calcite, clay etc., are prone to weathering. This makes them weak and unstable as it creates falls, inclined bedding planes, joints, or shear zones and thus become prone to landslides.

Climatic Conditions: The climatic conditions also determine the proneness to landslides. Regions which are sub humid or humid are more prone to landslides. As the climate changes the mountainous areas are more exposed and subjected to erosion and weathering of the material on the slope. This is expected to trigger more landslides.

Types of Vegetation: The type of vegetation also determines the stability of the slope. Vegetation helps to hold the material of the soil which increases the shear strength (SS) of the soil. It helps in retaining the soil cover firmly. The long roots increase the cohesiveness and thereby the strength of the soil. However, if the vegetation cover is not present the occurrence of rainfall may initiate a set of process like sheet erosion, rain splash erosion, and gully erosion, which ultimately results in failure of the slope to withstand. The vegetation cover protects the slope from direct impact of rainfall.

2.3.7.3.2 External Causes

External factors are the factors that do not directly cause landslides but are a triggering factor for the landslides to occur. This can be in the form of human influence, for example undercutting along the hill slopes, removal of trees, removal of the support at the foot of the slope, laying railway tracks, etc. Moreover, other factors such as vibrations which are manifested by earthquakes, blasting to explosives, volcanic eruptions can also lead to landslides.

2.3.8 Coastal erosion

The Coasts, like other landforms, are dynamic and are constantly modified by erosion and deposition. However, coastal erosion has become a matter of great concern. This is because it causes damage to vulnerable properties, and structures. Additionally, it also causes considerable loss of land.

Coastal erosion refers to the process in which coastal land gets eroded by wind, water and waves. This leads to the removal of sediments and causes the shoreline to retreat landwards. This happens through strong wave action, sea level rise or wear down of the coast due to flooding or carry away of sand, rocks or soils. The coastlines have always faced natural events, especially storms. However, when storm surges at high tides along with strong waves, particularly during tropical storms, it can be extremely dangerous. Figs. 2.46-2.47 show typical sand dune erosion and cliff erosions respectively.

Fig. 2.46: Sand dune erosion

Source:https://cwc.gov.in/sites/default/files/guidelines-%e2%80%9cprotection-and-control-coastal-erosion-india%e2%80%9d.pdf

Fig. 2.47: Cliff erosion

Source: (https://cwc.gov.in/sites/default/files/guidelines-%e2%80%9cprotection-and-control-coastal-erosion-india%e2%80%9d.pdf)

2.3.8.1 Causes of coastal erosion

The coastal erosion can be caused due to:

- Natural causes
- Man-made causes
- Combination of both

Natural causes

- **Environmental change:** The erosion is caused due to wave activity which depends on the wind. The wave activities increase due to cyclones and severe monsoon. If a Tsunami occurs, it can lead to accelerated coastal erosion.
- **Sea Level Change:** Due to global warming, sea levels are rising and the low-lying areas are getting inundated. Therefore, the land surfaces get exposed to the wave action, resulting in coastal erosion. It has also been observed that sea level rise rate varies from 1 to 2 mm per year along the Indian Coast whereas Global mean sea level rise rate is 3.2 mm per year.
- **Loss of sediment supply:** The sand moves continuously due to the action of the wind, waves or currents. During this process, it loses sediment. This causes loss in the sediment supply to the downdrift, thus causing erosion.

Man-made causes

Following are the man-made causes of the coastal erosion.

- **Construction of new structures:** Coastal structures such as Groynes, breakwaters, seawalls, jetties changes the morphology of the coast. This intercepts the transportation of natural sediment.
- **Sand mining and dune removal: Sand** is removed for the construction purposes from the coast. This has a huge impact on the coastline. Removal of dunes which act as natural barriers to Storm surge and Tsunami exposes the coastline resulting in the shoreline erosion.
- **Removal of coastal vegetation:** The coastal vegetation (especially mangroves, grasses and salt marshes), reinforces the soil and protects the shore from instability, as it attracts deposition and settlement. The removal of these vegetation exposes the soil bed and causes mud shore instability.

2.3.9 Soil erosion

Soil erosion occurs when the top layer of the soil which is also a fertile layer gets lost. This layer being very light can easily get carried away by the actions of wind and water.

Soil are the unconsolidated and loose materials derived from breaking down of rocks and form the fundamental part of the biosphere which supports life. Erosion is the process of detachment and removal of loose rock materials which is the topsoil of the field by the actions of wind or water. When these forces work, the soil moves to another region which can be near or far. However, erosion caused by natural processes without being interrupted by human activities is part of the natural geological process of the earth. Soil erosion occurs when the new soil is unable to form at the rate it degrades. Thus, soil erosion is an extreme form of degradation of soil in which natural processes of degradation are accelerated.

Soil erosion reduces crop productivity and can fill drainage channels as well as pollute watercourses.

2.3.10 Tornadoes

Tornadoes are funnel-shaped storms which are narrow, violently rotating updrafts of air that extend from a thunderstorm to the surface of the earth. The funnel shape of the tornado is similar to the shape of hurricane except that a tornado is much more slender i.e.,. Smaller in horizontal dimensions. Tornadoes rarely occur in India. However, when they do occur, they are very devastating and cause extensive destruction and damage.

2.3.10.1 Formation of a Tornado

Tornadoes can be generated by severe thunderstorms and hurricanes, with the former being the most frequent cause. It has been observed that thunderstorms are generally associated with a surface based warm and moist layer of air with a depth of approximately 1 km, a dry layer of cool air cantered above at about 2-4 km and a layer of high-speed jet stream cantered at about 10-12 km height. When the jet stream interacts with the dry layer of cool air, the warm most air ascends and produces a sinking mass of evaporatively cooled air. This creates appropriate conditions for the formation of tornadoes. A typical photograph of a tornado is shown in the Fig.2.48.

Fig. 2.48: Photograph Showing Tornado

Source: https://www.preventionweb.net/

2.3.10.2 Tornado intensity

The strength of a Tornado can be estimated from the degree of damage caused using the Enhanced Fujita scale given in Table 2.6.

Table 2.6: Enhanced Fujita scale

Enhanced Fujita Scale Number	3 sec gust speed (m/s)	Damage
0	29.2–38.1	Minor damage
1	38.3–49.4	Moderate damage
2	49.7–60.6	Considerable damage
3	60.8–73.9	Severe damage
4	74.2–89.4	Extreme damage
5	>89.4	Massive/incredible damage

Source: NWS, NOAA

2.3.11 Avalanches

Avalanche refers to a mass of ice, snow, associated debris such as rocks or vegetation moving rapidly down a slope under the influence of gravity in the snow-covered mountainous regions. This happens because the materials break loose from its location and swipe other materials along with them downwards. Avalanches are mainly of two types i.e., Loose snow avalanches and Slab avalanches. A typical photograph of an avalanche is shown in Fig.2.49.

Fig. 2.49: Photograph showing Avalanches

Source: https://ndma.gov.in/Resources/awareness/avalanche/visuals

2.3.11.1 Causes of avalanches

A steep slope, combined with a weak layer of snow cover triggers a movement. When the force of gravity is greater than its mechanical strength, then Avalanches will form. They may occur on any slope. Therefore, most of the avalanches which assume dangerous sizes originate when the angle of slope varies from 30 degrees and 45 degrees. There are several other factors which trigger Avalanches. These are earthquakes, wind, warming temperatures, vibrations by explosives and machines, rain, deforestation, construction activities, etc.

2.3.12 Thunderstorms and associated disasters

Thunderstorms and associated disasters are very hazardous and cause great loss to life and property.

2.3.12.1 Thunderstorms

Thunderstorms are defined as storms which are characterized by the lightning and its effect on the atmosphere. It is also known as an electrical storm which is a short-lived weather disturbance associated with thunder, lightning, strong winds, heavy rain or hail. A typical photograph of a thunderstorm is shown in Fig.2.50.

They form when there is movement or rapid rise of warm moist air. This warm moist air moves upwards (sometimes to heights of over 20 kilometers), to cool and form cumulonimbus clouds. The air which carries water droplets gets vertically lifted into the atmosphere, to form towering cumulonimbus clouds and thereby precipitation.

Fig. 2.50: Thunderstorm

Source: https://www.iitk.ac.in/nicee/IITK-GSDMA/W03.pdf

The columns of the cooled air eventually sinks downwards, striking the earth's surface with strong downdrafts and horizontal winds. Due to this, electrical charges get accumulated on particles of clouds. When this electric charge gets sufficiently large, lightning discharges occur. Furthermore, when this lightning passes through the air, it heats the air so intensely and quickly that shock waves are produced. These shock waves can be heard as rolls and claps of thunder. Thunderstorms are classified into two categories based on their intensity as given below: -

- **Moderate thunderstorm:** When there is a loud peal of thunder with associated flashes, moderate to heavy rains takes place, and maximum wind speed varies from 29 to 74 kmph, then it is categorized as a Moderate thunderstorm.
- **Severe thunderstorm:** When there is a continuous thunder and occasional hailstorm, and the maximum wind speed is greater than 74kmph, then it is categorized as a Severe thunderstorm.

2.3.12.2 Squall

Squall is a sudden and sharp increase in wind speed ranging from 29 kmph (I6 knots) to 40 kmph (22 knots) or even more. It lasts for at least one minute. Squalls can be classified into two categories based on their intensity as given below: -

- Moderate squall
- Severe squall

Moderate squall: When the surface wind speed (in gusts) reaches up to 74 kmph, then it is categorized as Moderate squall.

Severe squall: When the surface wind speed (in gusts) exceeds74 kmph, then it is categorized as Severe squall.

2.3.12.3 Dust Storm

Dust storms are seen in arid and semi-arid regions. They are also locally known as "aandhi". In this, large amounts of dry soil, sand, and dust are lifted from bare surfaces towards the atmosphere by strong winds. This process transports the materials from hundreds to even thousands of kilometers. Generally, they occur due to thunderstorms or cyclones.

2.3.12.4 Lightning

Lightning is also a weather-related disaster, associated with thunderstorms. It is a massive discharge of electricity in the atmosphere, some of which gets rapidly directed towards the Earth's surface. A typical photograph of lightning is shown in Fig. 2.51.

Fig. 2.51: Lightning

Source: Lightning | NDMA, GoI

2.3.12.5 Hailstorm

When solid ice falls down as precipitation, it is known as hailstones. Hailstorm is a thunderstorm that produces solid ice as precipitation known as hailstone. These Hailstones mainly consist of water ice. India gets moderate to severely affected by hailstones every year with approximately 29 hail days. It is among those countries in the world which experiences a very high frequency of hail.

2.3.13 Forest fire

Forest Fires refers to the uncontrolled and freely spreading fire. They are a threat to flora and fauna as they destroy the ecology and biodiversity of the region. This causes imbalance as it disrupts the habitat, endangers biodiversity and takes precious lives. While most of the forest fires occur due to human causes, rarely they can also occur due to Lightning. Forest fires are thus, one of the most destructive natural forces known to mankind.

Fire plays an important role in the forest ecosystem. This is because it naturally recycles the forest ecosystem and helps in the regeneration of the flora. The fire also helps in the removal of invasive weeds thereby promoting the growth of certain wildlife.

According to the Forest Survey of India, 2019, India 21.40 % of the forest cover in India is prone to fires. This has resulted in the destruction of large tracts of the forest lands.

2.3.13.1 Causes of Forest fire in India

There are mainly two reasons for causing the forest fires as under: -

- Natural causes
- Human made causes

Natural causes include lightning during thunderstorms, friction of rolling stones in the mountainous areas (if there is considerable combustible material), rubbing together clumps of dry bamboos, volcanic eruption, lack of moisture and dry vegetation, rise in temperatures due to global warming, etc., These are some of the natural causes of Forest Fires.

Human made causes include slash and burn shifting cultivation, need for feeding the fodder to cattle, to increase the production of tendu leaves, to conceal illicit felling, terrorizing wild animals to hunt them, careless traveling, protecting crops from wild animals, settling scores with the forest department, burning farm residue, etc.,

2.4 MAN-MADE DISASTERS

Man-made disasters are a result of human activities, or human negligence. Man-made disasters occur due to Chemical, Biological, Radiological and Nuclear Hazards (CBRN). Moreover, they may occur due to Violence, Civil Disorder, Conflict, Terrorism, Fire, etc., Additionally, they also take place due to poor planning, poor construction, overcrowding and accidents.

2.4.1 Chemical (Industrial) Disasters

The terms 'Industrial Disasters' and 'Chemical Disasters' are often used interchangeably. However, they are a subcategory of each other and are thus different from each other. Due to the rise and expansion in the number of industries in various sectors, more industries are exposed to hazardous chemicals. This is because industrial activity majorly concentrates on the use of hazardous chemicals for the manufacture and processing of various goods. The use of these chemicals also involves storage, handling and transportation.

This increases the number of people involved in the usage of such hazardous chemicals. Thus, this can result in explosion, fire, irreparable damage to the humans in and around the vicinity, emission, loss of life and property and adverse effects on the environment. The Bhopal Gas Tragedy, 1994 is one of the worst catastrophes, the world has ever seen, due to chemical hazards.

2.4.1.1 Causes of Chemical disasters

The following reasons may lead to the occurrence of Chemical disasters: -

- Fire
- Toxic release
- Explosion in a plant
- Poisoning
- Accidents in storage facilities of chemicals
- Accidents in treatment plants
- Improper waste management
- Accidents during the transportation of chemicals
- Misuse of chemicals
- Human error

2.4.2 Nuclear and Radiological Emergencies

Nuclear emergency/ Disaster is a result of release of radioactive materials, injurious radiations, or a combination of both. It occurs during the process of release of radiation or radioactive material either during the nuclear events which may include the explosion of a Radiological Dispersal Device (RDD), nuclear weapons, Improvised Nuclear Device (IND) or during the working of nuclear reactors.

2.4.2.1 Causes of Nuclear and radiological emergencies

The Nuclear and radiological emergencies may occur due to the following:

- Intentional use of nuclear weapons in the event of war
- Accidents in the nuclear power projects
- Accidents in handling radiation sources

2.4.3 Biological Disasters

Biological disasters take place due to the spread of diseases among living beings such as humans. animals and plants. They occur through microorganisms such as bacteria, fungi, viruses, and protein. The bioagents can be medical waste, samples of virus, or toxin, etc., This results in biohazards which threaten the health of living species including humans. They create severe harmful consequences for the health of the living species. For example, the world is facing a pandemic due to coronavirus (COVID-19).

COVID-19

The COVID-19 pandemic which began in 2019 due to the spread of an infectious virus among the humans known as coronavirus shook the world. It brought the world to a standstill as the pandemic killed millions. The first case was identified in the Chinese city Wuhan in December 2019. It was in March 2020, that the World Health Organization (WHO), declared the pandemic as a global concern. The disease is caused due to severe acute respiratory syndrome Coronavirus 2 (SARS-CoV-2). In India, the first case was reported in Kerala's Thrissur district on 30th January, 2020. The case of Covid-19 state wise in India till 31 May 2020 is shown in the Fig. 2.52.

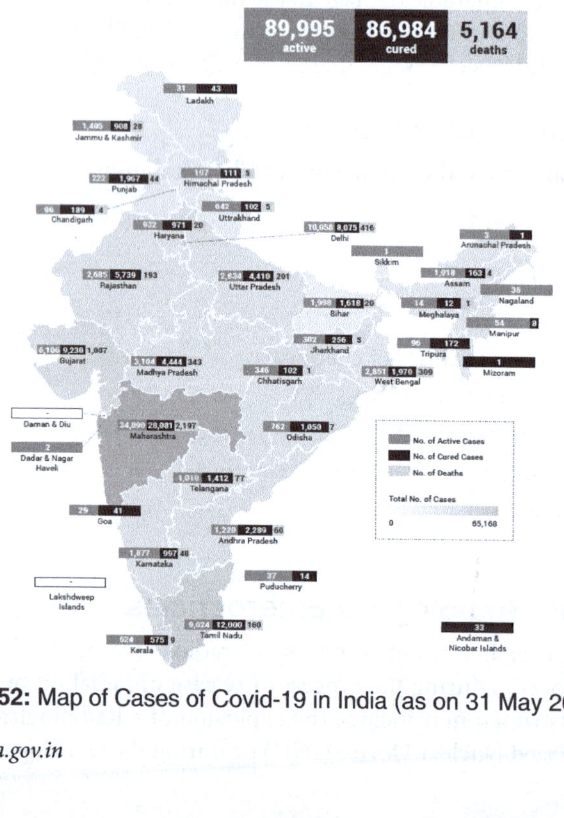

Fig. 2.52: Map of Cases of Covid-19 in India (as on 31 May 2020)

Source: NDMA,2020 web: ndma.gov.in

2.4.4 Accidents

There are mainly three types of transport related accidents:

- Road Accidents
- Rail Accidents
- Air Accidents

2.4.4.1 *Road Accidents*

The rapid expansion and development of road networks across the length and breadth of the country has exposed the users to the risks of accidents. Road accident is one of the most unfortunate things that could happen to a user. While most of the users are aware of the rules, they defy them causing crashes, etc. This happens mainly due to human error. Some of the common causes of road accidents include:

- Jumping Red Light
- Drunken Driver and Over Speeding
- Avoiding Safety Gears like Helmets, seat belts
- Non- compliance to the lane driving
- Overtaking in a wrong manner
- Harmful effects of the traffic on environment such as Noise, Air Pollution, Land Consumption, Safety, Degradation of the Aesthetics
- Overloading to save the cost of transportation
- Infrastructural deficits

This results in not only the accidents of the people involved in these activities but also several other people who might be present at that situation. They thus result in huge monetary losses because of injury, loss of productivity, and premature deaths. However, these accidents are usually not seen as a single unit and remain a hidden epidemic.

2.4.4.2 *Rail Accidents*

The definition of Railway Disaster as adopted by Ministry of Railways according to the DM Act 2005 is given as under: -

"Railway Disaster is a serious train accident or an untoward event of grave nature, either on railway premises or arising out of railway activity, due to natural or human-made causes, that may lead to loss of many lives and /or grievous injuries to a large number of people, and/or severe disruption of traffic etc, necessitating large scale help from other government/non-government and private organizations."

2.4.4.3 *Air Accidents*

Air accidents occur mainly due to the following reasons which include:

- Malfunction in equipmen
- Mid-air collisions
- Runway issues
- Weather
- Forced landings
- Crash due to poor visibility in mountainous terrain

Air accidents can occur at any time and location. Nevertheless, they often take place in the range of about 30 – 40 km radius of airports. Thus, it can be said that the places around the airport are most vulnerable. Additionally, a majority of the accidents happen during the landing and take-off as the path of flights gets congested. However, accidents also occur in remote locations that are inaccessible.

2.4.5 Stampede

Human stampedes have occurred throughout human history but with the rise in densely populated urban population, stampedes have increased in frequency. Stampedes can be described as a concerted, uncontrolled, sudden or rash impulse of the human crowd making an effort to get away from the perceived danger. However, this usually results in suffocation, death, injuries, trampling/stamping etc., The term crowd refers to the aggregate of people who gather, have homogeneity of thoughts and actions.

It has been observed that crowds gather for reasons such as religion, sports, festivities, or politics. This sometimes results in overfilling of the crowd beyond what the staff can manage and the space can accommodate.

2.4.5.1 Causes of Stampede

Stampede can occur because of the following reasons: -

- Lack of coordination
- Riots
- Fire
- Religious / other events
- Terrorist attack
- Free food distribution
- Power failure
- Sports events
- Entertainment events
- Natural disasters

2.4.6 Oil spills

Oil spills endanger the marine ecosystem, lakes, river systems, and even terrestrial habitat especially in areas where large scale oil drilling, refining, and transportation happens. The spills which are closest to the shore contribute to the maximum damage to the marine species as the oil can reach the shore, the earliest. The spills would not have time to disperse which can significantly affect the sensitive habitats of a variety of organisms.

Oil floats on water as it is lighter than water. When the marine organisms interact with this oil, they lose their ability to sustain in the given environment. So, their life gets threatened.

For example, Sea animals like fishes and whales come out to breathe from the air. During this process, the oil sticks to their body and they inhale it, leading to lung and heart disease. Similarly, juvenile turtles ingest them mistaking it as food and die. Additionally, oil sticks on the fur animals making them unable to insulate themselves, whose life gets threatened in cold water. Moreover, oil sticks to the feathers of birds who are not able to fly properly and when they use their beak to remove the oil, the oil gets ingested. Oil spills affect the physical, biological and chemical characteristics of both land and water.

2.4.6.1 Causes of Oil spills

Oil spills occur due to the following major reasons:

- Human error
- Technical faults
- Natural calamities
- Equipment failures
- Pipeline leak
- Planned releases

2.4.7 Terrorist attacks

Terrorism refers to those violent actions of a group or person that are aimed at creating fear of terror, killing innocent civilians, inflicting psychological trauma, damaging and destroying property, eliminating a culture, destabilizing the economy and society for gaining political, economic or religious aims. According to the FBI- "Terrorism is the unlawful use of force or violence against persons or property to intimidate or coerce a government, the civilian population, or any segment thereof, in furtherance of political or social objectives."

Terrorists adopt killing of a large group of people or property, through weapons of mass destruction, mass killing, hijacking, mass kidnapping, mass rape, shootings, robberies, narcotic materials, cyber weapons, nuclear and radiation weapons, biological pathogens agents. Cross border terrorism, separatists' wings, state sponsored groups, communalists.

2.4.7.1 Causes of Terrorism

- **Social-economic**- Factors such as poverty, lack of education, deprivation.
- **Political**- Dissatisfaction with the current set of government, encourages people to take to violence to inflict fear in the minds of the ruling class.
- **Strategic**–This is a strategy of the weak to create fear in the minds of people. This way they are able to change trends and patterns to evolve towards their goals.
- **Religious**- People associate their culture and emotions with Religion. Thus, terrorists selectively interpret the religious texts to influence people to work for their cause in the name of religion.

2.5 HAZARD AND VULNERABILITY PROFILE IN INDIA

India is the seventh-largest country in the world comprising an area of 32.87 lakh (3.3 million) sq.km. It is among the most affected countries by disasters. There are 36 states and UT's in India, out of which, 27 are prone to disasters. The Indian subcontinent is vulnerable to various types of disasters due to its unique physiographic and diverse geo climatic conditions, a large territory and a vast population comprising various socio-economic groups. India is vulnerable to a large number of natural disasters in varying degrees such as earthquakes, droughts, floods, thunderstorms, tsunamis, landslides, cyclones, avalanches, forest fires and manmade disasters including Chemical, Biological, Radiological, Nuclear (CBRN) disasters. Furthermore, India is experiencing a rapid rise in vulnerability due to changing climatic conditions, increasing population, development in hazard prone locations, industrialization, and unplanned urbanization, unscientific development practices.

The Indian landmass can be divided into the following regions, namely: -

- Himalayan Region
- Alluvial plains
- Peninsular region
- Coastal Region
- The desert region

These regions are prone to different types of disasters. Some of the regions are prone to multi hazards/ disasters. Himalayan regions are susceptible to earthquakes and landslides. Due to the plate tectonic movement, the region and adjacent alluvial plains are prone to earthquakes. Additionally, the plains are also prone to frequent flooding. The desert region of the country is mainly prone to droughts and famine. The western region of India, which includes Rajasthan, Gujarat and some parts of Maharashtra are vulnerable to droughts and are hit frequently by those. The coastal region is prone to cyclones, storms, and floods. Moreover, due to the tectonic activity in the ocean, coastal regions are also prone to tsunamis.

The Vulnerability atlas of India prepared by Building Materials & Technology Promotion Council (BMTPC) was first published in 1997. Recently, the third edition has been published in 2019. The hazard maps for the country have been given for the entire country which shows the boundaries of hazard zones state/ UT wise for winds, floods and earthquakes from which district wise vulnerable areas can be identified. This new edition also contains the maps for cyclones, thunderstorms and landslides. The Atlas is useful for assessing the level of risk that each area is exposed to. This can act as a tool for preparing disaster prevention, preparedness, mitigation and even relief plans especially for housing and infrastructures. Additionally, public servants like town planners, commissioners, urban planners, mayors, and various other executives can use them for formulating and implementing schemes like land zoning regulations, building bye laws and various other developmental schemes, according to the areas prone to hazards.

2.5.1 Earthquake

Approximately, 57 per cent of the land area of the country is prone to earthquakes that lies in the moderate (seismic zone III) to very high intensity (seismic zone V) zones according to the vulnerability atlas of India 2019. In these areas nearly 79% of the population of the country lives.

India has been classified into four seismic zones based on the level of intensities namely zone II, Zone III, Zone IV, Zone V as per the Indian Standard IS 1893 (Part 1): 2016. Earlier, in the version of 1970, the seismic zone map was divided into five zones name I, II, III, IV and V based on the level of intensities. However, in 2002 the map was revised and zone I was merged into Zone II. Zone III covers the maximum area of India which can likely experience a maximum intensity of VII, including Mumbai and Chennai whereas New Delhi lies in Zone IV. The earthquake hazard map of India is shown in Fig.2.53.

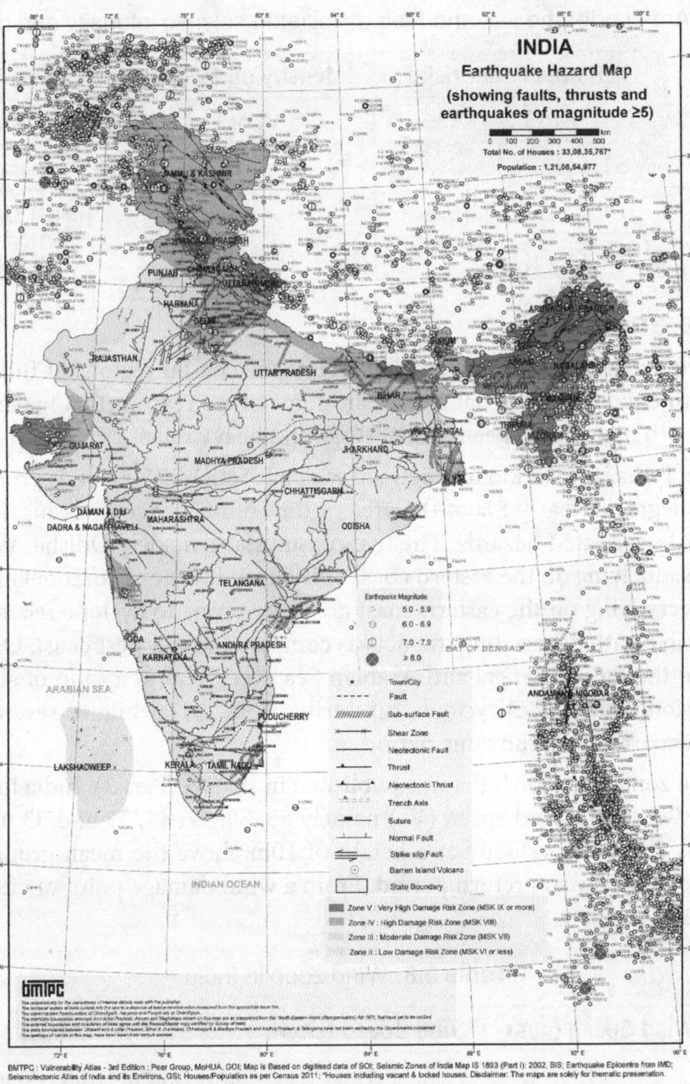

Fig. 2.53: Earthquake Hazard Map of India

Source: https://bmtpc.org/DataFiles/CMS/file/VAI2019/MAP/eqmap/EQ_JPG/EQ_INDIA.jpg accessed on Oct 02, 2022

Zone II indicates an intensity of MSK VI or less which is known as Low Damage Risk Zone. Zone III indicates an intensity of MSK VII which is known as Moderate Damage Risk Zone, an area of approximately 31.1% of India is liable to intensity VII on MSK scale which is similar to Jabalpur earthquake. Zone IV indicates an intensity of MSK VIII which is known as High Damage Risk Zone, an area of approximately 14.4% of India is liable to intensity VIII on MSK scale which is similar to Latur and Uttarkashi earthquakes. Zone V is the most vulnerable zone which indicates an intensity of MSK IX or more which is known as Very High Damage Risk Zone, an area of approximately 11.3% of India is liable to intensity IX or more on MSK scale. The area under the risk zones and their associated seismic intensity on MSK scale and damage risk are shown in Table 2.7.

Table 2.7: Area under the risk and their associated seismic intensity and damage risk

Seismic Zone	%of area under risk		Intensity on MSK scale	Damage Risk
Zone II	43.2		VI or less	Low Damage Risk
Zone III	31.1	56.8	VII	Moderate Damage Risk
Zone IV	14.4		VIII	High Damage Risk
Zone V	11.3		IX and more	Very High Damage Risk

2.5.2 Cyclone and Wind

Cyclone is one of the major natural disasters that affects the coastal regions of India. High population density, shallow continental shelf, and flat terrain are some of the reasons that make India vulnerable to cyclones associated with high wind speed, storm surge and heavy rains.

The coastline of India is 7,516 km in length, of which length of 5,700 km is prone to cyclone related disasters to varying degrees. Nearly 8% of the area of the country encompassing 13 coastal states and UT's are prone to cyclone related hazards. The five coastal states namely Odisha, West Bengal, Andhra Pradesh and Tamil Nadu, lying on the eastern coast of India and western coast of Gujarat and the Union Territory of Puducherry lying on the eastern coast are more prone to cyclone related hazards. The east coast is more vulnerable with devastating impacts as compared to the west coast. On an average, five to six cyclones occur in the Bay of Bengal and Arabian Sea every year at a ratio of about 4:1. In the east coast, 106 severe cyclones out of 273 cyclones hit during 1891-2017 while 16 severe cyclones out of 30 cyclones hit the west coast during the same period.

The wind speed zone maps for India was published in IS: 875 (Part 3). India has been divided into six wind zones based on basic wind speed (V_b) namely 55, 50, 47, 44, 39 and 33 m/s. This basic wind speed is based on 3s gust wind velocity at a height of 10m above the mean ground level in an open terrain i.e., Category 2 for 50 years return period. From a wind damage point of view, the damage risks are shown in Table 2.8.

Table 2.8: Wind zone in India

Wind Zone	Wind Speed (m/s)	Wind Speed (km/h)	Damage Risk
I	33	118.8	Low Damage Risk Zone
II	39	140.4	Moderate Damage Risk Zone–B
III	44	158.4	Moderate Damage Risk Zone–A
IV	47	169.2	High Damage Risk Zone
V	50	180	Very High Damage Risk Zone–B
VI	55	198	Very High Damage Risk Zone–A

According to the Vulnerability Atlas of India, 18% of the land area is prone to high wind velocity i.e., 50& 55 m/s. The coastal regions of India vulnerable to cyclones fall in the zone of 55&%50 m/s. New Delhi lies in 47 m/s zone, Mumbai lies in 44 m/s, Chennai and Kolkata lies in 50 m/s zone. This zoning is considered for designing the structures and risk and vulnerability classification of buildings. The wind hazard map for the country is shown in Fig. 2.54.

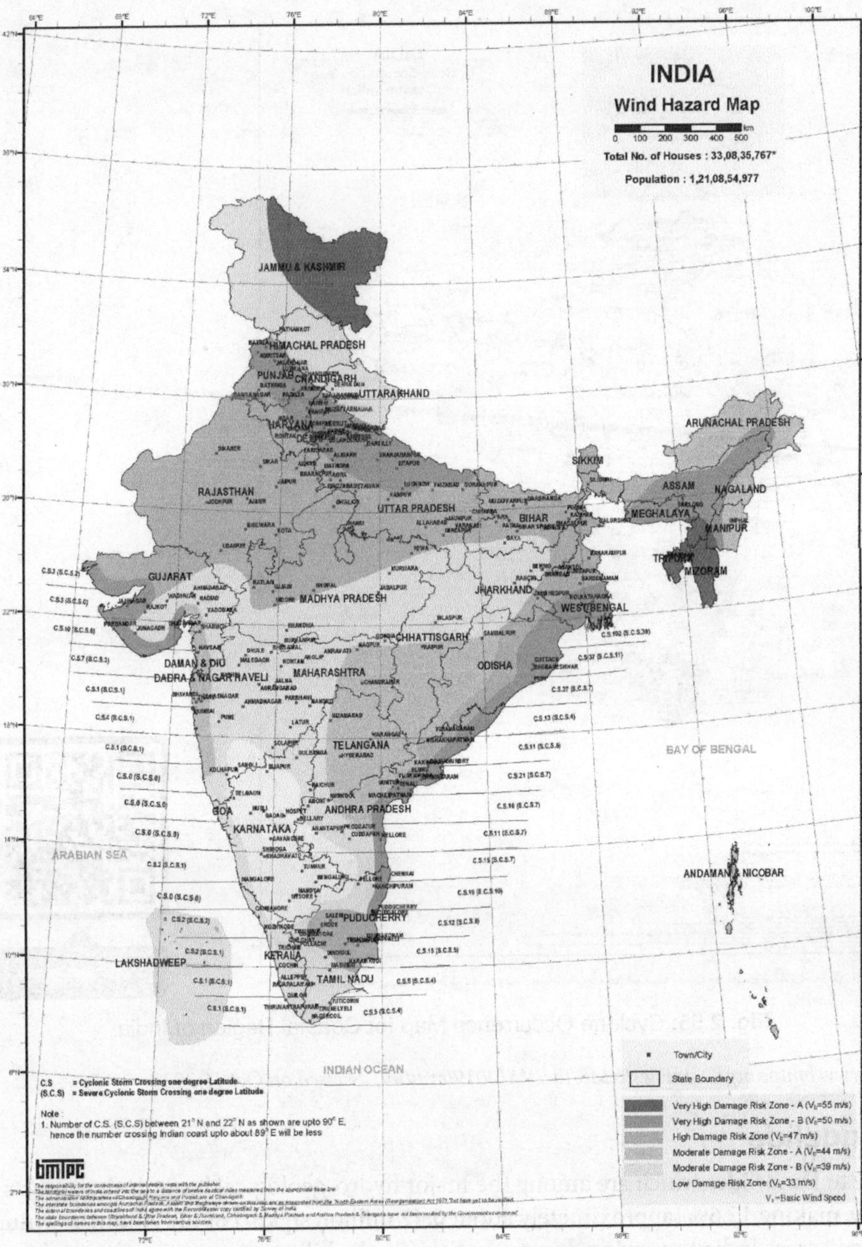

BMTPC : Vulnerability Atlas- 3rd Edition; Peer Group, MoHUA; Map is Based on digitised data of SOI, GOI; Basic Wind Speed Map National Building Code: 2016; Cyclone Data, 1891-2015, IMD. GOI. Houses/Population as per Census 2011; *Houses including vacant & locked houses. Disclaimer: The maps are solely for thematic presentation.

Fig. 2.54: Wind & Cyclone Hazard Map of India

Source: https://bmtpc.org/DataFiles/CMS/file/VAI2019/MAP/windmap/wind_jpg/WIND_INDIA1.jpg accessed on Oct 02, 2022

A cyclone occurrence map for coastal regions of India is shown in Fig.2.55. The map has been prepared on the basis of 3-minute average maximum sustained wind (in knots) data provided by IMD for the coastal districts affected by cyclones during the period of 1891-2008.

BMTPC : Vulnerability Atlas- 3rd Edition; Peer Group, MoHUA; Map is Based on digitised data of SOI, GOI; Maximum Sustained Wind (MSW) Data from IMD, GOI. Disclaimer: The maps are solely for thematic presentation.

VulnerabilityProfile

Fig. 2.55: Cyclone Occurrence Map for Coastal Region of India

Source: https://www.bmtpc.org/DataFiles/CMS/file/VAI2019/cy.html, assessed on Oct 16,2022

2.5.3 Landslide

India is prone to Landslides which are among the major hydro-geological hazards that affects large parts of the country, making 12.6% (approximately about 0.42 million sq.km) of the landmass vulnerable to it. It is distributed across India to varying degrees, especially the hilly terrain.

The major landslide prone areas are also the ones most affected by earthquakes i.e., Zone-IV and V. Thus, landslides are triggered here by earthquakes. For example, Uttarkashi Earthquake (1991), Chamoli Earthquake (1999), Kashmir Earthquake (2005), Sikkim Earthquake (2011) etc.,.

According to the Global Fatal Landslide estimate, during the period of 2004- 2016, India has a share of 20% in the global fatalities which is the highest among all the countries in the world.

The Landslide Hazard Zonation Map of India is shown in Fig.2.56. This map is useful for construction and development activities, regulation and mitigation of landslides.

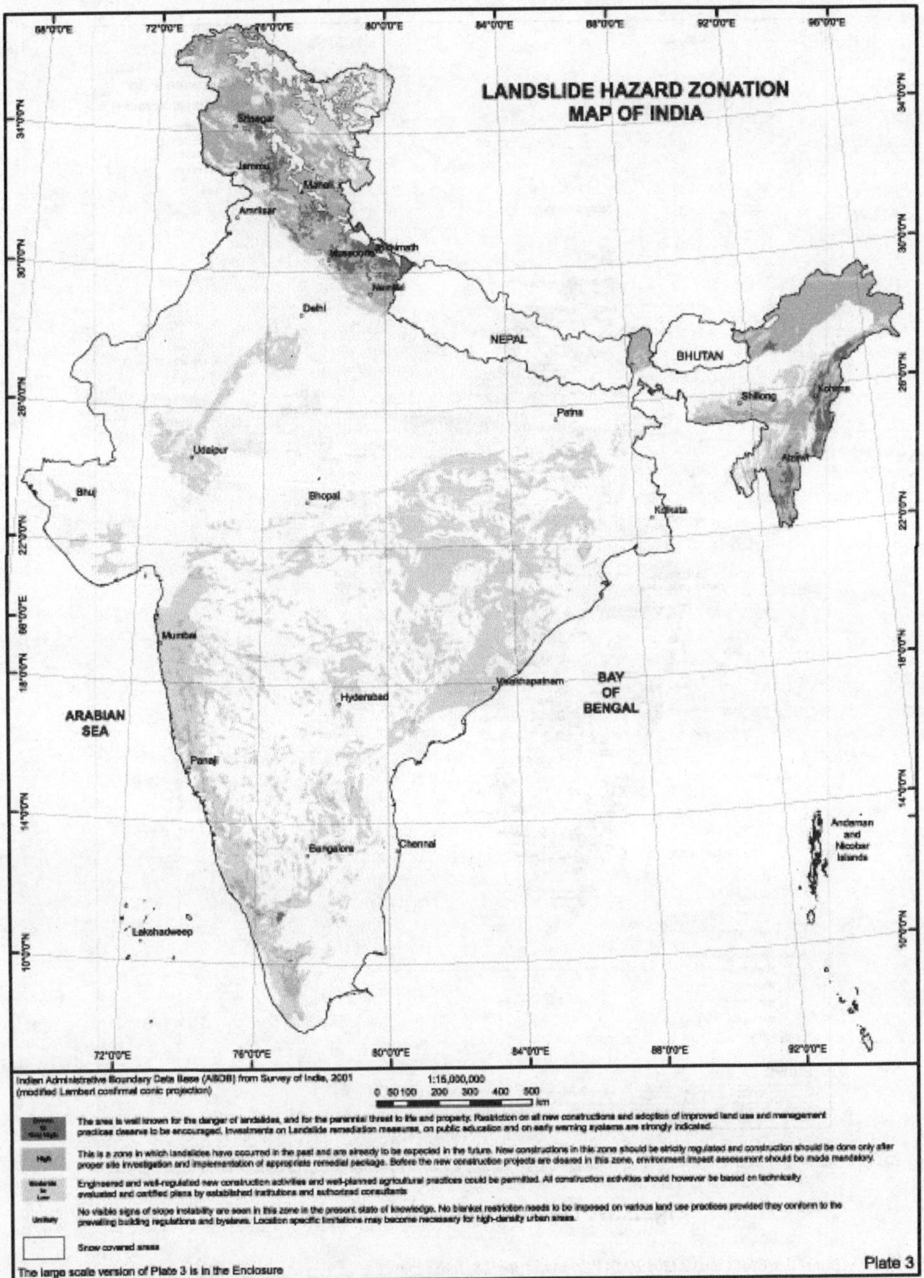

Fig. 2.56: Landslide Hazard Zonation Map of India

Source: https://bmtpc.org/topics.aspx?mid=56&Mid1=186

Landslide Incidence Map is given in the vulnerability atlas of India as shown in Fig.2.57. This map has been developed based on the 9000 (approx.) verified field data from GSI. Additionally, the Annual State Rainfall Normals (mm) in the base layer is also given in this map.

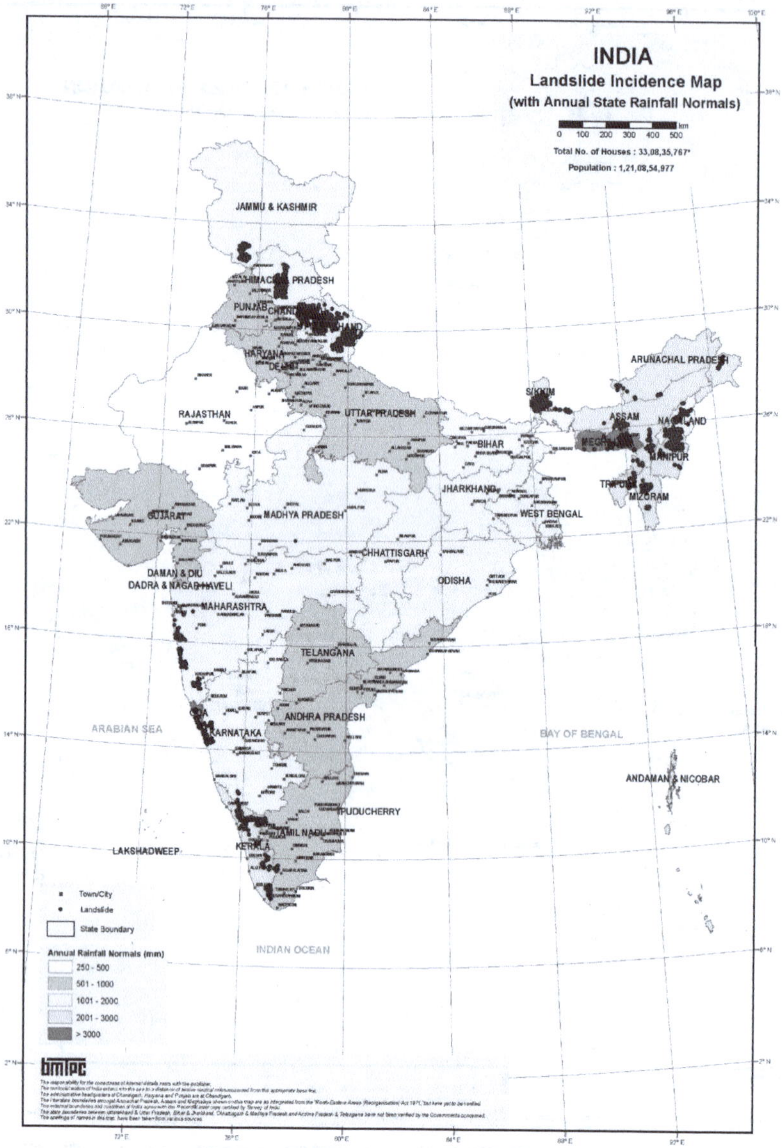

BMTPC: Vulnerability Atlas - 3rd Edition; Peer Group, MoHUA,GOI; Map is Based on digitised data of SOI; Landslide Incidence data GSI; Annual Rainfall data IMD; Houses/Population as per Census 2011;
* Houses including vacant & locked houses. Disclaimer: The maps are solely for thematic presentation.

Fig. 2.57: Landslide Incidence Map in India

Source: https://bmtpc.org/DataFiles/CMS/file/VAI2019/MAP/lsmap/ls_jpg/LS_India.jpg

2.5.4 Flood

India is among the most vulnerable countries affected by floods. This is due to the natural ecology of the country which is the monsoon system, river siltation, steep mountains that easily get eroded especially in the Himalayan regions. Nearly 12 percent of its land (i.e., 40 million hectares of land out of 329 mha) is vulnerable to floods and river erosion. As per the National Commission on Floods, it is possible to provide nearly 80 percent (i.e., 32 million hectares of land) a reasonable degree of protection.

On an average, 7.5 million hectares of land is affected due to floods every year. Flood is an annual feature of the Indo- Gangetic Brahmaputra plains. This not only causes damage to crops covering lakhs of hectares, renders many homeless but also kills a few hundred every year. The areas which are prone to flooding are indicated in the flood hazard map of India shown in the Fig.2.58.

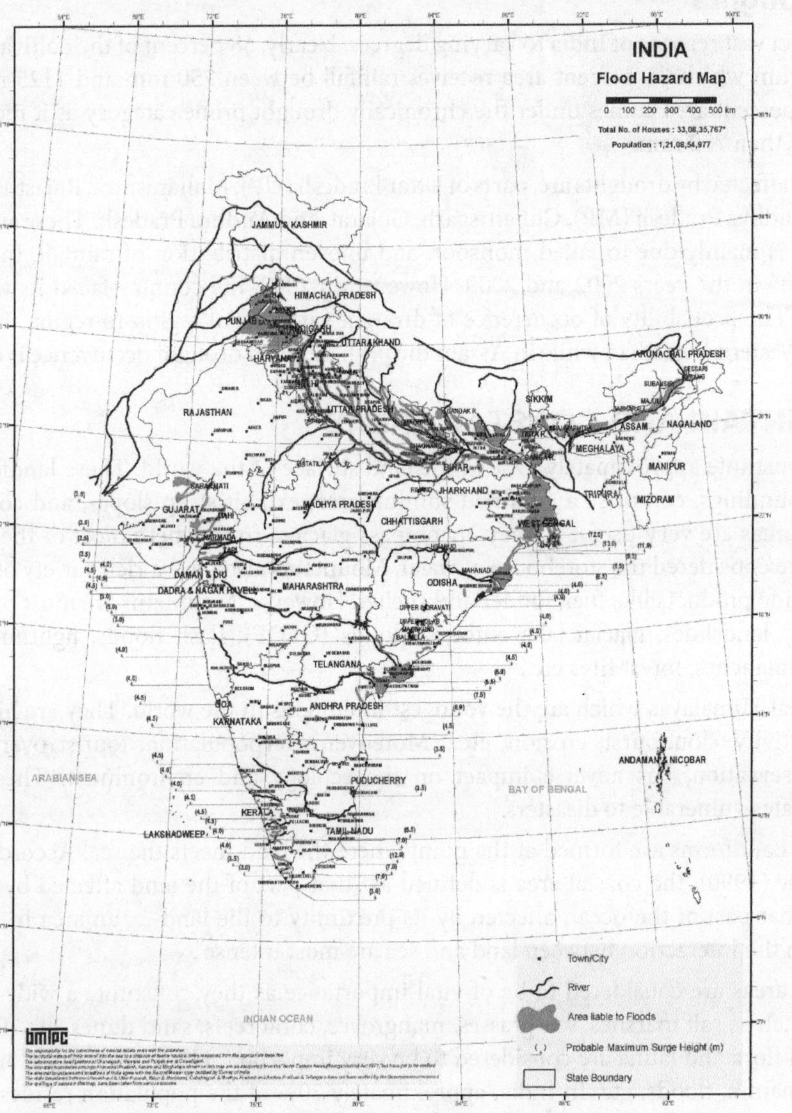

Fig. 2.58: Flood prone Map of India

Source: https://bmtpc.org/DataFiles/CMS/file/VAI2019/MAP/floodmap/flood_jpg/Flood-INDIA.jpg

Based upon the vulnerability of the floods, India can be classified into four regions namely-The Brahmaputra River Plains, The Ganga River Plains, The North-West River Plains, The Central India and Deccan Regions. Additionally, the Island regions of Andaman and Nicobar and Lakshadweep also face flooding, drainage congestion and erosion in the coast.

Twenty-three of the 35 states and union territories in the country are subject to floods and 40 million hectares of land, roughly one-eighth of the country's geographical area, is prone to floods and flood hazard zones are shown in the Fig. 2.58.

2.5.5 Droughts

Droughts affect vast regions of India to varying degrees. Nearly, 68 percent of the cultivable area is prone to drought, from which 35 percent area receives rainfall between 750 mm and 1125 mm per annum. However, 33 percent area comes under the chronically drought prone category as it receives an annual rainfall of less than 750 mm.

Regions affected by droughts are, parts of Uttar Pradesh (UP), Maharashtra, Rajasthan (chronically), Jharkhand, Madhya Pradesh (MP), Chhattisgarh, Gujarat, and Andhra Pradesh. These areas suffer severe distress. This is mainly due to failed monsoon and uneven distribution of rainfall. India experienced major droughts in the years 2002 and 2009. However, in 2002, the country faced its worst drought in twenty years. The probability of occurrence of drought varies from region to region. It is seen once in two years in Western Rajasthan while in Assam the probability of drought occurrence is once in 15 years.

2.6 MOUNTAIN AND COASTAL AREAS

Mountains constitute approximately 27% of the land surface of the world. These landforms are higher than its surroundings, comprise a confined summit area, exhibit steep slopes, and considerable local relief. These areas are very useful as they encompass glaciers from where most of the rivers originate and so they are considered the storehouse of water. Mountains also have a rich variety of flora and fauna and also provide products like fuel, fodder and shelter. However, Mountains are most prone to disasters and especially landslides, glacial lake outburst floods (GLOF), flash floods, lightning, earthquakes, hailstorms, avalanches, forest fires etc.,

The Great Himalayas which are the youngest mountains in the world. They are highly susceptible to seismic activity, cloudburst, erosion, etc.,. Moreover, overpopulation, tourist overflow, neglecting resource conservation, has adverse impact on the ecology and environment. These factors make Himalayan states vulnerable to disasters.

Coastal Landforms are formed at the point where the land meets the sea. According to Sorenson and McCreary (1990), the coastal area is defined as "that part of the land affected by its proximity to the sea and that part of the ocean affected by its proximity to the land ... an area in which processes depending on the interaction between land and sea are most intense".

Coastal areas are considered to be of vital importance as they constitute a wide range of coastal ecosystems such as salt marshes, sea-grasses, mangroves, coral reefs, sand dunes, etc. These encompass wide range of flora and fauna are considered to be very important. However, Coastal areas are prone to cyclones, tsunami's, floods, etc. In India, approximately 20% of the population resides in coastal areas and conducts developmental activities. This, puts pressure on the fragile coastal environment.

2.7 ECOLOGICAL FRAGILITY

Ecological fragility is the inverse of the ecosystem stability. These are important ecosystems which have unique resources and features. They might or might not be exposed to any disturbances. These include mountains, semi–arid lands, wetlands, small islands and certain coastal areas.

These encompass such local environments which are extremely sensitive to changes in air, water quality, temperature, and other environmental conditions. A minor change can significantly disturb and have harmful impacts, thereby reducing the functional capacities of the ecosystem.

Causes

- Natural- earthquakes, landslides, volcanic eruptions, floods, global warming, invasion of exotic species, variation in precipitation etc.,
- Anthropogenic- deforestation, construction activities, unplanned urbanization, industrialization, intensive agriculture, increased tourism. etc.,
- Some of the fragile ecosystems in India are: -
- Mountain Region- these have, Himalayas, evergreen to alpine forest, Western Ghats.
- Desert Region- Hot desert of Rajasthan and Rann of Katch, cold deserts of Ladakh
- Coastal areas – lagoons, estuaries, Mahanadi delta, sunder bans, coral reefs, forests in the North East
- Islands – Andaman and Nicobar, Lakshadweep

These fragile ecosystems are susceptible to degradation subject to a variety of factors such as climate change, anthropogenic factors including deforestation, pollution, etc. There is a need to adopt measures so as to preserve these ecosystems and thus promote sustainable development.

UNIT SUMMARY

- A disaster is a natural or anthropogenic phenomenon or a combination of both, which can lead to a disruption in the normal life, damage to the environment and property, thus requiring external assistance to cope.
- Disasters can be classified based on their source of origin into natural and human- induced/ anthropogenic disasters.
- Natural disasters occur due to natural phenomena. Examples of natural disasters are floods, earthquakes, landslides, cyclones, etc.,
- Man-made disasters are caused due to human negligence. Examples of man-made disasters are Chemical, Biological, Radiological, and Nuclear (CBRN) disasters, accidents, stampede, terrorist strikes etc.,
- Earthquake is a sudden motion of the earth due to release of strain energy by the collision or movement of tectonic plates underneath the surface of the earth.
- Flood means a rise in the level of water that results in the inundation of land which is usually dry along the coast or a river channel. This forces the people to move to relatively safer locations, and may damage property and other vital resources.
- Drought is an insidious hazard which is primarily caused due to either deficiency or absence of precipitation/rainfall from the expected, multiyear average for a region for an extended period of time/season.
- Tropical cyclones are generally known as "cyclones" used globally, that originate in the tropical region over the ocean. It is an intense vortex or a whirl with a swiftly rotating storm system in which wind speeds exceed or are equal to a minimum of 34 knots (62 kmph)
- A volcano refers to an opening on the Earth's surface that allows warmer material to escape from its interior. Volcanic eruptions can be threatening for life around its vicinity.

- A Tsunami is a series of ocean waves having extremely long wavelengths, generated by sudden displacement in the sea floor, caused due to earthquakes, landslides, or volcanic activity
- Landslide is defined as downward and outward movement of mass of rock, debris or earth under the effect of gravity and triggered by various factors.
- Coastal erosion refers to the process in which coastal land gets eroded by wind, water and waves. This leads to the removal of sediments and causes the shoreline to retreat landwards. This happens through strong wave action, sea level rise or wear down of the coast due to flooding or carry away of sand, rocks or soils.
- Soil erosion occurs when the top layer of the soil which is also a fertile layer gets lost. This layer being very light can easily get carried away by the actions of wind and water.
- Tornadoes are funnel-shaped storms which are narrow, violently rotating updrafts of air that extend from a thunderstorm to the surface of the earth.
- Avalanche refers to a mass of ice, snow, associated debris such as rocks or vegetation moving rapidly down a slope under the influence of gravity in the snow-covered mountainous regions.
- Thunderstorms are defined as storms which are characterized by the lightning and its effect on the atmosphere.
- Approximately, 57% of the land area of the country is prone to earthquakes that lies in the moderate (seismic zone III) to very high intensity (seismic zone V) zones according to the vulnerability atlas of India 2019.
- Nearly 8% of the area of the country encompassing 13 coastal states and UT's are prone to cyclone related hazards.
- Approximately, 12.6% of the land area of India is vulnerable to Landslides.
- India is among the most vulnerable countries affected by floods. Nearly 12 percent of its land is vulnerable to floods and river erosion.
- Droughts affect vast regions of India to varying degrees. Nearly, 68 % of the cultivable area is prone to drought.
- Coastal areas are considered to be of vital importance as they constitute a wide range of coastal ecosystems such as salt marshes, sea-grasses, mangroves, coral reefs, sand dunes, etc. However, Coastal areas are prone to cyclones, tsunami's, floods, etc.,
- Ecological fragility is the inverse of the ecosystem stability. These are important ecosystems which have unique resources and features. A minor change can significantly disturb and have harmful impacts, thereby reducing the functional capacities of the ecosystem.

EXERCISES

Multiple Choice Questions

Q.1 CBRN is a type of

a. Natural disaster   b. Human-made Disaster

c. Both   d. None

Q.2 How many disasters were identified by the High-Powered Committee (HPC)?

a. 32   b. 31

c. 35   d. 42

Q.3 Which of the following is not an example of Natural Disasters:-

a. Earthquakes b. Floods
c. Oil Spills d. Tsunamis

Q.4 The point inside the earth from which the seismic waves originate is called:

i. Focus
ii. Hypocentere
iii. Epicentr

a. and ii only b. i only
c. ii and iii only d. All the above

Q.5 In the context of earthquakes, which of the following are the fastest seismic waves?

a. P-Waves b. S- Waves
c. Love Waves d. Rayleigh Waves

Q.6 The magnitude of thc carthquake is measured on the scale which is known as:

a. Richter Scale b. Modified Mercalli Scale
c. MSK Scale d. All the above

Q.7 Which of the following types of floods takes places within the shortest span of time?

a. Riverine Floods b. Coastal Floods
c. Flash Floods d. Urban floods

Q.8 Which of the following describes the situation of an extreme flood?

a. HFL > L > DL b. L < WL
c. L > HFL d. DL > L > WL

Q.9 In the Antarctic ocean, cyclones are known as:-

a. Hurricane b. Willy-willy
c. Typhoon d. Tropical Cyclones

Q.10 The central part of the cyclone is known as its eye where

a. The pressure is the highest and temperature is the lowest
b. The pressure is the lowest and temperature is the highest
c. The pressure is the lowest and temperature is the lowest
d. The pressure is the higher and temperature is the highest

Q.11 Which of the following is the only active volcano in India?

a. Volcano Popa
b. Volcano Etna
c. Volcano of Barren Island
d. None of the above

Q.12 The shear strength of the slope material decreases with

a. The increase in slope b. The decrease in slope
c. Does not depend on the slope d. None of the above

Q.13 Slope movements occur when driving force is

A. Greater than the resisting force
B. Less than the resisting force

C. Equal to resisting forced.

D. In the context of Droughts, an area is said to experience severe drought situation if:

a. Rainfall is deficient from 26-50% b. Rainfall deficiency exceeds 75%

c. Rainfall deficiency exceeds 50% d. None of the above

Q.14 Which of the following will not lead to the occurrence of Tsunami?

a. Earthquakes b. Floods

c. Volcanoes d. Landslides

Q.15 Tropical cyclones do not develop near the equator because of which of the following:

a. The winds are too heavy and wet b. Excessive heat

c. Calm air d. Weak Coriolis force

Q.16 What percentage of India is prone to Cyclones?

a. 10% b. 8%

c. 12% d. 20%

Q.17 What percentage of India is prone to floods?

a. 12% b. 30%

c. 8% d. 15%

Q.18 What percentage of the cultivable area in India is prone to drought?

a. 57% b. 68%

c. 12% d. 8%

Q.19 A series of terror attacks took place in Mumbai in the November of which of the following year?

a. 2018 b. 2001

c. 2010 d. 2008

Answers of Multiple-Choice Questions

Answers of Multiple-choice questions				
2.1 **b**	2.2 **b**	2.3 **c**	2.4 **a**	2.5 **a**
2.6 **a**	2.7 **c**	2.8 **c**	2.9 **a**	2.10 **b**
2.11 **c**	2.12 **a**	2.13 **a**	2.14 **c**	2.15 **b**
2.16 **d**	2.17 **b**	2.18 **a**	2.19 **b**	2.20 **d**

Short and Long Answer Type Questions

Category I

1. What are exogenic and endogenic forces?
2. Differentiate between Natural and Man-made disasters.
3. Classify the Disasters based on their source of origin.
4. What are the causes of Earthquakes?
5. Explain Floods. What are the different types of floods?
6. Discuss the basic parts of a landslide.
7. Differentiate between intensity and magnitude of an earthquake?
8. What are plate tectonics?

9. How are the flood situations categorized in India?
10. How are the droughts classified?
11. Describe the major parts of a cyclone?
12. Give a brief description of the classification of Volcanoes?
13. Explain Tsunami. What is Tsunami Velocity?
14. What is the Human-made disaster?

Category II

1. Classify the Disasters based on their source of origin. Discuss in detail.
2. What are seismic waves? Differentiate between Body waves and Surface waves.
3. Define Landslide. What are the different causes of Landslides? Discuss in detail.
4. What are cyclones? Elaborate the favourable conditions for the formation of a cyclone?
5. How are the cyclones classified in India? Describe how it differs from the Saffir–Simpson Hurricane Wind Scale?
6. What is a Tornado? What are the factors that lead to the formation of a tornado?
7. What is a Thunderstorm? Describe in detail the disasters associated with thunderstorms.
8. Explain the vulnerability profile of India with respect to different disasters.

REFERENCES AND SUGGESTED READINGS

1. BMTPC (2019): Vulnerability Atlas of India, Ministry of Housing and Urban Affairs, Government of India.
2. CSIR (2020): Guidelines for "Protection and Control of Coastal Erosion in India" CSIR-National Institute of Oceanography, Goa.
3. Department of Agriculture and Cooperation (2009): Manual for Drought Management. Ministry of Agriculture, Government of India.
4. IMD (2021): Cyclone Warning in India: Standard Operation Procedure" India Meteorological Department
5. IS 1893 (Part 1) (2016): Indian Standard Criteria for Earthquake Resistant Design of Structures: Part 1 – General Provisions and Buildings, Bureau of Indian Standards, New Delhi.
6. MHA (2011): Disaster Management in India, Ministry of Home Affairs, Government of India.
7. Murty, C.V.R. (2005): IITK-BMTPC Earthquake Tips." Public domain. National Information Centre of Earthquake Engineering. http://nicee.org/EQTips.php
8. NDMA (2019): National Disaster Management Plan, Ministry of Home Affairs, Government of India.
9. NDMA (2019). "Home Owner's Guide for Earthquake and Cyclone Safety" Ministry of Home Affairs Government of India.
10. NDMA (2018): Guidelines for Preparation of Action plan–Prevention and Management of Thunderstorm & Lightning/ Squall/Dust/Hailstorm and Strong Winds, Ministry of Home Affairs, Government of India
11. NDMA (2010): National Disaster Management Guidelines: Management of Tsunamis. Ministry of Home Affairs, Government of India.

12. NDMA (2008): National Disaster Management Guidelines – Management of Cyclones, Ministry of Home Affairs, Government of India.
13. NDMA (2008): National Disaster Management Guidelines – Management of Floods, Government of India. GOI
14. NDMA (2007): National Disaster Management Guidelines – Management of Earthquakes. Ministry of Home Affairs, Government of India.
15. Parkash Surya (2020): Training Module on Comprehensive Landslides Risk Management. National Institute of Disaster Management, New Delhi. https://nidm.gov.in/PDF/pubs/LandslidesModule_2020.pdf
16. Parkash Surya (2019): Landslide Preparedness Guidelines for Safety of Buildings on Slopes; published by National Institute of Disaster Management, Ministry of Home Affairs, Government of India. https://nidm.gov.in/PDF/pubs/Landslide_Preparedness_Guide_.pdf
17. https://nidm.gov.in/PDF/Disaster_geo.pdf
18. https://www.preventionweb.net/files/2156_VL323106.pdf
19. https://www.adrc.asia/countryreport/IND/2018/India_CR2018A.pdf

03 DISASTER IMPACTS

UNIT SPECIFICS

The salient objectives of this unit are to familiarize the students with the following:

- *To understand the impacts of Disasters.*
- *To elucidate the different types of Disaster related impacts.*
- *To understand the demographic aspects related to disaster.*
- *To describe the mental health scenario and psychosocial reactions as a consequence of disasters.*
- *Ability to comprehend the global and national disaster trends.*
- *To explain the urban disaster scenario and Climate Change.*

In this unit, the impacts of disasters such as physical, social, economic, environmental, etc., are discussed. Furthermore, the demographic aspects of vulnerability are discussed in detail. The chapter also discusses the mental health and psychological consequences of disasters. Then, the impact of climate change and urban disasters are elaborated. Henceforth, the chapter elucidates the global and national disaster trends.

A number of multiple-choice questions are given as well as questions of short and long answer types are marked in two categories following lower and higher order of Bloom's taxonomy. A list of references and suggested readings are given in the unit so that one can go through them for practice. It is important to note that for getting more information on various topics of interest some QR codes have been provided in different sections which can be scanned for relevant supportive knowledge.

RATIONALE

This unit helps students to gain insights on various aspects of disaster related impacts. It explains the various types of disaster impacts which are discussed at length to develop the understanding of the subject matter. Disaster impacts millions of people globally, and causes havoc in terms of human life and misery. The post disaster situation is very complex and needs to be understood from various points in order to be able to arrive at appropriate disaster management plans. However, disasters not only cause these visible damages such as death and destruction but also leaves a trail of human suffering in terms of mental agony, emotional disturbance, uprooting of the social balance in society, withdrawal from society for the survivors. One of the most important concern is to understand that Climate Change is a continuous phenomenon which has increased risks as it is aggravating disaster frequency and intensity. It is also increasing immense pressure on the resources and is revealing infrastructural vulnerabilities which are now needing to be retrofitted or rebuilt to adapt to the changed climate. The chapter also discusses the global and national disaster trends.

PRE-REQUISITES

NIL

UNIT OUTCOMES

List of outcomes of this unit is as follows:

U3-O1: Realize the need to study disaster impacts

U3-O2: Describe the demographic aspects related to disaster

U3-O3: Explain the Psycho-Social and mental health issues in disaster

U3-O4: Explain the global and national disaster trends

U3-O5: Describe Climate Change and urban disaster scenario

Unit-3 Outcomes	EXPECTEDMAPPINGWITHCOURSEOUTCOMES (1-Weak Correlation; 2-Medium correlation; 3-Strong Correlation)					
	CO-1	CO-2	CO-3	CO-4	CO-5	CO-6
U3-01	2	2	1	2	1	2
U3-02	-	1	3	2	2	2
U3-03	-	1	1	2	1	-
U3-04	1	2	2	1	2	2
U3-05	-	-	2	1	1	1

3.1 INTRODUCTION

Disasters impact millions of people globally, through both natural and human made causes. They may take the form of floods, earthquakes, hurricanes, fire, tornadoes, or even terrorist attacks. Disasters may involve a full range of losses including physical, social, political, economic, health, ecological or environmental. Disasters impact people's health through loss of life, injury, ill-health, disability or trauma. Furthermore, as these disasters disturb the established order, they result in huge economic losses like damage to property and infrastructure, disruption of supply chain, loss of jobs, etc, Moreover, they can alter the environment through habitat destruction, ecological stress and loss of biodiversity, water scarcity, food scarcity, etc. Disasters may also have political implications where the power balance can shift and people's confidence in the system can get eroded. Additionally, they can have several indirect impacts such as loss of attendance in schools if schools get damages and other allied impact. Thus, it can be clearly stated that disasters have negative effects. However, it can also bring an opportunity to "Build Back Better" with itself. The general characteristics of disaster impacts relate to:

- Loss of life, property and environment.
- Disturbance in the normal pattern of life.
- Migration both short term and even long term.
- Civil unrest, leading to law and order difficulty.

Disaster Impact

- Post-Traumatic Stress Disorder (PTSD).
- Adverse impact on economic and social structure.
- Falling apart of infrastructure, transport and communication.
- Disruption in the supply chain of the goods that the community needs like food, clothes, medicines, and even shelter.
- Collapse of the economy and social structure.
- Epidemiological threats.

3.2 TYPES OF DISASTER IMPACTS

The following are the Impact of Disasters as given below and shown in Fig. 3.1.

- Economic Impacts of Disasters
- Social Impacts of Disaster
- Physical Impacts of Disaster
- Ecological impacts of Disasters
- Environmental Impacts of Disasters

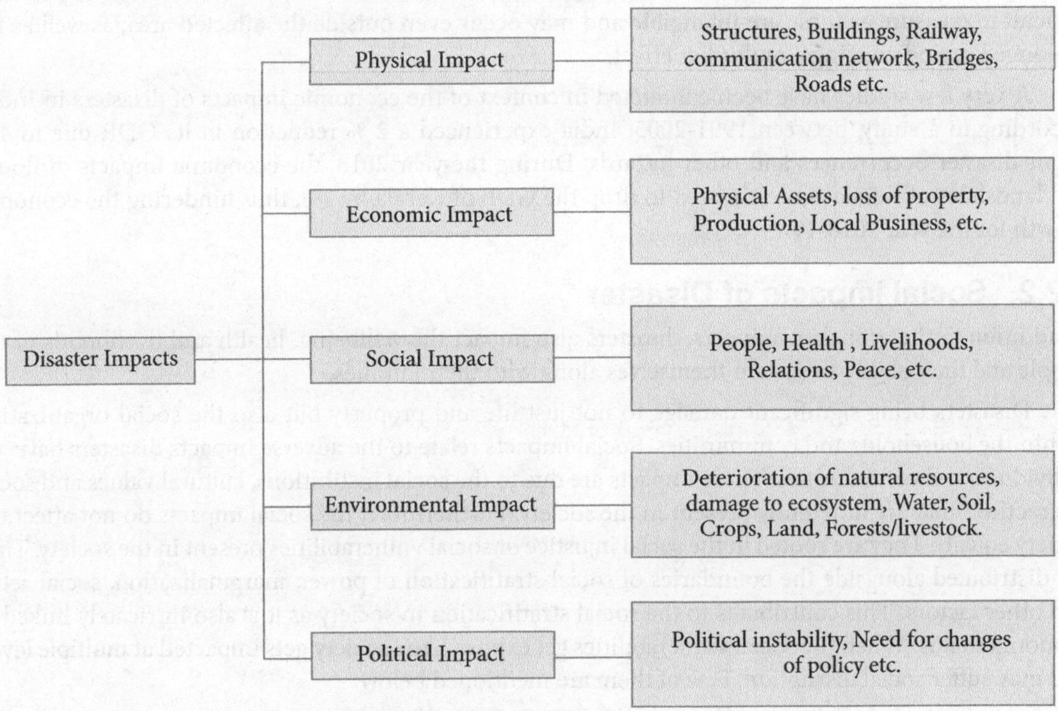

Fig. 3.1: Impact of Disasters

3.2.1 Economic Impacts of Disasters

The disaster affects both rich and poor. However, it is the poor who are worst affected, as they are least capable to cope with the disaster themselves. Poor are hit the hardest as it impacts them not only directly but also indirectly in terms of various costs that they have to incur for the disaster impacts.

The total economic losses comprise both direct and indirect costs. The direct costs are the ones which can be directly measured in terms of monetary loss of partial or total damage of the physical assets in the region of disaster occurrence. For example, the physical assets include social infrastructure (hospitals, schools, homes, commercial and governmental buildings), economic infrastructure like roads, transport, energy, telecommunications, electricity supplies), productive capital and stock variants such as (inventories, crops, livestock, industrial plants). These are tangible as they can be easily assessed just after the event.

Indirect economic losses include lower output due to loss of productive capital or infrastructure and disruption in the supply- chain for goods and services. This can lead to lower quantity supplied by the producer and hence rise in prices, leading to economic disruption. Higher prices can also hurt the economic sentiments leading to instability in the stock markets thereby affecting businesses. Other indirect costs relate to increased medical expenses. Comprehensively, this reduces the purchasing power of many people, thus lowering demand for goods and services in the long run. This can also lower the demand for labor (thus increasing unemployment) and capital and henceforth earnings. Damages and losses along with reconstruction costs can exceed the government's budget. This can mean lower levels of development and poverty for many. However, there are few positives at one end of the supply chain where the demand for labor increases as a result of rehabilitation. Indirect economic losses are however difficult to measure as these are intangible and may occur even outside the affected area, as well as for prolonged period creating a multiplier effect.

A very few studies have been conducted in context of the economic impacts of disasters in India. According to a study, between 1991-2005, India experienced a 2 % reduction in its GDP, due to 431 major disaster occurrences and other hazards. During the year 2018, the economic impacts of floods and landslides of Kerala was estimated to drop the GDP of Kerala by 2%, thus hindering the economic growth for the year 2018-19.

3.2.2 Social Impacts of Disaster

In addition to the economic impacts, disasters also impact the wellbeing, health and livelihoods of the people and their ability to sustain themselves along with their families.

Disasters bring significant damage to not just life and property but also the social organization within the households and communities. Social impacts relate to the adverse impacts disasters have, on individuals and communities. These impacts are due to the social institutions, cultural values and social interactions that are inherently present in the society. Furthermore, the social impacts do not affect the society equally. They are rooted in the social injustice or social vulnerabilities present in the society. They are distributed alongside the boundaries of social stratification of power, marginalization, social setup and other factors. This contributes to the social stratification in society as it is also intricately linked to economic status. When the social vulnerabilities get exposed, the society gets impacted at multiple levels and may suffer social disruption. Few of them are mentioned below: -

- Caste and Communal Discrimination
- Sexual Abuse
- Social Exclusion
- Problem of Social networking.
- Adverse effects on women.
- Social problems of Scheduled Castes/ Tribes
- Social composition

- Roles and relations among different social groups.
- Social capital and cohesion (violence, communalism, crime and social unrest)
- Migrating in search of work
- Withdrawal of children from school.

At the level of households, the gender roles take a turn, usually in the form of women getting affected the most. At the level of community, the disaster impacts the social composition of the affected communities, and changes the roles and relations among different social groups, especially gender. This impacts the social capital and cohesion, which includes risks of violence, crime, and social unrest. It can even alter the way we live, relate with each other, play, work and cooperate within and among the society.

The impacts also include how different social groups are able to cope from the impacts of the disasters including migrating in search of work, reducing expenditure, children not being attend the school, etc.

For example, During the Kerala Floods of 2018 livelihoods were lost, impacting the households economically which led to instability in the lives of many. Similarly, during the Indian Ocean Tsunami of 2004, it was estimated that the job loss was around 2.7 million in India. This was true especially for those who had little access to assets and risk transfers.

3.2.3 Physical Impact of Disasters

Just after the disaster event has occurred, the physical impacts can be seen in the form of casualties such as injury, deaths and destruction of life and damage to property. These impacts can be easily measured and are the first to be reported as these impacts are directly visible. Losses due to damage to physical infrastructures such as buildings, houses, railways, roads, communication network, electricity, water supply, etc., animal husbandry and crops are crucial factors for measuring the physical impacts. The rate of physical impacts that can be seen are higher in developing countries. The damage to property affects various types of services such as residential, community services, industrial, commercial, critical infrastructure. The damage to the physical infrastructure can affect two arenas, structure and content. For example, an earthquake can trigger a fire, if the electric components get destroyed. Similarly, an industry where chemical or radioactive material is present can contaminate the environment if the physical infrastructure is damaged. More than 500,000 houses and 6,700 healthcare facilities and electricity infrastructure were damaged during cyclone Fani in the year 2019.

3.2.4 Political Impact of Disaster

Politics is an integral part of disasters as it requires efficient management on part of the government. The government is the largest stakeholder in this regard, as it not only responds to it, but also prepares for it and works to prevent it in future from occurring. Every disaster impact is not only expected to draw prompt responses from the government especially for those who are affected but also for those who might get affected in future. Thus, the role of government may get highly contested from those in opposition, media and others and may lead to politicization. This creates tumultuous situations for the political systems of a nation, sometimes making it undergo extreme shocks not only due to the disaster shocks, but also shocks due to political transformations, which may translate into instability and question the political legitimacy.

These shocks wreak havoc on the socio-economic systems as well and worsens the citizens' insecurity and increases their demands. Moreover, disaster also reduces the capacity of the governments to respond.

Government's role is very important because its decisions affect the lives of its citizens. Government has special powers which are needed to run the country during such a scenario. At the same time, they are also under immense pressure to perform better according to the needs of the people and time.

Here are few of the challenges that the government might face while responding to or preparing for the disaster impacts. These are: -

- Lack of leadership.
- Limited access to political representation and thus power.
- Lack of resources with local and national institutions.
- Lack of participation in community affairs.
- Lack of educational background.
- Lack of social support.
- Rise of social activism against the government.

Disaster impacts might introduce a new set of victims and grievances which can shuffle the government's political agendas and political participants.

Disasters may affect people by changing the way they think: People might help each other during a disaster situation. Similarly, if the government responds well or vice-a-versa, it might affect the public opinion about the government. In this context, it can be said that the political impacts of disasters can be experienced by a person directly or indirectly. However, it is to be noted that people may even be affected by disasters through mediated ways. This occurs through various ways such as traditional newspapers, media. Furthermore, recently there has been a spur of social media-based news which has caught the attention of a large number of people.

3.2.5 Ecological impacts of Disasters

The Ecological impacts of disasters relate to, the natural resource depletion and degradation as a result of extreme events. Extreme events such as chemical explosion, bioterror etc., can lead to insufficient access to safe water, clean air, sanitation, waste management especially in urban areas which are densely populated. This can also trigger socio-economic vulnerability of the affected communities. These contribute to poor environmental conditions such as soil degradation, food scarcity, and loss of biodiversity. This can also threaten livelihoods of people especially for those who are dependent upon earnings through land-based products namely agriculture, marine, forests, pastures. In totality, this leads to scarcity of natural resources which reduces the coping capacity and resilience of the people to face any disaster. These all factors can eventually lead to economic destitution, social discord and forced migration.

During the occurrence of the Indian Ocean tsunami, the affected community witnessed habitat destruction, damage to livelihoods, water logging, damage to agriculture, disruption to fishing. It even affected the marine ecosystem including coral reefs, flora and fauna, mangroves, sea-grass, etc., The fisherman colonies of semi-urban areas and urban areas also got encroached along with areas which were supposed to be the protected areas in the coastal regulatory zones. (CRZ).

3.2.6 Environmental Impacts of Disasters

The impact of disasters damages environmental sustainability because it affects the environmental resources. This also poses a challenge to achieve the Millenium Development Goal (MDG7- Ensuring Environmental Sustainability).

Environment provides a number of vital services such as natural capital for the existence and well-being of humans. Disasters can directly damage the environment through damage to the natural infrastructure and ecosystem or indirectly through poor management after the occurrence of the disasters. Disasters themselves and in its post intervention phase can incur far reaching impacts on the environment and is one of the fundamental causes for its degradation. Thus, the environment and disasters are intrinsically linked not only in the context of developing countries but also in the developed countries like the US, Japan, etc., Degradation of the natural resource base leads to alteration of natural processes, alters humanity's resources, ecosystem damage, loss of biodiversity which affects the sustainability of the environment. Thus, disasters and environmental vulnerability are linked as degradation decrease overall resilience and coping strategies. As the environment consists of everything around us, it impacts not only the natural environment but also the human-made environment. The potential environmental impacts that different disasters can create upon the environment are given in Table 3.1

Env. Impacts

Table 3.1: Potential Environmental Impact of Different Disasters

Disasters	Potential Environment Impacts
Earthquake	– Industrial Chemical releases – Natural Gas leaks – Building waste debris – Contamination of water – Hazardous waste
Droughts	– Loss of biodiversity – Habitat destruction – Dry up water resources leading to water scarcity – Poor quality of soil leading to food scarcity – Risk upon the endangered species – Wetland degradation
Flood, Storms, Hurricanes, Typhoons Cyclones	– Ground and surface water contamination – Surface runoff or rapid drainage leading to loss of topsoil· – Damage or loss of ecosystem (coral reefs or mangroves)
Forest fires	– Loss of Biodiversity – Loss of ecologically sensitive areas – Deforestation, Air and water pollution
Landslides	– Ground and surface water contamination – Damage/deterioration to ecosystems – Damage to agriculture and other land use functions

Adapted from: DEWGA, 2008

Moreover, the disasters can also disrupt the Urban environment by destruction of important structures, especially those connected to our culture or work. Additionally, other infrastructures such as oil and gas pipelines, roads, bridges, transmission lines etc., can also be impacted. Thus, disasters impact the environment and vice versa. These inter-dependencies and interactions affect the ecosystem, biodiversity and people.

3.3 DEMOGRAPHIC ASPECTS

Demography relates to the systematic study of population. The term is derived from the Greek word's demos i.e., people and *graphein* i.e., describe, meaning "describing the people in a particular area". It analyzes the trends in population change including distribution in gender, age, disability, and other factors. Demographic data becomes important for planning and implementing during the Disaster Risk Reduction (DRR) activities. It helps in understanding not only the distribution but also helps in analyzing and evaluating the social causes behind it. When disasters occur, they do not discriminate between people but people do. The coping capacity of people depends upon the social, political, economic, cultural environment.

According to the Census 2011, the total population of the country is 1,210,854,977 people. The average density is 382 persons per sq km. In 2017, it was estimated that the population has reached around 1,339 billion, among whom approximately 31.6% of the population resides in urban India. This population however is not distributed equally across states. For example, 47.7% of the population of Kerala resides in Urban regions and the Union Territories (UT) of Chandigarh and Delhi remain the most urbanized UT's with 97.5% and 97.25% respectively. However, the state of Himachal Pradesh has one of the least populated urban areas with only 10% of its population residing in urban areas.

The inequalities across caste, class, or gender not only discriminate, while addressing the challenges of planning, response, or recovery but also alienate the vulnerable group from the decision-making process. Disaster management could become biased by being blind to such existing inequalities.

This topic highlights the significance of DRR to tackle inequalities in the coping capacities by acknowledging that some sections are more vulnerable than others during disasters due to their position in the social system.

In fact, the Disaster Management (DM) Act 2005 laid down by the Government of India (GoI) prohibits any form of discrimination related to caste, class, community, descent, sex or religion in all its forms and manifestations during activities of Humanitarian Assistance Disaster Relief (HADR), Disaster Risk Reduction (DRR) to the affected people. According to the National Policy of Disaster Management (NPDM 2009), the socially marginalized such as Women, economically weaker sections (EWS), Scheduled Castes (SC) and Scheduled Tribes (ST) tend to suffer more during the disasters. The Sustainable Development Goal (SDG) 10.2 targets to "empower and promote the social, economic and political inclusion of all irrespective of age, sex, disability, race, ethnicity, origin, religion or economic or other status" by the year 2030.

Inclusive Disaster Management implies that there should be dignity, rights and opportunities for all, thereby contributing to resilience, while also acknowledging diversity across gender, disability, age and various other factors. According to NDMP 2019, disaster management in India should lay emphasis on inclusion for DRR as under: -

- Gender-based Vulnerabilities
- Sexual and Gender Minorities
- Scheduled Castes and Scheduled Tribes (SC&ST)
- Elderly

- Children and
- Persons with Disabilities (PWD)

3.3.1 Gender-based Vulnerabilities

Gender implies social roles and responsibilities that a society associates with male and female. It is different from 'sex' which refers to biological attributes of belonging to a particular gender. It is more of the social roles assigned that perpetuates, reinforces, and increases gender inequality than the biologically ascribed status.

A gendered aspect to DRR helps to focus upon the vulnerabilities and capacities of each gender to prepare, prevent and recover from Disasters.

Women are generally considered to be more vulnerable during disasters than men. This is because; It has been observed that there are increased instances of abuse against women, violence against women, divorce rates in the aftermath of disasters. Due of lack of privacy, women are at an increased risk of facing sexual assault. Access to basic sanitation also takes a back seat due to scarcity of various resources. Young women and girls are also at a risk of getting married earlier or getting entrapped by traffickers.

Many times, women are not part of the decision-making process during the relief and recovery phase. This is because they either do not hold positions of power or do not have enough resources such as land in their name. This makes it difficult for them to bring a gendered aspect in disaster relief and reconstruction. Women who are single, widows or heading the family, find it difficult to access financial help and information for recovery and reconstruction as neither of their family members participate in the decision making. In many situations, due to pre-existing social vulnerabilities and conditioning, women usually tend to demand less during the relief, recovery or reconstruction process. This amplifies the already existing vulnerabilities and socio-economic stress.

Women need to be mainstreamed through participation in the planning and implementation of disasters, to become active contributors in building resilience. The Sendai Framework for Disaster Risk Reduction (SFDRR 2015-2030) emphasizes the need to involve women in the decision-making process in the lead roles, not only in the reconstruction phase after the disaster has occurred but also in the planning phase.

For promoting gender equity, houses and especially reconstructed houses should be registered in the name of both wife and husband. Women who are single and widows, and do not have land in their names should also be given shelter. This makes them feel confident, safe and secure. Owner Driven Reconstruction (ODR) can be promoted where women can take the lead role in monitoring the implementation of such technology which promotes safe housing.

Programs and schemes shall be designed in a manner which empowers women financially either through income generating schemes, social security measures or self-employment opportunities. Women Self Help Groups (SHG's) should be promoted, this can encourage livelihood opportunities. Vocational training is also an important aspect of this. This needs to be imparted in the form of enhancing skills such as masons, trading local products, carpenters, etc. This can go a long way, in helping women gain access to resources, promote gender equality and reduce vulnerabilities. Thus, making DRR more inclusive.

3.3.2 Sexual and Gender Minorities

It has been observed that disasters do not affect every individual equally. People with various kinds of disadvantages are more vulnerable to disasters as compared to people who are at an advantageous position. Gender minorities are people who belong to genders other than Male or Female, whereas Sexual minorities are those who have different sexual orientation. These groups of people are disadvantaged is terms of accessing opportunities and thereby receive reduced services and resources. Moreover, they are also socially and economically vulnerable. This is because they not only have reduced access to opportunities and resources but also face stigma and discrimination. These factors also deprive them of disaster response and mitigation programs, thus making them even more vulnerable. Additionally, the disaster management efforts including legal and institution ones often ignore the needs of these groups of people. Several case studies conducted in recent times have shown that sexual and gender minorities are more adversely affected by disasters as they are highly marginalized. Thus, it is important that the DRM policies incorporate their issues and needs and make them a part of implementation of Disaster Risk Reduction (DRR) efforts.

3.3.3 Scheduled Castes and Scheduled Tribes

The scheduled castes (SC) and Scheduled tribes (ST) are recognized in the Constitution of India, as historically disadvantaged people needing affirmative actions and policies. They usually live on the hazard prone areas lying either in the floodplains, unstable hillsides, coastal tracts which are unsafe, and which lie on the marginal lands of rural or urban areas. These areas are also majorly deprived of the basic services such as access to sanitation, water, safe housing, toilets, health services, quality education, and other basic amenities. The unsafe housing that they reside in are not disaster resilient and hence their poverty becomes one of the key challenges to DRR. In urban areas, their residence is usually on the open lands or small huts which are unauthorized lands. These uncertain living spaces, combined with chronic poverty, hazardous living conditions, and lack of access to basic amenities makes disaster resilience, mitigation and adaptation difficult in such areas. The women of these communities suffer even more. The inherent system that prejudices against SC's and ST's make them more vulnerable especially during evacuation, disaster relief distribution, reconstruction, recovery.

Accordingly, efforts need to be made to not allow any discrimination in any DRR activities or while providing humanitarian assistance. Thus, while making such DRR efforts, caste related issues and challenges need to be kept in mind so as to achieve sustainable development for all.

3.3.4 Children

Children are vulnerable due to their physical nature as well as mental immaturity and inability to understand the surrounding. The first legally binding document to adopt the rights of the children is the United Nation's Convention on the Rights of the Child (UNCRC) 1989. It underscores that the children have the right to have adequate water, shelter, food, and education. They need to be able to grow in a supportive and safe environment. They should also be free from abuse, trafficking, neglect, and sexual exploitation.

During disasters, children may face trauma due to trafficking, gender violence, isolation, anxiety, losing their parents, separation from their families, and may end up in child labour, beggary, etc.,. They may also face issues such as interruption in their education, poor access to sanitation, food and nutrition, and recreational activities. They thus need special attention and support as they are in their developmental age. The disasters may erode the support system and bring chaos in their life. This could traumatize them affecting their physical and mental health.

So, it is important to provide appropriate interventions to ensure that the children are able to cope up with the disasters and live a life full of nurture and care. Adequate provisions also need to be made at the level of community or schools to bring awareness about the disaster situations and strategies in emergency response. This can go a long way in helping their parents as well, when they get back home and share the knowledge. Thus, special provisions for children need to be made in the DRR, relief, recovery, adaptation and mitigation planning to make sure that they get adequate attention and support to ensure their well-being.

3.3.5 Elderly

Approximately, 10 % or 700 million people throughout the world have aged over 60. By 2030, people in the age bracket of 60 would be more than in the bracket of children under 10. This implies that the world is aging. However, this also makes DRR planning for elderly very crucial. The elderly have particular physical and emotional needs. The older population needs adequate attention apart from several basic facilities. This coupled with more extreme disasters and climate events adds to risks and vulnerability of the older people. They need to be prioritized while developing plans for disaster management. This is because when disaster occurs, they can get forgotten in the crowd as they are usually among the last in the line. This happens because they have impaired physical mobility along with psychological vulnerability. They may also have diminished sensory awareness and poor health conditions. Added to this, the elderly is also limited by social and economic capacity as well as capability to adapt and respond.

After the disaster has occurred, the needs of the elderly should be taken care separately, keeping in mind their specific needs and concerns and the fact that they are more vulnerable as compared to others. There is a need to have community-based support for senior citizens so that they are mainstreamed in their communities. The local community should be educated on such measures to help and support senior citizens. The district DRR plan should reflect the list of measure for senior citizens who are living without any support of family. The district officers should also work on setting up temporary arrangements for taking care of their personal needs such as medicine, food, shelter, etc.,

3.3.6 Persons with Disabilities

According to the UN Convention on the Rights of Persons with Disabilities (UNCRPD) "Persons with disabilities include those who have long-term physical, mental, intellectual or sensory impairments which in interaction with various barriers may hinder their full and effective participation in society on an equal basis with others". Moreover, the Dhaka Declaration which was adopted in December 2015 on Disability and Disaster Risk Management realizes: "the significance of linking Sustainable Development Goals (SDGs) with disability inclusive Disaster Risk Management (DRM) on the interpretation that, "inclusion builds the resilience of the whole of society, safeguards development gains and minimizes disaster losses".

According to the census 2011, the people belonging to the PWD segment are 2.2% of the total population or 2.68 crore. Of these, 44% of them are females while 56% of them are males, whereas the female male percentage in the total population is 49% and 51% of India respectively.

The persons with disability have less capacity to deal with the disasters. This implies that they are at higher risk than others. Additionally, they often belong to the poorest class of people. Hence, they are particularly vulnerable to disasters, as they live-in poor-quality houses which lack adequate sanitation and facilities, thus making the living conditions hazardous. They are often ignored during aid distribution. They sometimes might even become barriers for themselves due to the negative attitudes which might develop as they are not part of the mainstream.

Other barriers that exist are: -

- *Natural Environments*- Cliffs, hills, etc.,
- *Social Environment*- Economic, Political, and Legal factors.
- *Socio-cultural factors*- Attitudes, beliefs, discrimination such as unequal access to shelter, food distribution, and livelihood opportunities.
- *Built space*- inaccessible water systems, sanitation systems, shelters, information and communication. This makes non-availability of early warning systems to PWDs.

According to a survey conducted by United Nations International Strategy for Disaster Reduction (UNISDR) in 2013, it has been found that there is a need to prioritize inclusiveness of PWD in Disaster Risk reduction (DRR) efforts. This will foster involvement of PWDs in DRR-related activities. Thus, DRR efforts should focus on addressing the vulnerabilities of PWD specifically among others keeping in mind their needs and concerns and the fact that they are more vulnerable as compared to others. Special attention should focus towards leaving no one behind.

There is a need to have community-based support for PWD so that they are mainstreamed in their surroundings. The local community should be educated on the measures to help and support senior citizens. The PWD should have a buddy-based support system who can be informed about their needs and priorities. The district DRR plan should reflect the list of measure for such PWD's who are in need of special care. The district officer should also work on setting up temporary arrangements for taking care of their personal needs such as medicine, food, shelter, etc.

3.4 MENTAL HEALTH &PSYCHO-SOCIAL ISSUES IN DISASTERS

Disasters either man made or natural, bring loss of life, injury and damage to property. These disasters leave a trail of human suffering and misery, emotional trauma, mental agony, stress of survivors because of death of near and dear ones and damage to their assets and property. It has been observed that the people experience emotional reactions and stress after the disaster occurrence as a 'normal response to an abnormal situation'. When hopes, dreams, and assumptions get shattered, they cause psychological impact of varying degrees on the lives of individuals and communities. This can cause long term mental health and psychological problems.

Psychosocial care

The affected community will require interventions not only for the material and logistical assistance but also for Psycho- Social care and Mental Health support.

So, while planning for disaster recovery, it should be kept in mind that years after the damage has been restored the mental agony and trauma of the survivors might continue. Therefore, it is important to identify such people and provide early counseling to prevent such prolonged distress and agony.

A significant portion of the survivors would also experience decline in social functioning because of the inability to cope from distress by themselves. They will require adequate psycho-social support and mental health care.

Thus, Psycho-Social Support and Mental Health Services (PSMHS) should be an essential part of Disaster management plans whether it is man-made or natural. The terms Psycho-social support/care and mental health services are different but often used interchangeably.

Psycho-social support aims to address an extensive range of psycho-social problems through comprehensive interventions such as actively listening to the survivors, helping them restore their day to day functioning, getting them connected to near and dear ones, and promoting social cohesion among survivors in the aftermath of disasters. Whereas mental health services aim to address clinical psychological signs through medical interventions such as diagnosis and management of manifest stress, identifying symptoms of mental disorders. These services require expertise of psychologists, psychiatrist, psychotherapist, mental health professionals, etc.

Most importantly, it is crucial to bring awareness about the personal coping strategies, normal reactions to the disasters and knowing where and when to seek help prior and even in the aftermath of the disasters. These elements can essentially decrease the duration and intensity of post disaster distress.

Thus, the principal aim of any Psycho-Social and Mental Health intervention is to achieve the wellbeing of the communities affected by disasters. The severity of social disability and psychological distress depends upon the magnitude of the trauma. Disasters like tsunamis and earthquakes may leave a major trauma for a large number of people. Whereas disasters which are less severe may leave lesser trauma for people affected by it. However, man-made disasters such as terrorist activities, communal riots, and, Chemical, Biological, Radiological; Nuclear (CBRN) disasters create more distress than natural disasters.

The significant psycho-social consequences of disasters include:

- Worsening of pre- existing social problems (pre-disaster) such as facing discrimination and marginalization because of belonging to a particular group, extreme poverty, and political oppression.
- Emergence of new social problems due to disasters such as separation from family, damage to resources, destruction of the structure of community, homelessness, increase in gender related violence, unemployment.
- Humanitarian aid induced Social problems such as loss of traditional support mechanism, undermining of the community structure.

Similarly, The significant mental health consequences of disasters include:-

- Worsening of pre- existing problems (pre-disaster) such as alcohol abuse, severe mental disorder.
- Emergence of new problems due to disasters such as non-pathological distress, grief, depression including post-traumatic stress disorder (PTSD).
- Humanitarian aid induced problems such as lack of information regarding food distribution and related anxiety.

Thus, mental health and psycho-social problems in complex emergencies encompass far more than the experience of disaster induced depression or PTSD. A selective focus on only these two problems will be inappropriate. Coordination will be required from all stakeholders. Henceforth, there is a need to integrate all the actors/ agencies involved in facilitating and extending support because health workers are limited during such situations.

3.4.1 Common Psychological Reactions to Disaster

It should be understood that for a majority of survivors, distress reaction ranging from mild to moderate form is normal and may not be a cause of worry as it is transitory. However, it becomes a concern, if it overwhelms the capacity of the survivors to cope with the new situations. Thus, it should be labeled pathological only if it exceeds a tolerable limit, is prolonged, or interferes with regular functioning.

Survivors react with grief for losing loved ones, possessions and home and also experience poor concentration, depressed mood, etc., The reactions to traumatic situations depend not only on the circumstances but also on the personality of each individual.

The common reactions to disasters can be classified into emotional, psychosomatic, cognitive, behavioral and attitudinal effects. These reactions are shown in the Table 3.2.

Table 3.2: Common disaster-related stress reactions

Emotional reaction	Psychosomatic reactions	Cognitive reaction	Behavioral and attitudinal reaction
– Fear	– Sleep disturbance	– Confusion	– Disruptions in social relationship
– Panic Attacks	– Nausea	– Memory problems	
– Shock	– Muscle tension	– Recurring dreams or nightmare	– Poor motivation and concentration
– Anger	– Palpitation	– Trouble Concentrating or	
– Sadness	– Headaches	– remembering things	– Lethargy
– Guilt	– Diarrhea	– Repeated thoughts	– Hopelessness
– Helplessness	– Breathing difficulties	– Flashbacks	– Increased conflict with family
		– Difficulty in making decision	
		– Shortened attention	
		– Confusion	

Source: Psycho-social Care in Disaster Management, NIDM

3.4.2 Common Reactions to Disasters in Different Age Groups of Children

Children experience a variety of feelings and reactions. The reactions exhibited by children differ from the ones expressed by adults. Children lack the conceptual and verbal capacity to cope effectively with sudden stress. Children have limited capacity and are not able to understand the totality of the situation to be able to process about what has happened. The adolescents among them may exhibit a few behaviors which are more risk-taking than usual such as use of drugs, reckless driving, etc.,. They may not be able to discuss those with their families. When disasters occur, they disrupt the normal functioning of the society, disrupt peer relationships and school life, thus hampering the healthy psychological as well as personality development of the children.

Since children have specific needs as they adapt to the given circumstances, they require special attention and care to meet their needs. When symptoms of stress continue, they might need the help of a mental health professional. Therefore, there is a need to recognize the common psycho-social reactions which may be exhibited by children of various age groups before planning any type of psycho-social interventions. The psychological reactions in different age groups of children due to disasters are shown in the Table 3.3.

Table 3.3: Reactions to Disasters in Different Age Groups of Children

Age Range	Reactions
Pre-school age (1-5 years)	– Helplessness – Clinging and demanding – Fear and anger – Fear of darkness or sleeping alone – Increased aggression – Irritation, Moodiness, – Temper tantrums & Crying – Scary nightmares – Regressive behaviour (thumb sucking, wanting to be carried, bed-wetting)
School age (5-11years)	– Headache – Stomach aches – Lack of self-competency – Isolation – *Fear of recurrence of the event* – Behavioral problems – Disinterest or difficulties in school work- disturbs others, worrying, being tense, undisciplined, refusal to go to school – Regression to behaviors like thumb sucking etc – Nightmares or Sleeplessness – Difficulty in following routines – Emotional problems like apathy, anxiousness withdrawal from, society, depression – Fear of darkness / sleeping alone / separation from parents – Aggression – Understand loss and become very anxious
Adolescents (13-18 years)	– Seeks isolation, becomes less communicative. – Irritability – Aggression–fights, destructive, argumentative – Sleeplessness or increased sleep – Dropping out of school or work – Inability to concentrate – Increased risk taking behaviours . Increase substance abuse – Angry, frustrated and may feel very helpless – Feelings of hopelessness, feeling of neglect and isolation – Depression due to loss – Try to get involved in activities to get a sense of control like rescuing and organising at the camps – Avoidance of trauma related thoughts, feelings and activities – Disobedience, specially towards authority and parents – Guilt for not being able to do enough or for having survived – Aches and pains due to stress. – Feel different or alienated because of their experiences – Behavioural problems like–aggression, lying, stealing

Source: NIMHANS: Training of trainers Module on disaster psycho-social care -2004

Those children are considered to be particularly vulnerable in a disaster situation who have the following conditions: -

- have lost one or both the parents
- have been rendered disabled after the disaster occurrence
- whose parents have remarried
- are unaccompanied minors
- are girls
- those who require critical medical facilities

The National Disaster Management Authority (NDMA) released the National Guidelines on Psycho-social Support and Mental Health Services (PSMHS) in 2009. The guidelines emphasize the need for effective and efficient qualitative service delivery to the survivors of disasters to address the consequent psychological and mental health problems.

The National Institute of Mental Health and Neuro-Sciences (NIMHANS) in India is the apex center for mental health and neuroscience education. It has contributed immensely in facilitating psycho-social support for the people affected by disasters through various initiatives. Its fundamental aim is to create a pool of trained human resources who can offer psycho-social support for disaster management.

3.5 TRENDS IN DISASTERS

Trends in disasters are indicators which provide the disaster and emergency managers to analyze the risk and vulnerability scenario. Systematic collection of the disaster data helps governments and agencies to arrive at decisions in order to be able to plan for DRR, Mitigation, adaptation, relief and recovery.

Disaster trends

The global trend of disaster occurrence from 1900 to 2000 is shown in Fig. 3.2. It is clear from the figure that the occurrence of disasters is increasing since 1900. However, at present the disaster occurrence has increased tenfold as compared to the occurrence of disasters in 1960's.

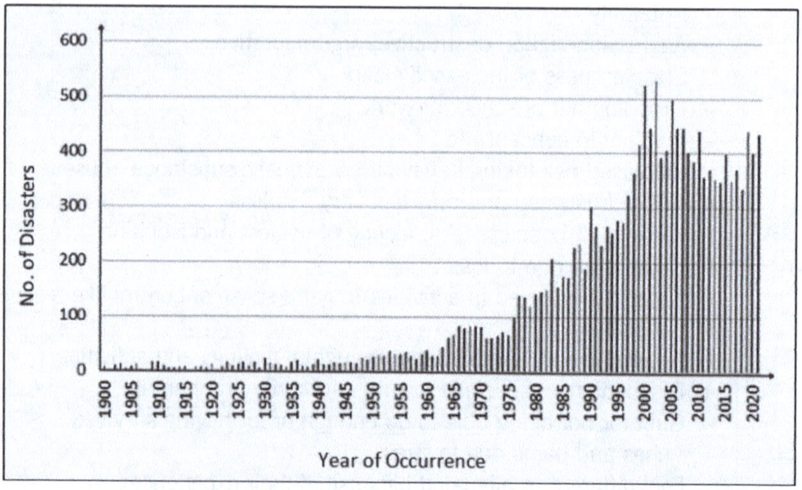

Fig. 3.2: Number of disaster occurrence from 1900-2020

EM-DAT/CRED,2022

According to the Emergency Event Database (EM-DAT), 432 natural disasters have occurred in 2021. These disasters killed 10,492 people, and affected 101.8 million people. Total economic losses were approximately 252.1 billion US$. During 2021, the Asian continent witnessed 40% of all the disasters which caused 66% of the total number of deaths and 49% of the deaths making it the most disaster-prone region in the world. This was particularly evident in countries such as Indonesia with 28, India with 19, China with 17 and Philippines with 14 number of disaster occurrences.

The number of occurrence of disasters was significantly higher at 432 in 2021 as compared to 357, which is the annual average occurrence of disasters during the period of 2001-2020. It is clear from the figure (Fig.3.3) that floods were the most dominant of disaster events in all these years. However, the year 2021 witnessed 223 flood occurrences as compared to 163 annual average flood occurrences, during the period 2001-2020.

Storms were the second most dominant disasters after floods. The number of storm occurrences was higher in 2021 with 121 such occurrences as compared to an annual average of 102 storm occurrences during 2001-2021 as shown in Fig. 3.3.

In the year 2021, a number of 28 earthquakes were reported, whereas 27 earthquake events occurred during 2001-2021 on an average. During 2021, worldwide 15 droughts were witnessed. This is almost similar to the annual average occurrence of droughts in the years 2001-2020. Wildfires were also higher in number in 2021 (19 events) as compared to 11 average occurrences during 2001-2020 (Fig. 3.3).

A very few extreme temperature events were reported in 2021 (three such events) as compared to an average of 21 events per year between 2001-2020 (Fig.3.3)

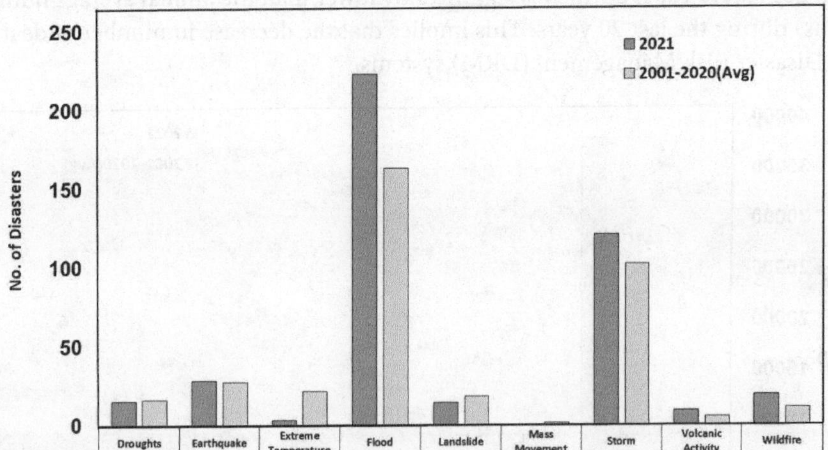

	Droughts	Earthquake	Extreme Temperature	Flood	Landslide	Mass Movement	Storm	Volcanic Activity	Wildfire
2021	15	28	3	223	14	0	121	9	19
2001-2020(Avg)	16	27	21	163	18	1	102	5	11

Fig. 3.3: Comparison of disaster occurrence in 2021 with the annual average data of 2001-2020 (EM-DAT/CRED,2022)

As discussed above, floods and storms continue to show the highest frequency in terms of occurrences and thereby considerable amount of economic losses. It has been reported that the total economic loss was 252 billion US$ in 2021. The economic losses in 2021 due to different types of disasters are compared with the annual average losses during 2001-2020 as shown in Fig. 3.4. It is clear from the figure that the economic losses in 2021, due to disasters continue to show a rising trend, making the year 2021 as the fourth most damaging year in term of economic losses in last 20 years.

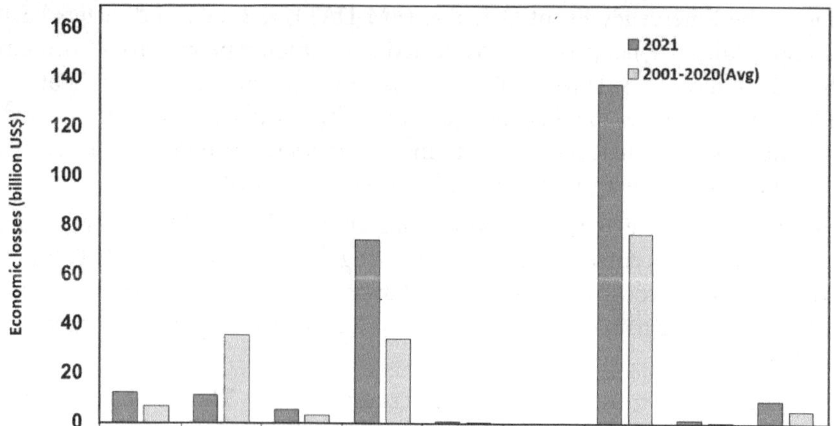

	Droughts	Earthquake	Extreme Temperature	Flood	Landslide	Mass Movement	Storm	Volcanic Activity	Wildfire
2021	12.1	11.3	5.6	74.4	0.5	0	137.7	1.3	9.2
2001-2020(Avg)	6.7	35.4	3.1	34.1	0.3	0	77	0.1	5

Fig. 3.4: Comparison of Global Economic Losses in 2021 with the annual average data of 2001-2020 (EM-DAT/CRED,2022)

The numbers of deaths from different type of disasters in 2001 are compared with the number of deaths during 2001-2020(annual average) as shown in figure 3.5. It is evident from the figure that the no. of deaths from disasters are decreasing in spite of an increase in frequency of disaster occurrences. The total deaths in 2021 were 10, 492 which is significantly lower than the annual average number of deaths (61, 212 deaths) during the last 20 years. This implies that the decrease in number of deaths is possibly due to better Disaster Risk Management (DRM) systems.

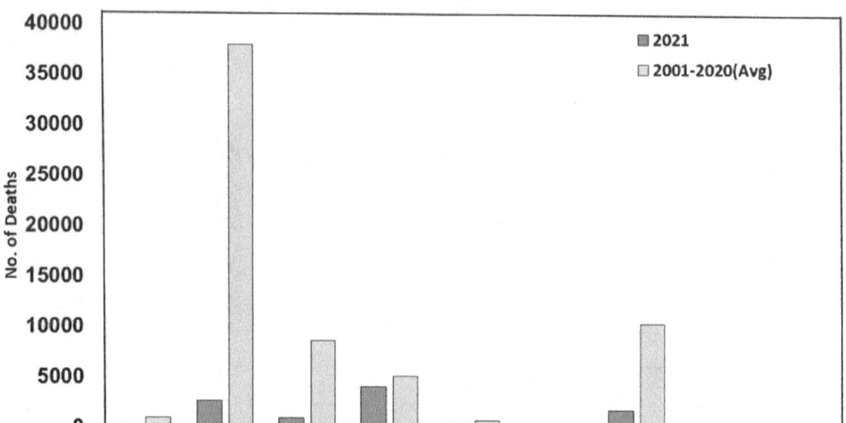

	Droughts	Earthquake	Extreme Temperature	Flood	Landslide	Mass Movement	Storm	Volcanic Activity	Wildfire
2021	0	2742	1044	4143	474	0	1876	85	128
2001-2020(Avg)	1059	37942	8684	5185	884	37	10442	89	77

Fig. 3.5: Comparison on No. of Deaths in 2021 with the annual average data of 2001-2020 (EM-DAT/CRED,2022)

The number of affected people (millions) in 2021 is compared to the 2001-2020 annual average type in Fig. 3.6. The figure indicates that the number of affected people has decreased in 2021(193.4 million) as compared to 101.8 million people affected during the period 2001-2021 per year.

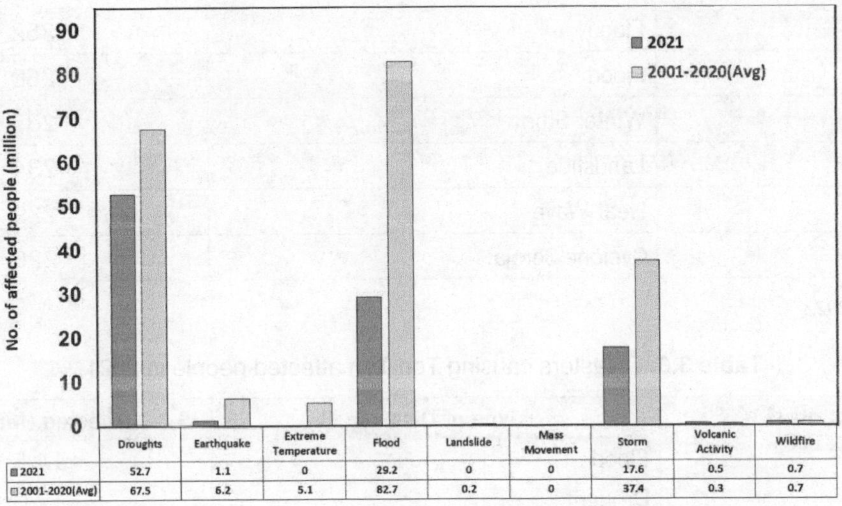

Fig. 3.6: Number of affected (million) by disaster type: 2021 compared to the annual average (EM-DAT/CRED, 2022).

Comparison of occurrence of disasters, number of deaths, affected people and economic losses in 2021 with annual average of 20 years (2000-2020) are shown in the Table 3.4.

Table 3.4: Comparison of occurrence of disasters, number of deaths, affected people and economic losses

	2001-2020 (Annual average)	2021
Occurrence of disasters	347 <	432
Number of deaths	61212 >	10492
Number of affected (million)	193.4 >	101.8
Economic losses (billion (US$)	153.8 <	252.1

It is clear from the table that with the increase in occurrence of disasters, economic losses are increasing but the number of deaths and affected people are decreasing.

The following disaster occurrences caused the highest mortality, affected the largest number of people, and caused the maximum economic losses in the year 2021, which are given in the Tables 3.5-3.7 respectively.

Table 3.5: Disasters causing Top Ten mortality losses in 2021

Country	Type of Disaster	Mortality
Haiti	Earthquake	2575
India	Flood	1282
Canada	Heat Wave	815
Philippines	Typhoon Rai	457

China	Flood	352
Afghanistan	Flood	260
USA	Winter Storm	235
India	Landslide	234
USA	Heat Wave	229
Indonesia	Cyclone Seroja	226

Source: CRED,2022

Table 3.6: Disasters causing Top Ten affected people in 2021

Country	Type of Disaster	Affected (Million)
China	Flood	14.5
South Africa	Drought	12.0
Afghanistan	Drought	11.0
Philippines	Typhoon Rai	10.6
Iraq	Drought	7.0
Somalia	Drought	5.6
Ethiopia	Drought	5.5
Syrian Arab Republic	Drought	5.5
Iran	Drought	2.6
Kenya	Drought	2.1

Source: CRED,2022

Table 3.7: Disasters causing Top Ten Economic losses in 2021

Country	Type of Disaster	Economic Losses (Billion)
USA	Hurricane Ida	65.5
Germany	Flood	40.0
USA	Winter Storm	30.0
China	Flood	16.5
USA	Drought	9.0
Japan	Earthquake	7.7
France	Cold Wave	5.6
USA	Tornado	5.2
USA	Wildfire	3.3
China	Drought	3.1
USA	Storm	3.1
India	Flood	3.1

Source: CRED,2022

Globally, floods account for 44% of the total disaster occurrences during 2000-2019, making it the most frequent type of disaster. Furthermore, the storms account for 28% of the disaster events worldwide, making it the second most commonly occurring disaster.

Similarly, earthquakes (including tsunamis) and volcanic activity account for 9%, extreme temperatures for 6%, droughts for 5% and wildfires for 3% of the total disaster occurrences globally. The distribution of the percentage of occurrence of disasters and number of disasters are shown in Figures. 3.7-3.8 respectively.

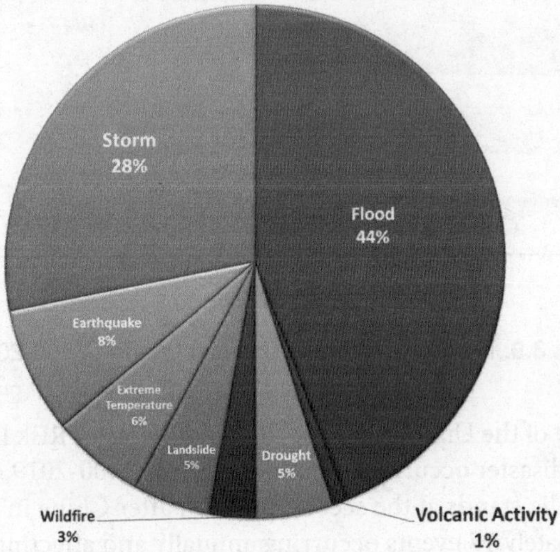

Fig. 3.7: % of occurrence of disasters during 2000-2019

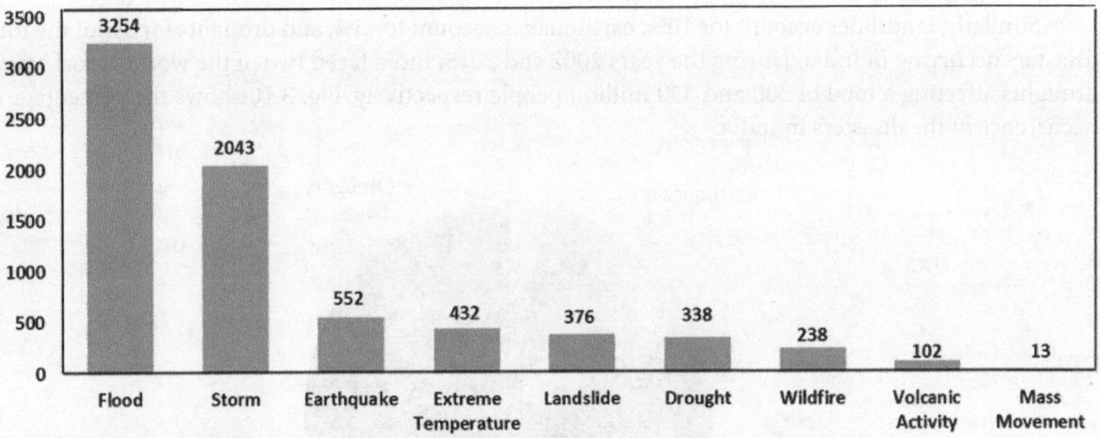

Fig. 3.8: Number of Occurrence of disasters during 2000-2019

Source: CRED&UNDRR, 2020

India due to its varied geographic position, inter-tropical convergence point, and seismicity, episodes of heat waves, droughts, floods, and heavy monsoon rains makes it one of the most disaster affected country. It is highly exposed to natural disasters such as floods, earthquakes, cyclones, landslides and droughts, etc.,

During the period 2000-2019, it was reported that India faced 321 catastrophic events. India stands at the third position after China (577 events) and United States of America (U.S) (477 events) in terms of number of natural disaster occurrences, as shown in Fig.3.9.

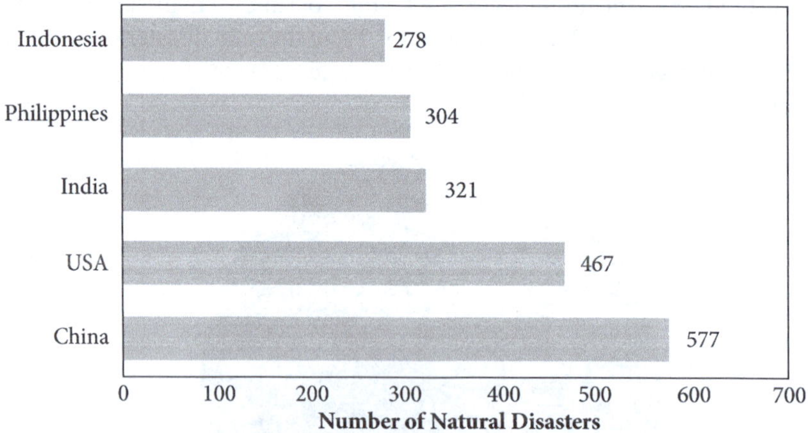

Fig. 3.9: Number of Natural Disasters during 2000-2019

Source: CRED&UNDRR, 2020

According to the report of the United Nations Office for Disaster Risk Reduction (UNDRR), floods account for 52% of the total disaster occurrences in India during 2000-2019, making it the most frequent type of disaster. Globally, India stands at the second position after China in terms of worst hit countries due to floods with approximately 17 events occurring annually and affecting 345 million people.

Furthermore, the cyclones account for 30% of the disaster events, making it the second most commonly occurring type of disaster in India.

Similarly, landslides account for 10%, earthquakes account for 5%, and droughts for 3% of the total disasters occurring in India. During the years 2002 and 2015, India faced two of the world's most severe droughts affecting a total of 300 and 330 million people respectively. Fig. 3.10 shows the percentage of occurrence of the disasters in India.

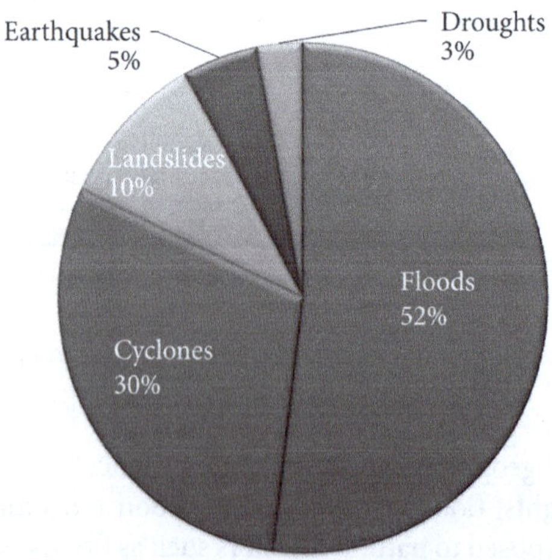

Fig. 3.10: % of occurrence of Natural disasters in India (2000-2019)

During the same 20-year period, these disasters killed 79,732 numbers of people, affected more than 100 crore people and caused economic losses of nearly 80 billion USD in India. The top ten deadliest disasters occurring during the period 2000-2019 worldwide are shown in Table 3.8.

Table 3.8: Ten Deadliest Disasters (2000-2019)

Disaster	Country	Year	Number of Deaths
Earthquake & Tsunami	Indian Ocean	2004	226408
Earthquake	Haiti	2010	222570
Storm	Myanmar	2008	138366
Earthquake	China	2008	87476
Earthquake	Pakistan	2005	73338
Heat Wave	Europe	2003	72210
Heat Wave	Russia	2010	55736
Earthquake	Iran	2003	26716
Earthquake	India	2001	20005
Drought	Somalia	2010	20000

Source: CRED&UNDRR, 2020

3.6 CLIMATE CHANGE AND URBAN DISASTERS

The word climate implies long term weather patterns in an area. Climate is changing rapidly due to the rise in global temperature primarily as a result of industrialization, urbanization, agricultural activities, deforestation, land use changes and similar developments which involve emission of Green House Gasses (GHG's). The effects of Climate Change are felt globally, largely impacting urban life. Cities are one of the largest contributors to Climate Change as their activities generate Greenhouse Gasses in large quantities. According to estimates, 75% of the global CO_2 emissions are emitted by cities among which buildings and transports, have the largest share. In recent years, it has become evident that climate change is real and the climate is rapidly changing the urban landscape. Climate change intensifies the risks of disasters in various visible ways such as damage to the ecosystem, degradation of the environment, rise in frequency and intensity of extreme events such as cold waves, heat waves , floods, cyclones, droughts, rise in sea levels, etc.,. However, with shifting precipitation and temperature patterns there are certain invisible impacts as well, which includes effect on urban ecology, pricing, food and water supply, vector borne diseases, etc,. Henceforth, disasters and climate change are closely interrelated. Climate Change augments disasters and disrupts access to clean water, sanitation, and livelihood and food security. The IPCC Assessment Report (2012) also highlights that climate change will lead to changes in the duration, frequency and spatial extent of disasters leading to a possibility of unprecedented extreme events.

Climate Change is also revealing infrastructural vulnerabilities. Infrastructures of various kinds are exposed by varying levels to different kinds of climatic changes and related extreme events

Warming of the planet is making cities warmer than their rural counterparts as cities have more concretization. Urban areas are the centers of economic activity where the population is concentrated along with various types of infrastructure and built environment to carry out various activities. Additionally, cities utilize water, electricity, sewers-system, hospitals, parks, schools, shops, and transportation in large amounts to serve their population, since the population has the purchasing power. The second and third tier cities are even more at risk of climate related impacts due to lack of institutional and infrastructural capacities, lack of revenue, and rapidly expanding population. Several factors attract people from rural areas to work in urban areas and earn a better living. These are the areas where most of the development, infrastructure, resources, and people are concentrated and are ever expanding. When disaster strikes in such an area, it is likely to face adverse consequences of Climate Change. The process of urbanization and development makes disaster risk in cities more prominent. This increases the carbon footprint of the urban areas. When disasters affect the urban regions, it is termed as "Urban Disasters".

India in particular is highly vulnerable to urban disasters and climate change. This is due to its diverse terrain, rapid use of natural resources, urbanization, industrialization and economic growth. Some of the main factors that make cities vulnerable to disasters are: -

- Density of population
- Poor infrastructure
- Technological disasters
- Chemical accidents
- Industrial explosions
- Inappropriate construction
- System failures
- Spillage in water, air and ground.
- Unplanned developments
- Rapid growth
- Concentration of political, economic or human resources

Urban Disaster

The coastal communities of urban areas are mainly exposed to tropical cyclones. Urban populations living in the low-lying coastal areas and floodplains are under greater risk from the impacts of Climate change. This is because urban areas have large population density and greater livelihoods dependent on them. Thus, there is a need to conduct multi-hazard risk adaptation process in coastal cities encompassing the following: -

- Temperature and precipitation variability assessment
- Urban drought mapping
- Flooding and extreme rainfall mapping
- Cyclone and storm surge mapping
- Sea-level rise analysis
- Environmental health risk assessment

The consequences of climate change along with sectors affected by it and related impacts with potential mitigation and adaptation strategies are shown in Fig. 3.11.

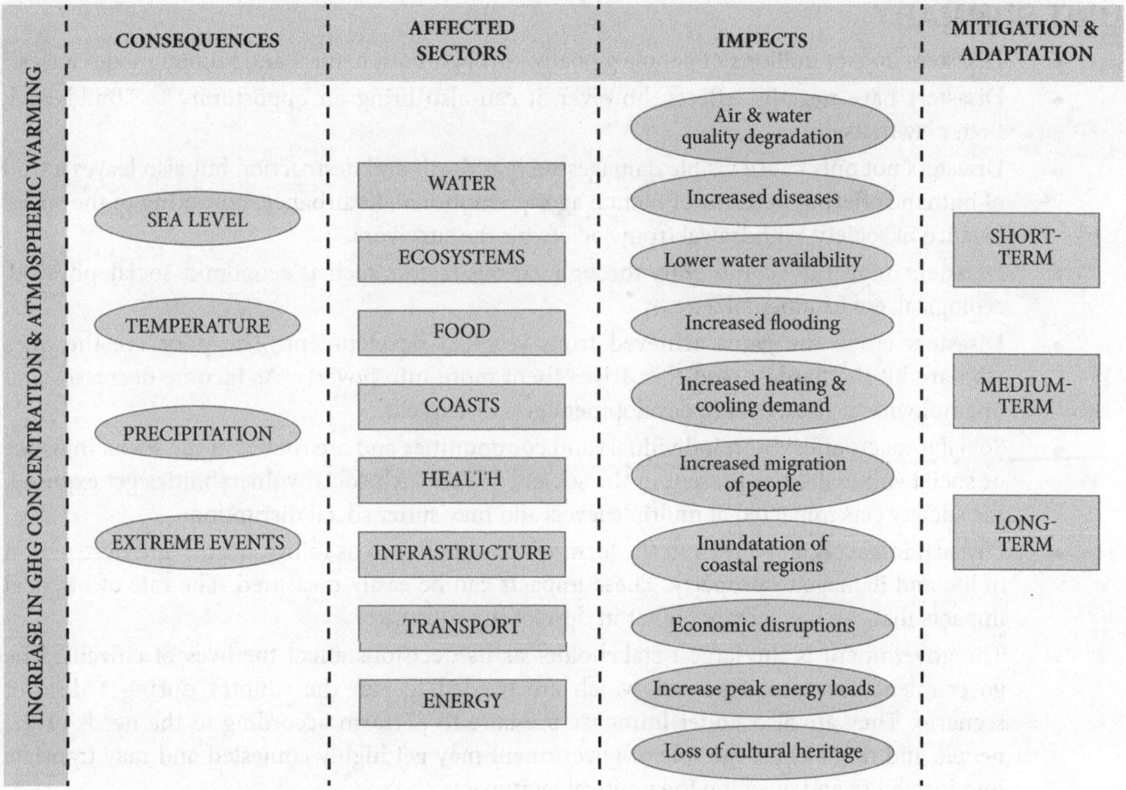

Fig. 3.11: Consequences of Climate Change and its related impacts on various sectors

Source: Climate Resilient Cities, 2008 Primer

The disasters thus are increasing in frequency and intensity, exposing the urban areas to face extreme events in both developing and developed locations. However, cities in the developing countries have low resilience and are more vulnerable. These cities are rapidly growing and exposing more people, resources to disasters. This leads to increase in vulnerability to various disasters.

This requires that urban disaster management should play a proactive role while making developmental plans. Mainstreaming DRR in urban development plans will ensure a sustainable and safe development. Land should be considered as a living entity as it sustains life. Urban planning needs to be based on urban watershed management. This implies that societal requirements should be complemented with environmental requirements. India in particular should focus on Urban disaster management as it is expected to see 100 metropolitan cities by 2035, but unplanned developments could cause huge impacts on not just the economy, environment but also human health. The worst affected would be the poor who would live in high risk areas and have fewer resources to protect themselves.

Thus, the combined pressures of increasing urbanization, climate change, and related factors impact various sectors such as infrastructure, energy, transportation, health, food, water, coasts, and ecosystems. Climate action including climate proofing, especially retrofitting the available buildings and new construction of climate resilient buildings and infrastructure to ensure resilience is a potential action for building climate resilient cities. Thus, DRR initiatives must be integrated with climate change adaptations (CCA).

UNIT SUMMARY

- Disasters impact millions of people globally, through both natural and human made causes.
- Disasters have negative effects; however, it can also bring an opportunity to "Build Back Better" with itself.
- Disasters not only cause visible damages such as death and destruction but also leaves a trail of human suffering in terms of mental agony, emotional disturbance, uprooting of the social balance in society, withdrawal from society for the survivors.
- Disasters impact the community through various factors such as economic, social, physical, ecological, environmental, etc.,.
- Disasters erode the gains achieved from years of development. The poor are the ones who are hit the hardest, and this drives them more into poverty. As income decreases and unemployment rises, overall development gets disrupted.
- Social impacts affect both individuals and communities and are rooted in the social injustice or social vulnerabilities present in the society. When such social vulnerabilities get exposed, the society gets impacted at multiple levels and may suffer social disruption.
- Physical impacts can be seen in the form of casualties such as injury, deaths and destruction of life and damage to property. These impacts can be easily measured. The rate of physical impacts that can be seen are higher in developing countries.
- The government is the largest stakeholder as its decisions affect the lives of citizens. The government has special powers which are needed to run the country during a disaster scenario. They are also under immense pressure to perform according to the needs of the people and time. Thus, the role of government may get highly contested and may translate into instability and question the political legitimacy.
- The Ecological impacts of disasters relate to, the natural resource depletion and degradation as a result of extreme events. This leads to scarcity of natural resources which reduces the coping capacity and resilience of the people to face any disaster.
- The environment and disasters are intrinsically linked. Disasters can directly damage the environment through damage to the natural infrastructure and ecosystem or indirectly through poor management after the occurrence of the disasters. These interdependencies and interactions affect the ecosystem, biodiversity and people.
- Demography means describing the people in a particular area". Demography analyzes the trends in population change including distribution in gender, age, disability, and other factors. Demographic data becomes important for planning and implementing during the Disaster Risk Reduction (DRR) activities.
- Gender implies social roles and responsibilities that a society associates with male and female. A gendered aspect to DRR helps to focus upon the vulnerabilities and capacities of each gender to prepare, prevent and recover from Disasters.
- According to the Indian Constitution, the scheduled castes and Scheduled tribes are historically recognized as disadvantaged people. They usually live in the hazard prone areas, deprived of basic facilities, combined with chronic poverty and hazardous living conditions. This makes disaster resilience, mitigation and adaptation difficult in such areas.
- Children are vulnerable due to their physical nature as well as mental immaturity and inability to understand the surrounding. They should also be free from abuse, trafficking, neglect, and

sexual exploitation. Appropriate interventions are required to ensure that the children are able to cope up with the disasters.

- The elderly has particular physical and emotional needs. They may have impaired physical mobility along with psychological vulnerability. The needs of the elderly should be taken care of separately, keeping in mind their specific needs and concerns.
- The Persons with Disability (PWD) have less capacity to deal with the disasters. This implies that they are at higher risk than others. Thus, there is a need to have community-based support for PWD so that they are mainstreamed in their surroundings.
- Warming of the planet is making cities warmer. Urban areas are the centers of economic activity. This process of urbanization and development makes disaster risk in cities more prominent.
- People often experience emotional reactions and stress after a disaster occurs. However, it becomes a concern, only if it overwhelms the capacity of the survivors to cope. In such cases Psycho-Social Support or Mental Health Services or both should be provided.

EXERCISES

Multiple Choice Questions

Q.1 *Indirect economic losses are:*

a. Intangible
b. Tangible
c. Both
d. None of these

Q.2 Which is MDG 7?

a. Eradicate extreme poverty and hunger
b. Improve maternal health
c. Ensure environmental sustainability
d. Develop a global partnership for development

Q.3 Psychosocial support refers to

a. Actively listening to the survivors
b. Helping them restore their day to day functioning
c. Getting them connected to near and dear ones
d. All of the above

Q.4 Psychosocial support can be provided by which of the following: -

a. Psychologists
b. Psychiatrists,
c. Mental health professionals
d. Anyone trained in this area in the community
e. Doctor

Q.5 Which of the following is not a physical impact of disasters? -

a. Buildings
b. Communication network
c. Livelihood
d. Roads

Q.6 Which of the following is not a potential Environmental Impact due to Earthquake:

a,. Natural gas leaks
b. Building waste debris
c. Hazardous waste
d. Poor quality of soil

Q.7 Demography is derived from the following:

a. Greek word
b. Latin word
c. French word
d. Spanish word

Q.8 Demography analyzes the trends in the distribution of which one of the following:

1. Health status
2. Gender
3. Behavior

a. Both 1 and 2
b. 3 only
c. 2 only
d. None of the above

Q.9 The Sustainable Development Goal (SDG) 10.2 targets to

a. By 2030, progressively achieve and sustain income growth of the bottom 40 percent of the population at a rate higher than the national average
b. By 2030, empower and promote the social, economic and political inclusion of all, irrespective of age, sex, disability, race, ethnicity, origin, religion or economic or other status
c. Adopt policies, especially fiscal, wage and social protection policies, and progressively achieve greater equality
d. Adopt policies, especially fiscal, wage and social protection policies, and progressively achieve greater equality

Q.10 The first legally binding document (United Convention on the Rights of the Child) was adopted in: -

a. 1999
b. 1989
c. 2009
d. 2019

Q.11 What do you mean by Global Warming?

1. Rise in the average temperature of the oceans.
2. Decrease in average temperature of the atmosphere of the earth.
3. Lowering of CO2 in the environment.
4. Increase in average temperature of the atmosphere of the earth.

a. 2 only
b. Both 1 and 3
c. Both 1 and 4
d. All of the above
e. None of the above

Q.12 The second and third tier cities are even more at risk of climate related impacts. This is due to which of the following: -

a. Institutional and infrastructural capacities
b. lack of revenue
c. stagnant population
d. All of the above

Q.13 India is particularly vulnerable to Climate Change due to which of the following factors: -

1. Its diverse terrain
2. rapid use of natural resources
3. Inappropriate construction
4. urbanization, industrialization and economic growth

a. 1 and 3 only
b. 1, 2 and 3 only
c. All of the above
d. None of the above

Q.14 A Disaster is termed as an "urban disaster"

a. When it strikes in an urban area.

b. When it impacts the infrastructure of the affected area

c. When it hits the coast of the urban region

d. All of the above

Q.15 Which is the most commonly occurring disaster throughout the world.

a. Earthquakes b. Floods

c. Cyclones d. Landslides

Q.16 Which is the most commonly occurring disaster in India.

a. Earthquakes b. Floods

c. Cyclones d. Landslides

Q.17 Which was the deadliest disaster in the year 2021.

a. Earthquakes b. Floods

c. Landslides d. Cyclones

Q.18 Which country is the worst affected by floods globally?

a. India b. USA

c. China d. Germany

Answers of Multiple-Choice Questions

Answers of Multiple-choice questions				
3.1 **a**	3.2 **c**	3.3 **d**	3.4 **d**	3.5 **b**
3.6 **d**	3.7 **a**	3.8 **c**	3.9 **b**	3.10 **b**
3.11 **c**	3.12 **b**	3.13 **c**	3.14 **a**	3.15 **b**
3.16 **b**	3.17 **a**	3.18 **c**		

Short and Long Answer Type Questions

Category I

1. What is MDG 7?
2. Which is the first legally binding document to adopt the rights of the children?
3. What do you mean by EM-DAT?
4. How do children react when they encounter a disaster?
5. What do you mean by Build Back Better (BBB)?
6. What are the ecological impacts of a disaster?
7. How do natural disasters affect the environment?
8. What makes India one of the most disaster-prone countries in the world?
9. What makes women more vulnerable to disasters?
10. Explain the meaning of the term "Demography". How does it help Disaster Managers in Disaster Risk Reduction (DRR)?

11. What is the relationship between Disasters and Climate Change?
12. While Elderly people do not have swift physical mobility, children do have. Why, then, both elderly and children are equally vulnerable to Disasters?

Category II

1. Vulnerability influences the impacts of disasters and threatens the people. Discuss different types of impacts with reference to Disasters.
2. Who are the persons with disability (PWD)? What are the factors that make them vulnerable to Disasters?
3. What are various types of psychosocial reactions commonly experienced by the survivor after the occurrence of a disaster?
4. With reference to Psycho-Social Support and Mental Health Services (PSMHS), what measures should be adopted to mitigate the impacts of trauma on the disaster survivors.
5. Describe Climate Change and its related consequences on cities?
6. What are the trends in disaster occurrences globally and nationally in the last 20 years?
7. Delineate the future strategies for disaster risk reduction in an urban area to achieve the goal of sustainable development.

REFERENCES AND SUGGESTED READINGS

1. Bandyopadhyay & Chandrani (2014): Training Module on Urban Risk Mitigation. NIDM, New Delhi.
2. CRED. 2021 Disasters in numbers. Brussels: CRED; 2022. https://cred.be/sites/default/files/2021_EMDAT_report.pdf
3. CRED&UNDRR (2020): Human Cost of Disasters 2000-2019
4. DEWGA. (2008): Linking Disaster Risk Reduction, Environment Management and Development Practices and Practitioners in Asia Pacific Region: A review of opportunities for integration. Disasters Environment Working Group for Asia.
5. Gupta, A.K., Nair, S.S., Wajih, S.A., Chopde, S., Gupta, G. and Aggrawal, G. (2014):.Mainstreaming Climate Change Adaptation and Disaster Risk Reduction into District Level Development Plans. NIDM New Delhi.
6. Gupta, A.K., Jafar, E., Bhardwaj, S., Tyagi, N., Mahajan, V., Sethia, R., Parveen, U. and Bindal, M.K. (2022): Climate Proofing Disaster Relief and Recovery. NIDM, Delhi.
7. ISDR (2008): Climate Resilient Cities 2008 Primer, Reducing Vulnerabilities to Climate Change Impacts and Strengthening Disaster Risk Management in East Asian Cities.
8. MHA (2011): Disaster Management in India, Ministry of Home Affairs, Government of India.
9. NDMA (2009): National Disaster Management Guidelines, Psycho-Social Support and Mental Health Services in Disasters, Ministry of Home Affairs, Government of India.
10. NDMA (2019): National Disaster Management Plan, Ministry of Home Affairs, Government of India.
11. NIMHANS (2004): Training of trainers Module on disaster psycho-social care.
12. New South Wales (NSW) (2000): Health, Disaster mental health response handbook. North Sydney, NSW: NWS Health.Sekar, K.; Pan, S., Jaykumar, C., Girimaji, S. and Kumar, & Kishore K. V. (2005): Tsunami Psycho-social Care for Children, NIMHANS Publications, Bangalore.

13. Sekar, K.; Pan, S., Jaykumar, C., Girimaji, S. and Kumar, & Kishore K. V. (2005): Tsunami Psychosocial Care for Children, NIMHANS Publications, Bangalore
14. Sujata Satapathy (2009): Psychosocial Care in Disaster Management: A Training of Trainers (ToT) Module, NIDM Delhi
15. UNDRR (2020): Disaster Risk Reduction in The Republic of India: Status Report 2020. Bangkok, Thailand, United Nations Office for Disaster Risk Reduction (UNDRR), Regional Office for Asia and the Pacific.

04 DISASTER RISK REDUCTION

UNIT SPECIFICS

The salient objectives of this unit are to familiarize the students with the following:

- *To understand the different phases in Disaster Management.*
- *To explain the different terms of the Disaster Management cycle.*
- *To describe the concept of Early Warning System.*
- *To understand the structural and non-structural mitigation measures.*
- *To understand the concept of vulnerability and capacity assessment*
- *To elucidate the various legislations laid down for disaster management in India.*
- *To describe the roles and responsibilities of various stakeholders in managing disaster.*

In this unit, the different phases of the disaster management cycle are discussed in detail. It further discusses the importance of Early Warning Systems in managing Disaster. An overview of structural and non-structural measures for various disasters are elaborated. The concept of Vulnerability and Capacity Assessment is presented. Furthermore, the various policies and legislations and Disaster Risks Program in India are explained so as to give the reader an insight into the Disaster Management System of India. Additionally, the components of Disaster Relief which includes water, health etc., and roles and responsibilities of various stakeholders of Disaster Management are discussed in detail.

A number of multiple-choice questions are given as well as questions of short and long answer types are marked in two categories following lower and higher order of Bloom's taxonomy. A list of references and suggested readings are given in the unit so that one can go through them for practice. It is important to note that for getting more information on various topics of interest some QR codes have been provided in different sections which can be scanned for relevant supportive knowledge.

RATIONALE

This unit helps students to gain insights about the Disaster Management cycle. It explains the different phases of disaster to develop an understanding of the different situations in a disaster management program. This understanding of the disaster management cycle helps the students gain insights into the different ways in which the disasters can be managed. An introduction about the concept of Early Warning Systems is elucidated. An overview of the mitigation measures of various disasters is presented which helps the reader to understand the various structural and non-structural strategies for managing the disasters. Moreover, the chapter further discusses the various policies and legislations and Disaster Risks Program in India so as to give the reader an insight into the Disaster Management System of India. Thereafter, the roles and responsibilities of various stakeholders of Disaster Management and the components of disaster relief are discussed in detail. This will help those involved in disaster management evolve better practices in their Disaster Risk Reduction efforts.

PRE-REQUISITES

NIL

UNIT OUTCOMES

List of outcomes of this unit is as follows:

U4-O1: Understand the different phases of Disaster Management.

U4-O2: Understand the mitigation measures of various disasters.

U4-O3: Understand the method of Vulnerability and Capacity assessment.

U4-O4: Comprehend the policies and legislations of disaster management in India.

U4-O5: Understand the roles and responsibilities of various stakeholders.

Unit-4 Outcomes	EXPECTED MAPPING WITH COURSE OUTCOMES (1-WeakCorrelation;2-Mediumcorrelation;3-StrongCorrelation)					
	CO-1	CO-2	CO-3	CO-4	CO-5	CO-6
U4-01	3	1	2	1	2	1
U4-02	1	1	1	2	3	1
U4-03	-	-	2	1	1	3
U4-04	-	-	-	3	1	1
U4-05	2	1	-	2	1	1

4.1 INTRODUCTION

The objective of Disaster Management is to reduce or prevent the potential losses due to impact of hazards. It requires an effective response mechanism, rapid and effective recovery measures. All measures related to Disaster management which are required to be discharged by the policy and administrative officers are represented on a disaster management cycle.

According to Disaster Management (DM) Act 2005, Disaster management is "A continuous and integrated process of planning, organising, coordinating and implementing measures which are necessary or expedient for the following:

- Prevention of danger or threat of any disaster
- Mitigation or reduction of risk of any disaster or its severity or consequences;
- Capacity building;
- Preparedness to deal with any disaster,
- Prompt response to any threatening disaster situation or disaster;
- Assessing the severity or magnitude of effects of any disaster;
- Evacuation, rescue and relief;
- Rehabilitation and reconstruction

4.2 DISASTER MANAGEMENT CYCLE

Disaster Management integrates all the measures, activities and programs which are performed before, during and after the occurrence of a disaster, to avoid or prevent the losses from a disaster or recover from its impacts. All activities related to Disaster management can be divided into three phases:

- Pre–Disaster phase
- During Disaster phase
- Post-Disaster phase

Pre–Disaster Phase: During this phase, proactive steps are taken so as to prevent or reduce the human, property, environmental losses due to hazards. This ensures that disasters do not occur on the first hand and if they do, the losses are minimized through mitigation. Mitigation and preparedness are the risk reduction measures which are taken during the pre-disaster phase.

During Disaster Phase: During this phase of disaster, initiatives and measures are taken to make sure that the needs of people affected by disasters are met to reduce the suffering. Response is the risk reduction measure which is taken during the occurrence of disaster.

Post Disaster Phase: After a disaster has taken place, recovery measures are taken to rapidly recover and rehabilitate the affected communities. The recovery efforts should be taken in such a way that ensures that the originally vulnerable conditions are not reproduced. Thus, disasters can be taken as a chance to Build Back Better (BBB). Reconstruction and Rehabilitation are the risk reduction measures which are taken during the post-disaster phase.

These three phases of disaster can be represented in a disaster management cycle which provides the framework and direction to the different actors such as government agencies, non- governmental organizations, businesses, and civil society. The framework helps in planning for all the three phases of disaster management to reduce the impact of disasters. Therefore, the disaster management cycle covers all aspects of disaster management, i.e., prevention, mitigation, preparedness, response, recovery, and building back better. The Disaster management cycle is shown in Fig.4.1.

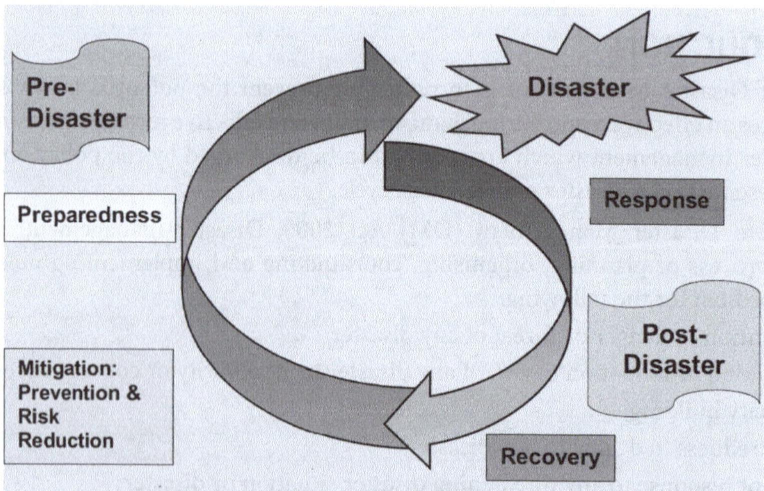

Fig. 4.1: Disaster Management Cycle

Source: NDMP,2019

Activities/measures which can be taken for proper disaster management and planning are shown in the Fig. 4.1. These are

- Pre-Disaster Phase- Mitigation (Prevention and Risk reduction) & Preparedness,
- During Disaster Phase- Response
- Post Disaster Phase- Recovery (Rehabilitation and Reconstruction)

These terms are discussed below: -

Prevention

If any area, community, or region is prone to any hazard (earthquake, cyclone, flood, etc.), then the first aim is to prevent the occurrence of hazards, if possible or completely avoid/prevent the adverse impact of hazards through the precautions/actions taken in advance. These are some examples to prevent the adverse impacts of hazards:

- Construct embankments or dams
- Land-use regulations
- Avoid construction in seismic/landslide/flood prone region

For example, fire risk can be avoided completely. However, it is not always possible to prevent hazards or completely avoid the losses or damages due to impact of hazards, in such situation's prevention turns into mitigation.

Mitigation

Sometimes impacts of hazards like earthquakes, cyclones, landslides, etc. cannot be prevented completely. In such situations, measures are taken to minimize the losses or damages due to hazards in advance.

Mitigation, thus, means to take all the measures (Structural and non-structural) to minimize/reduce the impact of hazards. Examples of mitigation measures are hazard resistant construction, land use planning, various engineering measures, public awareness, etc. The structural and non-structural measures are described in subsequent sections.

Preparedness

Preparedness involves programs, activities and measures to ensure that there is an efficient response to disasters. The aim of preparedness is to build the capacities of governments, organizations, and communities that are needed to handle all types of emergencies and plan how to respond during disaster. The measures include preparedness plans, rehearsals, training and awareness programs, early warning systems, temporary evacuation of people from the highly affected areas, reserves of food, equipment, water, medicines etc.

Response

During the onset of a disaster, it is expected that the community or the system is ready to respond to the impact of hazard. Response measures are taken just after a disaster so as to provide prompt assistance to the people affected by disasters. These measures include evacuation of affected people, warning to vulnerable populations, rescue and search operation, providing emergency service, temporary shelter, and food, medical facilities, etc. A quick and effective response requires adequate planning and preparedness.

Recovery (Reconstruction and Rehabilitation)

After the occurrence of a disaster, such activities and measures are taken to return the community to normal situation. Recovery measures include rehabilitation and reconstruction which starts just after the immediate response to the emergency phase. Recovery measures are both long term and short term. These include reconstruction, temporary housing, livelihood, providing financial support, psychological support, medical care, health, safety and education, etc.

Reconstruction is a long-term measure which includes construction of physical structures, replacement of damaged buildings, the full restoration of all services, etc. The measure should be applied on the "Build Back Better (BBB)" principle.

Rehabilitation is a short-term measure which includes restoring the basic facilities and services of a community affected by a disaster for the society to function. It includes psychological support, financial support, livelihood support, etc., to bring society back to normalcy.

4.3 STRUCTURAL AND NON-STRUCTURAL MEASURES

Natural hazards cannot be prevented but damage and disruption due to natural hazards can be minimized by proper disaster management and planning. Mitigation measures which are an important part of disaster management mainly focuses on eliminating or reducing the risk from the hazards. Mitigation measures can be classified into:

- Structural Measures
- Non-structural Measures

Structural Measures

Structural measures are defined as any physical construction, i.e., natural or artificial to decrease or eliminate the losses due to disasters. It is the implementation of engineering methods to build hazard resistant structures to protect from hazards. The examples of structural measures are earthquake-resistant construction, ocean wave barriers, flood levies, dams, and evacuation shelters.

Non-structural measures

Non-structural measures are defined as the measures which include policies and laws, plans and regulations, building codes, land use planning, laws and their enforcement, public awareness, training and education, warning system, financial measures, and good management practices. These are useful to minimize the risk and impact from the hazards. Non-structural measures do not include physical construction.

4.3.1 Structural and Non-structural measures for specific disasters

Structural and Non-structural measures are followed for specific disasters as they relate to specific hazards. Some of major disasters are discussed below:

4.3.1.1 Earthquake

The structural and non-structural measures used for Earthquake resilience are discussed below:

Structural measures

- Structures and Buildings must be designed as per building bye laws and IS Codes to withstand ground shaking.
- Improving the building design and construction practices.
- Analysing the soil properties before construction.
- Retrofitting of the existing buildings to strengthen their resistance to earthquake forces.

Non-structural measures

- Public awareness and Education: Training programs should be conducted for Engineers, Architects, Contractors, Builders, Policy makers, Masons, Government functionaries, NGO's, etc.
- Community preparedness: Community preparedness plays an important role in disaster mitigation measures. It includes educating the communities with evacuation maps, shelters and encouraging them to maintain food reserves.

4.3.1.2 Flood

The structural and non-structural measures used to safeguard against flood are discussed below:

Structural Measures

The following structural measures which are useful to reduce the losses caused due to floods. are:

- Reservoirs, Dams, and other Water Storage
- Embankments
- Channel Improvements
- Drainage Improvement
- Diversion of Flood Water// Interlinking of Rivers
- Catchments Area Treatment/Watershed Management
- Sea Walls
- Coastal Protection Works
- Anti-Erosion Works

Flood Mitigation

Reservoirs, Dams, and other Water Storage

Reservoirs, Dams and other water storage whether they are natural or manmade can reduce the intensity of flood or flood peaks in the river. Reservoirs, dams, and tanks can store water during the flood. The water thus stored is released after the critical flood condition is over. Water stored in the reservoirs, dams can also be used for power generation, irrigation purposes, drinking water needs and other purposes.

Embankments

The embankment system is the one of the structural measures of flood in which the river gets confined to its existing course and therefore restricts the flood flow, thereby reducing the damage. This measure was used extensively in the past because of it being an inexpensive and quick method of flood protection. Generally, embankments are constructed with earth but in developed areas, concrete or masonry floodwalls are also constructed.

Channel Improvements

The objective of channel improvement is to increase their carrying capacity through stabilized river channel and reduced bank erosion. This measure is adopted to a very limited extent due to constraint of topographical condition and high cost.

Drainage Improvement

The aim of Drainage improvement is to prevent congestion and flooding in downstream areas. This can be achieved by improving the capacity of existing channels or constructing new channels to facilitate the continuous draining of water and thus prevent flooding.

Diversion of Flood Water/Interlinking of Rivers

In this flood control measure, flood waters are discharged into natural or artificial constructed channels which may be lying within or outside the floodplain. This flood control measure is effective to prevent flooding in urbanized areas. The Interlinking of Rivers is also a flood control measure for division of flood.

Catchments Area Treatment/ Watershed Management

In this measure, protection is provided to catchment areas through measures such as afforestation. The measures of watershed management which includes increasing the vegetative cover through conservation of soil cover, afforestation and structural works like diversion channels and detention basins, check dams, etc. These measures are helpful in controlling the flood.

Sea Walls/Coastal Protection Works

The construction of seawalls and other coastal protection works serve as effective measures to prevent the flooding from the sea water and also helps to prevent erosion of land in the coastal region.

Anti-Erosion Works

Alluvial rivers are characterized by their meandering nature. They raise problems of erosion from concave bends and deposition at other locations. This leads to loss of valuable land. Anti-erosion works are generally used for protection of towns, industrial areas, railway lines and roads, etc.

Non-structural measures

Non-structural measures are important aspects to reducing the impacts of Flood. These also reduce the adverse effects on the environment. Non-structural measures to reduce or prevent the impacts of flood are:

- Flood Plain Zoning
- Flood Forecasting and Warning
- Flood Proofing
- Flood Insurance
- Control of flood plain development
- Adherence to Coastal Zone Regulations

Flood Plain Zoning

The aim of flood-plain zoning is to identify zones which are likely to be affected by floods based on the flood frequencies or probability level for the region of interest. It is useful to regulate land use for various developmental activities in order to minimize or prevent the damages due to floods.

Flood Forecasting and Warning

Flood forecasting and warning is one of most significant non-structural measures for flood control. This system has been developed by the Central Water Commission (CWC) in India and the CWC is responsible for forecasting floods and issuing warnings in India. The CWC issues flood forecasts at 325 stations according to the Standard Operating Procedure (SOP's).

Flood Proofing

It is defined as "the modification of buildings and structures and their immediate surroundings to reduce damage during flooding." These measures include raised platforms for shelter to population, raised platforms for houses and buildings, etc.

Flood Insurance

Flood insurance provides immediate and temporary relief due to damage caused by flood. This measure differs from the other non-structural measures of flood. While other measures enable cost reduction due to flood damage, Insurance doesn't reduce the long term-cost of flood damage.

Control of flood plain development

Floodplains are generally low-lying areas next to waterways. These lands are subjected to flooding periodically. To protect these areas from the flood, following techniques can be used:

- Zoning
- Floodplain regulations
- Building Codes
- Development policies

Adherence to Coastal Zone Regulations

The Ministry of Environment, Forest and Climate Change (MoEFCC) issued a Coastal Regulations Zone (CRZ) Notification, 2019. The aim of this regulation is to protect ecologically sensitive coastal regions from flooding. Enforcement of this notification will save the community and reduce the impact of floods.

4.3.1.3 Cyclone

Cyclones affect the coastal areas which can cause huge damage to life and property. There are structural as well as non-structural ways to reduce the impact of cyclones.

The structural measures for mitigating the effects of cyclones include:

- Cyclone shelter construction
- Culverts, road links and bridges construction
- Drains, canals and water tanks construction
- Embankments for saline water
- Towers for communication and networks for power transmission etc.

Cyclone shelter construction

During cyclones, it has been observed that the loss of life is primarily due to the lack of cyclone shelters in the coastal regions. So, there should be provision of safe cyclone shelters for the protection of life. The shelters can include buildings, places of worship, schools, community halls, etc.

Culverts, road links and bridges construction

The coastal villages should be connected with the help of all-weather roads for emergency evacuation. The conditions of roads, bridges, and culvert should be audited by the authorised agencies for smooth functioning of operations related to disaster management during cyclones. Roads, bridges, culvert should be constructed for the last mile connectivity.

Drains, canals and water tanks construction

The network of canals and drains plays a very important role in reducing the impact of cyclones. They are involved in the receipt, accommodation and return back of surge waters into the sea. Coastal canals may also be used as an alternate to roads for evacuating the people from affected areas during a cyclone or flood. The surface water tanks are used in lowering the effect of cyclones as well as storm surges.

Embankments for saline water

Coastal areas are vulnerable to inundation due to the cyclones related impacts such as rainfall and storm surges. Construction and renovation of Saline Embankments is one of important structural measure for the protection of coastal areas.

Towers for communication and networks for power transmission etc.

It has been recommended that towers should be constructed for the 100-year return period of the cyclone's wind velocity. This should be based on failure of communication and transmission towers in past cyclones.

Non-structural measures

Non-structural measures are used to reduce cyclonic risk through effective mitigation policies and strategies. These measures consist of

- Early warning systems
- Systems for communication as well as dissemination
- Creating awareness and capacity building
- Developing shelter belts
- Coastal zones management
- Hazard mapping

Early warning systems

Early warning systems installed along the coastlines can significantly contribute to forecasting techniques. It can help in early evacuation of people.

Systems for communication as well as dissemination

Systems for communication as well as dissemination of information plays a significant role in minimizing the impacts of cyclones.

Creating awareness and capacity building

Trained human resources are necessary for effective disaster management. Capacity building is a continuous process which equips the stakeholders such as the officials, the community to perform their duties effectively during the cyclones. Awareness program should be conducted in the cyclone prone region about how to respond to cyclone warning and what to do, what not to do during cyclones.

Developing shelter belts

Shelter belts which include plantations of trees along the coastal line can enable breaking of wind-and tide. Improvement of the vegetation also prevents soil erosion.

Coastal zones management

As discussed earlier, it is not possible to prevent the cyclones from occurring, but the losses to life and damage to property can be considerably reduced by coastal zone management. Measures include proper planning for identifying the vulnerable communities and building infrastructure within safer areas in coastal regions, etc., Thus, it is essential to initiate a plan of action for coastal areas. The Coastal Regulation Zone (CRZ) must be followed for all activities to minimize the losses due to cyclones.

Hazard mapping

A hazard map depicts the regions which are vulnerable to cyclone-based probability of wind speeds/ return period. Hazards map can be developed based on the meteorological records of the wind speed, frequency of flooding etc. These maps are useful to estimate the severity of cyclonic wind speed, flood, etc. and accordingly the estimated damages. Therefore, the maps are useful for planning cyclone mitigation strategies in coastal regions.

4.3.1.4 Landslide

Structural and non-structural measures for the landslides given below:

Structural measures

These are the structural measures which are implemented of existing landslides which are near to public structures.

- Buttresses
- Sub-drains
- Shear keys
- Retaining walls
- Soil reinforcement, etc.

Non-Structural Measures

Some are the non-structural measures are:

- Proper Land Use Measures
- Afforestation
- Awareness Generation
- Proper Land Use Measures
- Insurance

Proper Land Use Measures

Land use planning must be based on land use regulations and building codes to minimize the damage due to landslides. New construction or development should be discouraged in the hazards areas where appropriate remedial measures have not been applied.

Afforestation

Increasing vegetative cover is the one of cheapest and most effective ways to prevent mass movement. This also helps in preventing excessive runoff and soil erosion. Therefore, afforestation should be undertaken in landslide prone areas.

Awareness Generation

People should be educated about the signs which are used in landslide prone areas. This will enable taking personal safety measures.

Insurance

Insurance supports people whose houses get damaged by the impacts of hazards. While constructing new buildings, it includes standards for site selection and construction techniques.

4.4 EARLY WARNING SYSTEMS

Early warning systems (EWS) have become a major component of disaster risk management. They help in saving lives and reducing the number of casualties and economic losses due to the impact of natural hazards. EWS is a set of capacities that enable generation and dissemination of warning information about extreme events such as cyclones, floods, drought, etc., timely. This ensures that the communities can prepare and thus act timely so as to reduce the losses. However, it is necessary that such warnings that are issued are simple, and understandable to the people in context. Moreover, for the effectiveness of the system, it should be integrated with risk assessment and action plan.

As per the UNDRR, early warning system can be described as "an integrated system of hazard monitoring, forecasting and prediction, disaster risk assessment, communication and preparedness activities systems and processes that enables individuals, communities, governments, businesses and others to take timely action to reduce disaster risks in advance of hazardous events."

The Indian Ocean Tsunami, 2004 caused huge economic losses and loss of lives in India and Asia-Pacific. It was realized that losses to lives could have been reduced if there were appropriate systems for early warning. Therefore, after the Tsunami, India focused its attention towards building EWS in India. The world has also recognized the importance of multi-hazard EWS and the Sendai Framework for Disaster Risk Reduction (SFDRR) has also incorporated the EWS as in its targets i.e., "Substantially increase the availability of and access to multi-hazard early warning systems and disaster risk information and assessments to people by 2030".

Disasters may not occur in isolation and accompany one another i.e., a Tsunami may follow an earthquake or a landslide may follow a flood. Therefore, a multi hazard and integrated early warning system is an effective tool to communicate the exact situation. This will ensure that disaster impacts are reduced. A country like India which is highly vulnerable to multiple hazards can significantly benefit from the Multi-hazard EWS. The integrated EWS is shown in Fig. 4.2.

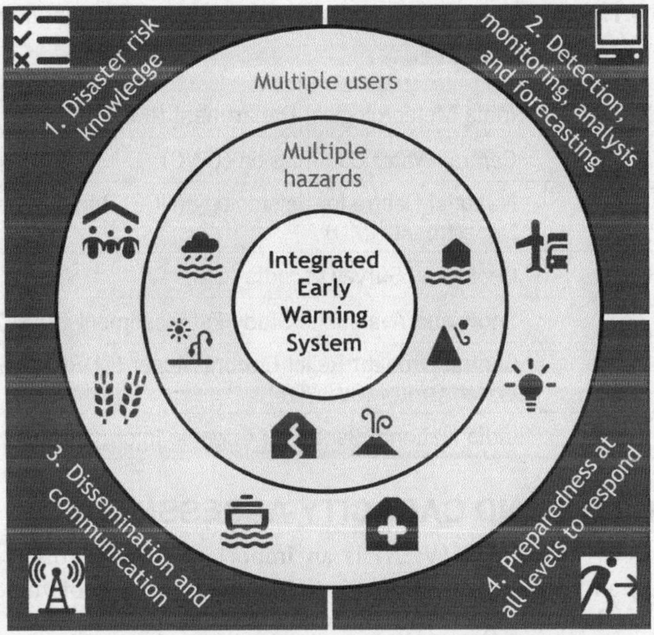

Fig. 4.2: Integrated Early Warning system (WMO,2019)

Effective early warning system is integration of elements which are: -

- Disaster Risk Knowledge
- Detection, Monitoring, Analysis and Forecasting
- Disseminating and Communication
- Response

EWS

Disaster Risk Knowledge: Disaster risk knowledge gives essential information to build mitigation and prevention measures and design early warning systems.

Detection, Monitoring, Analysis and Forecasting: Early warning systems i.e., equipment, communication links, simulators, ICT tools, etc, can enable in monitoring the possible consequences of hazards.

Disseminating and Communication: Effective communication systems deliver warning messages/ alerts to the local, regional agencies and people about the locations which are likely to be affected by hazards. The warning messages so issued should be reliable, clear, and understandable by authorities and people. Additionally, it requires a lot of social and cultural awareness to spread appropriate information to specific recipients such as People with Disability (PwD), elderly, children etc.,.

Response: Response involves performing such activities and adopting such measures at all the stages to be able to respond to the warnings received. Likewise, awareness generation and educational programs are significant measures of disaster mitigation.

All the four elements of the EWS need to be well coordinated across all the sectors to ensure that the system performs efficiently. Additionally, feedback mechanisms should also be in place to enable continuous monitoring. The nodal agencies responsible for providing EWS for each disaster is shown in Table 4.1.

Table 4.1: Nodal Agencies for Natural Hazards Early Warning/Forecast

Hazards	Agency
Cyclone	India Meteorological Department (IMD)
Floods	Central Water Commission (CWC)
Earthquake	National Centre for Seismology (NCS), India Meteorological Department (IMD)
Landslides	Geological Survey of India (GSI)
Avalanches	Snow and Avalanche Study Establishment (SASE)
Drought	Central Drought Relief Commissioner (CDRC) and Crop Weather Watch Group (CWWG)
Tsunami	India National Centre for Oceanic Information Services (INCOIS)

4.5 VULNERABILITY AND CAPACITY ASSESSMENT

Vulnerability and capacity assessment (VCA) is an important pillar of disaster management. The purpose of vulnerability and capacity assessment is to identify the causes of vulnerability and measure the capacities to cope in the existing situation. It is a continuous process which enables assessing the preparedness and mitigation measures which can be taken. Thus, it is a part of the Pre-disaster stage of the disaster management cycle.

4.5.1 Vulnerability Assessment

It is defined as "the conditions determined by physical, social, economic and environmental factors or processes which increase the susceptibility of an individual, a community, assets or systems to the impacts of hazards".

The process of vulnerability assessment involves identifying the vulnerable community and vulnerable infrastructure. This means that those populations who are vulnerable would be identified such as women, Persons with Disability (PwD), children, elderly, mentally challenged, poverty-stricken people living in vulnerable locations. Additionally, vulnerable infrastructure would be identified like kutcha houses, communication lines, roads, telephone lines etc. It assesses the vulnerable population and assets of the community. The tools for vulnerability assessment are given below:

- Transect Walk
- Problem Tree
- Livelihood Analysis
- Focus Group Discussion (FGD)
- Vulnerability mapping

VCA

Transect Walk: This is a systematic walk to explore the area by observing, listening, interviewing and identifying the land use zones, spatial differences, vulnerable areas, evacuation sites. It helps intervening organizations to have a first-hand knowledge about the location and thereby produce transect diagrams. An example of transect walk is shown in the Fig. 4.3.

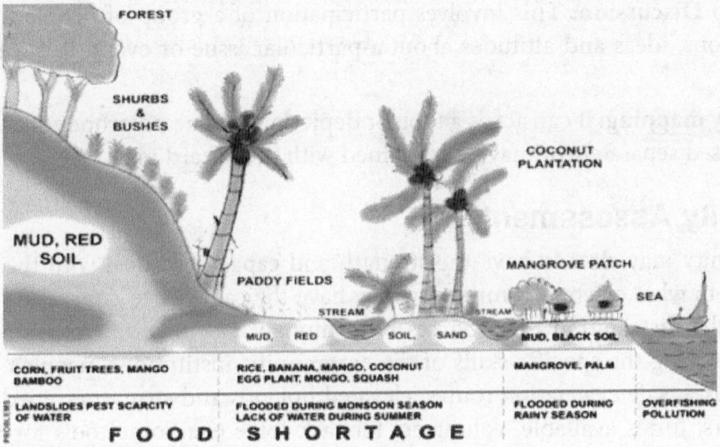

Fig. 4.3: Example of Transect Walk

Source: https://nidm.gov.in/PDF/Modules/NIDMSDMP_22.pdf)

Problem Tree: It is a pictorial representation showing a relationship between vulnerabilities and its root causes and their effects. The Trunk represents key vulnerability, the roots depicts the causes while the leaves signify the effects. This tool enables in getting a quick glance of the vulnerabilities of a hazard and how they might turn into a disaster. An example of Problem Tree is shown in the Fig. 4.4.

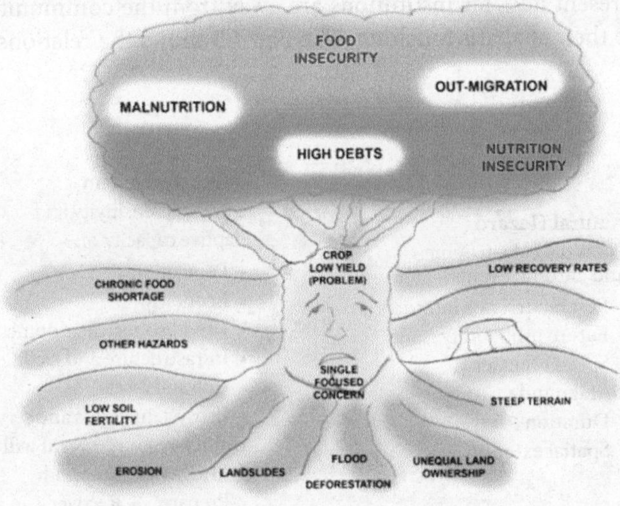

Fig. 4.4: Example of Problem Tree

Source: https://nidm.gov.in/PDF/Modules/NIDMSDMP_22.pdf

Livelihood Analysis: It analyses different ways in which people are able to sustain themselves and the impacts of various hazards on different households and groups. It is done through mapping the resource accessibility, effectiveness of DRR measure, livelihood diversity, individual adaptive capacity. Moreover, it tries to understand the livelihood strategies, behaviour, vulnerability, decisions and risk perception of people from various socio-economic backgrounds. This enables studying the vulnerability in the context of livelihoods.

Focus Group Discussion: This involves participation of a group of people to understand their perceptions, opinions, ideas and attitudes about a particular issue or event. It is a form of qualitative research.

Vulnerability mapping: It can act as a tool for depicting the hazard prone zones of the community. This map can be used separately or may be combined with the hazard map.

4.5.2 Capacity Assessment

The local community may already have the strength and capacity to deal with the disaster. This tool helps in analyzing to what extent a community may have the capacity to cope using its resources. This involves plotting the distribution of resources both human and material, access and its assessment. For example, identifying the specific skills of the community, institutions, people's knowledge, strong buildings, safe houses, safe evacuation routes, elevated uplands and structures, medical and sanitation facilities, swimmers, funds available, volunteers for task force etc. Some tools for Capacity/Resource Assessment are mentioned below:

Chapatti Diagrams: This is also known as Venn Diagram. This tool helps in identifying the relationships that exist in a society. It can enable understanding of the working of various institutes/organizations working in the field of disaster management and their areas of interest and importance, capacities. It also enables us to carry out comparison, draw similarities, classify information, and bring out differences.

The size of the chapati corresponds to the importance of the institution. Additionally, the chapatis which are far away represent how far institutions are away from the community. The institutions that work together will have their chapatis touching. The Fig. 4.5 shows the relationship of risk with hazard and vulnerable system.

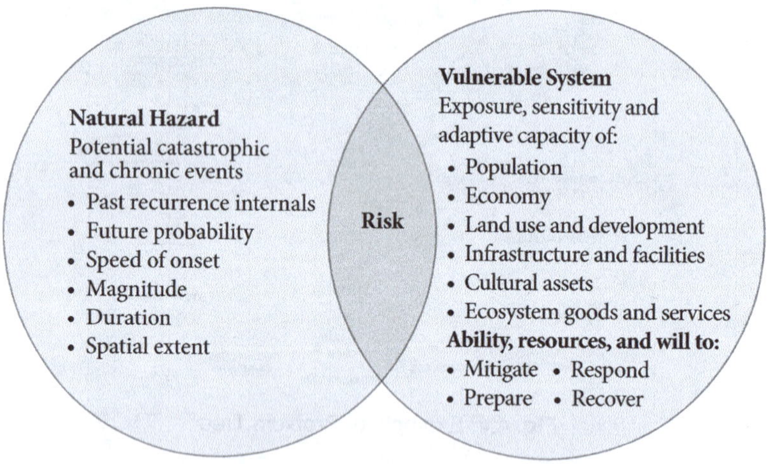

Fig. 4.5: Relationship of risk with hazard and vulnerable system

Source: https://pubs.usgs.gov/fs/2011/3008/fs2011-3008.pdf

Resource Mapping: It is a tool for identifying or locating resources such as health units, water points, schools, etc., Which helps in quick response during/post disaster.

Resource Matrix: It is a tool which depicts general information about the human and material resources in a matrix format.

4.6 COMPONENTS OF DISASTER RELIEF

Communities which are affected by disasters require immediate relief which involves food, water, health, shelter and waste management, sanitation, etc.,.

4.6.1 Food

Scarcity and availability of the food articles is often considered to be an immediate need of any disaster. The delivery of the food articles gets obstructed because of various challenges like disruption in food distribution supply chain, and unavailability of food stocks. In such scenarios, special food relief schemes and plans are initiated, which focus on the following objectives:

- Determination of the food needs on daily basis
- Assessment of the nutritional requirements of the sufferers.
- Setting up a plan regarding the delivery of the food articles to the victims at different time phases on a daily basis.

4.6.2 Water

Water is one of the most important post- disaster emergencies. One could last for quite a few days without having food; but couldn't resist thirst. Water distribution system of an area may get affected due to Earthquakes, Tornadoes, Floods, Hurricanes and all other types of natural disasters. This creates a huge detrimental impact on the drinking water supply system.

Thus, a proper management and planning system must be in place to ensure the drinking water supply to the affected places. Special consideration must be given to eradicate post- disaster scenarios where safe drinking water is not available due to some contamination.

Precautions to be followed for using the water in outdoor facilities such as a shelter homes during emergencies are mentioned below:

- Water derived from moving water bodies such as streams, natural springs, rivers and even from rainwater can be used for drinking as well as other purposes.
- Water with shady colour and bad odour must be avoided.
- If the water is salty in nature, then it can only be used after its distillation.
- In case of floods, people must avoid drinking from natural water bodies.

4.6.3 Health

The Healthcare sector is the first responder during any disaster. Disasters can result in the direct or indirect impact on the health of people of the affected Community. The functioning of the healthcare systems can also get impacted because of the overburden and scarcity of resources during emergencies. The main objectives of the Health system is to save maximum lives after the disaster occurrence.

For responding in such scenarios, a proper channel of communication must be there between the different units of the system so as to respond effectively and efficiently. Moreover, since the health workers play a vital role in taking care of the victims they must be properly trained to deal with such situations.

Furthermore, during the post-disaster scenario, the risk of spreading communicable diseases increases. Thus, an effective risk management system must be established and implemented. NGOs play an important role in spreading awareness and setting – up the Healthcare Information System (HIS), ensuring to reduce the mortality rate by keeping control on Non – communicable and communicable diseases.

4.6.4 Shelter

The prime function of shelter is to provide a temporary – based living space for the victims. In other words, it can be treated as a short-term living arrangement. In a post-disaster situation, the provision for establishing and providing a shelter comes under the authority of the Local Government. Sometimes, a provisional refuge is also developed for the disaster victims. Thus, Shelter protects people from exploitation, danger, and suffering. The shelters must be safe and provide people with their needs so as to help victims feel at home.

4.6.5 Sanitation

For preventing and spreading of any disease after the disaster, proper sanitation and hygienic conditions must be maintained, especially in the areas where temporary shelters are installed. Most of the disasters have a direct impact on the sanitation as they destroy the water distribution system as well as sewage treatment system of a particular area. The main problem arises when both of the systems collapse and merge. Such a situation can be considered as a critical situation for the occurrence of water-borne diseases.

Various types of diseases that have a high chance of occurrence during the aftermath of a disaster. After a disaster hits an area, several measures must be taken by the local authorities/Government to maintain a hygienic environment. Some of the measures may include:

- Protecting the supply of water from any kind of contamination.
- Ensuring that all the people in the temporary shelter must have proper arrangements for storing of water.
- Provision of soaps and sanitizers for cleaning their hands on regularly basis.
- Arrangements must be provided in / nearby of the temporary shelters for the purpose of excretion in a hygienic space.
- Spreading awareness amongst the people for proper utilization of water and food articles; and also keeping themselves away from getting infected.

4.6.6 Waste Management

After a disaster occurs, a lot of waste is generated which includes debris from the buildings, industrial wastes, and human wastes; both in solid and liquid form. Additionally, if any chemical – based industry is affected, it is quite probable that chemicals and poisonous gasses may get released. Some of the other waste that can be generated as a result of natural disasters include vegetation waste, electronic waste, and animal waste. Such types of waste must be differentiated from the normal classification of waste so as to manage them separately for safe disposal of the same.

Probability is quite high for the release of hazardous waste in case any chemical – based industry is highly affected by the disaster, which includes release of chemicals and poisonous gasses. The amount of waste generated due to the occurrence of natural disasters cannot be forecasted accurately. One of the major sources of generation of waste during post – disaster situations is the food provided by centres, which gather a huge amount of waste at one single position. Such types of waste can be minimized by adopting a well post – disaster waste management plan, which will work efficiently in its implementation of collecting and disposal of waste far away from the place of temporary shelters.

4.7 ROLES AND RESPONSIBILITIES OF VARIOUS STAKEHOLDERS

Disaster Management is a comprehensive subject, which requires integration of various stakeholders to be able to efficiently manage disasters. Accordingly, they play important roles and responsibilities. These are mentioned below: -

- Government
- Community
- Local Government
- Non-Government Organizations (NGOs)
- Trainers
- International Agencies
- Media

4.7.1 Government

Government has the primary responsibility in managing disasters. It plays a significant role in crisis management. It provides a central, coordinated action plan of all the Ministries, Organizations and Departments to address the risks associated with Disasters.

The Government of India has enacted the Disaster Management Act 2005, which created National Disaster Management Authority (NDMA) and National Disaster Response Force (NDRF). Some of the important functions of the government are:

- Design and Implement policies on Disaster Management.
- Recommend the provision of funds for disaster mitigation.
- Establish communications and coordination at all the levels.
- Coordinate at the International level.
- Supplement the efforts of the state government

At the state level, State Disaster Management Authority (SDMA) has been set up and at the District level, District Disaster Management Authority (DDMA) has been set up for Managing Disasters as per the DM Act,2005.

4.7.2 Community

The impact of Disasters is felt at the community level. So, the community is referred to as "disaster fronts". The community is the First Responder before the arrival of any support. The impacts of the disasters are related with the culture, traditions, socio-economic conditions, and climate of the region. The communities are at the forefront and thus they should be able to manage the risks and respond to the threats that may threaten their wellbeing.

The people at the grassroots should understand the risks that they face because of disasters and be well versed in taking actions against such risks. Involving the community in creating disaster planning and decision making helps in building capacities and transferring of resources to the community.

4.7.3 Local Government

Local self-government institutions play an important role in matters of immediate concern. They play a vital role as a sequel to the 73rd and 74th Amendment Act. They are the first authority to handle disasters at the grassroot level. Therefore, they work in harmony with the state governments to respond to disasters or even issue early warnings. Some of the Important functions of the Local Government are: -

- Generating awareness and educating the community on disaster preparedness measures.
- Identifying the needs of the people by identifying the vulnerabilities through community involvement
- Identify the resource gap and building capacities.
- Creating and maintaining synergies with NGO's/CBO's.
- Converging the efforts of the local institutional structures which implement measures relating health, education, Livelihood, social justice, etc.,
- Implementing Disaster Management Plans.

4.7.4 Non-Government Organizations

These are organizations which are registered under the Society's Registration Act,1860, meant for non-profit companies. NGO's act as links between the affected community and disaster management agencies. NGOs work at the grass roots as well as advocacy level. Before the onset of disasters, they are involved in disaster preparedness activities which also aim at sustainable development. Moreover, during disasters, they can perform all the activities of rescue and relief. They also work in the post- disaster phase by involving in rehabilitation and reconstruction. Thus, they perform roles at the levels of disaster cycle, which makes them a significant part of the government's support in their role of managing disasters. Some of the Important functions that make the NGO's unique are: -

- They can respond promptly as they share links with the community.
- They know the community well and so their efforts can be very effective and fruitful.
- They can provide customized relief to people in distress.
- They can involve the community as they are familiar with the local language and traditions.
- They constitute a wide range of people, comprising activists, people, professionals who can manage disasters in a wide variety of ways.

4.7.5 Trainers

Training is a significant way for ensuring that the community is better prepared for disasters. Training provided to the community leaders and agents is done by trainers. These trainers provide awareness including activities which identify the vulnerability and capacity of the people. They also design the possible awareness activities for improving the capacities of the people. Moreover, they ensure that the training material is visible to the community. This way the training can enable communities to not panic and respond to disasters efficiently.

4.7.6 International Agencies

International agencies such as the United Nations, Red Cross, Oxfam, Department for International Development (DFID), United States Agency Rehabilitation, Reconstruction and Recovery for International Development (USAID) play a significant role in contributing to managing Disasters throughout the world. They conduct Disaster response, mitigation, prevention, rehabilitation and recovery operations. Some of the important functions of the International organizations are: -

- Provide resources and support to the communities and countries affected by disasters.
- Provide aid and coordinate relief efforts such as shelter, food, medical assistance and care.

- Promote Resilience and Disaster Risk Reduction (DRR) through capacity building and training programs.
- Act as a link between the international community and the affected countries to help mobilize funding and other resources.

4.7.7 Media

Media plays a significant role in Disaster Management. It has an all-inclusive role encompassing all the phases of Disasters i.e. Pre-Disaster, Post Disaster and During Disaster.

Before the Disaster- It can influence the different stakeholders including the government to take up Disaster Risk Reduction measures by exposing the vulnerability, or inefficient expenditures of an area. Moreover, it can help in creating Early Warning alerts during emergencies. It also helps in awareness of generation.

During Disasters- It helps in creating self confidence among people, covering and informing about the factual data thereby helping various organizations, spreading Do's and Don'ts. It also gives a glimpse to the outside world about the situation.

After Disasters- the media helps in gathering help from people, helps people connect to their near and dear ones, and keeps a watch on anti-social activities. Additionally, it counters the negative reporting and propaganda.

4.8 POLICIES AND LEGISLATION FOR DISASTER RISK REDUCTION

In India, the move towards a legal framework was started in 1999. A High-Powered Committee (HPC) was set up by the Central Government under the Chairmanship of Mr. J.C. Pant, Secretary, Ministry of Agriculture to develop India's holistic approach towards different disasters. The report of the committee was submitted in 2001. Finally, the Bill became the Disaster Management Act, which was passed by the Indian Parliament in 2005. Disaster management Act, 2005 provides an institutional framework for managing disasters in India.

4.8.1 Disaster Management Act 2005

The Disaster Management (DM) Act, 2005 provides the core legal and institutional framework at the national, state and district levels for the effective management of disasters. Salient features of DM Act, 2005 are given as under:

- It establishes a National Disaster Management Authority (NDMA) at the National Level under the chairmanship of the Prime Minister.
- It establishes State Disaster Management Authorities (SDMA's) at the State Level under the chairmanship of Chief Minister.
- It establishes District Disaster Management Authorities (DDMA's) at the District Level under the Chairmanship of Collectors/District Magistrates.
- Set up the National Institute of Disaster Management (NIDM) for providing training and capacity building.
- Set up the National Disaster Response Force (NDRF) for responding during the relief operations.
- Makes provisions for the National Disaster Mitigation Fund
- Preparation of National Policy on Disaster Management by NDMA

A legal institutional framework of India is shown in Fig. 4.6. The Ministry of Home Affairs (MHA) is the nodal ministry for coordinating overall Disaster Management in India.

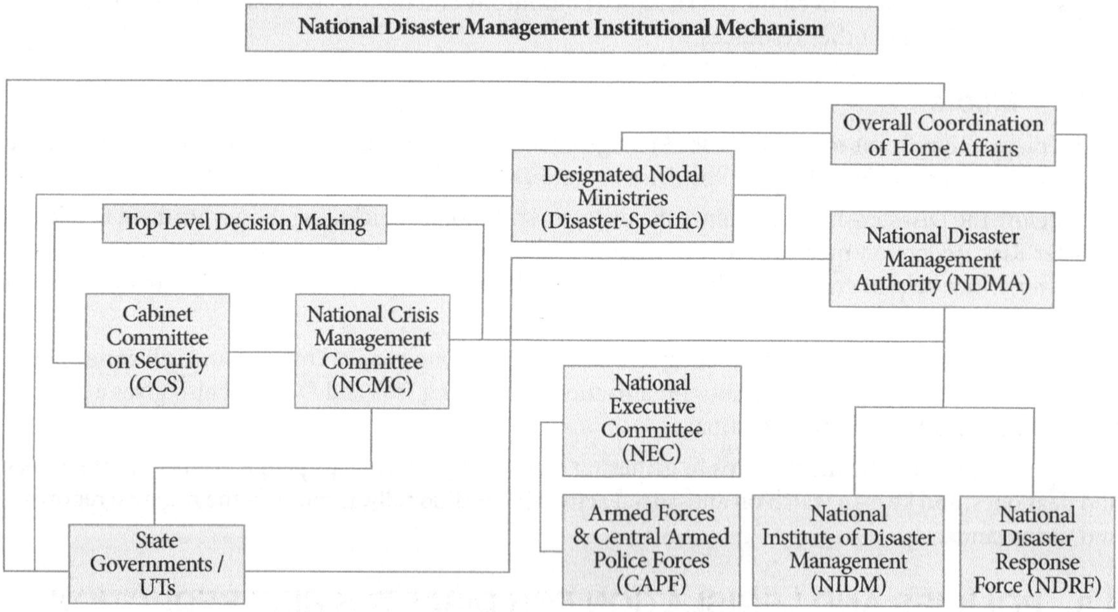

Fig. 4.6: Legal and Institutional Framework

Source: NDMP,2019

4.8.2 National Disaster Management Authority

The National Disaster Management Authority (NDMA) is the apex body for Disaster Management in India. The Prime Minister of India is the Chairperson of the NDMA. The structure of its organization comprises of, one-member secretary, three members and five joint secretaries.

4.8.2.1 Mandate of NDMA

The mandate of NDMA is to lay down policies and guidelines on disaster management. These policies and guidelines are to be followed by various Ministries and Departments of the Govt. of India (GOI) to take steps for disaster risk reduction. It has also been given the responsibility to draw measures and guidelines that should be followed by various State Level Authorities so as to make the State Plans. It also undertakes such measures for the management of disasters, as are necessary for carrying out their responsibilities, available on NDMA website are given as under: -

- Lay down policies on disaster management
- Approve the National Plan
- Approve plans prepared by the Ministries or Departments of the Government of India in accordance with the National Plan
- Lay down guidelines to be followed by the State Authorities in drawing up the State Plan
- Lay down guidelines to be followed by the different Ministries or Departments of the Government of India for the purpose of integrating the measures for prevention of disaster and mitigation of its effects in their development plans and projects

- Coordinate the enforcement and implementation of the policy and plan for disaster management;
- Recommend provision of funds for mitigation purposes
- Provide support to other countries affected by major disasters as determined by the Central Government
- Take other measures for the prevention, mitigation, preparedness and capacity building for dealing with the threatening disaster situation
- Lay down broad policies and guidelines for the functioning of the National Institute of Disaster Management.

4.8.3 State Disaster Management Authority

The DM Act, 2005 provides for the constitution of State Disaster Management Authorities (SDMAs). The SDMA's are chaired by the Chief Minister of the concerned state. In the Union Territories SDMA is chaired by the Lieutenant Governor and co-chaired by the Chief Minister of the concerned state. A legal institutional framework of the state level in India is shown in Fig.4.7.

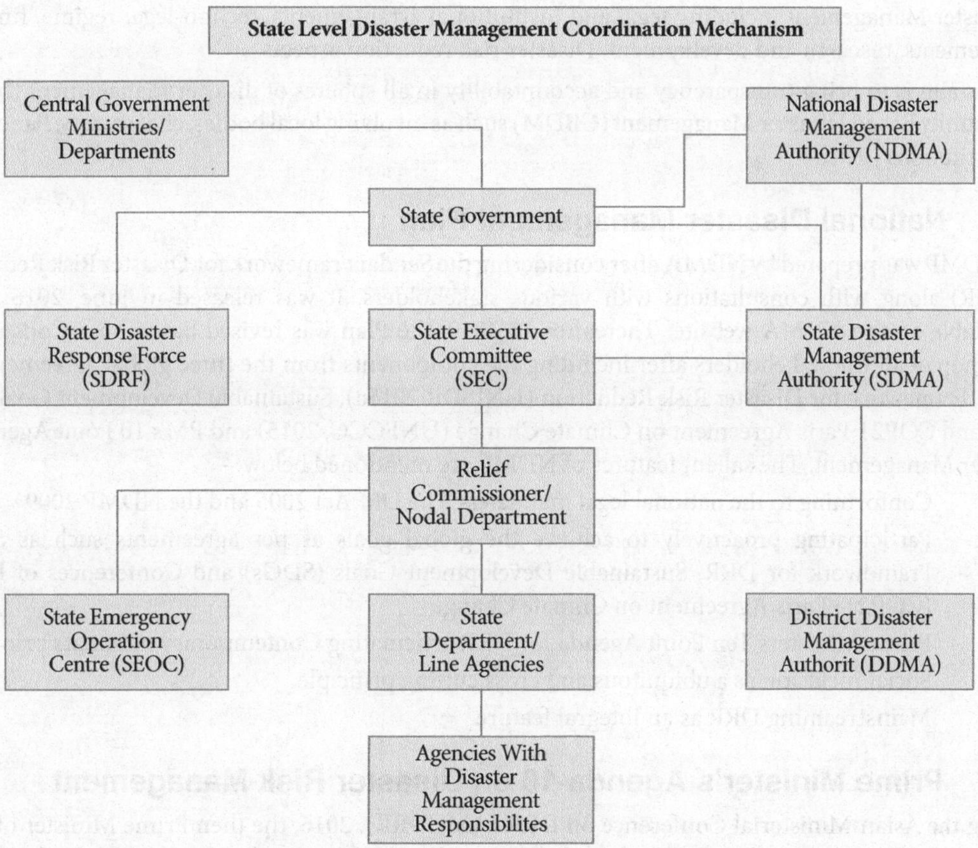

Fig. 4.7: State level Institutional Framework

Source: NDMP,2019

4.8.4 District Disaster Management Authority

District Disaster Management Authority (DDMA's) are constituted in every district of the states as per the section 25 of the DM Act. The District Magistrate/ District Collector/Deputy Commissioner heads the Authority as Chairperson and the elected representative of the local authority is the Co-Chairperson. However, in the tribal areas, the Chief Executive Member of the District Council of Autonomous District is designated as Co-Chairperson.

NDMP

4.8.5 National Policy on Disaster Management

After the enactment of the DM Act, 2005 subsequent formulation of the National Policy on Disaster Management (NPDM,2009) took place. It was based on the Hyogo Framework for Action (HFA), 2005–2015.

The policy emphasized on a shift from response centered approach to proactive disaster management approach with stress on Prevention, Preparedness and Mitigation. It comprehensively covers every aspect of Disaster Management including legal and institutional arrangements, techno-legal regime, financial arrangements, research and development, Disaster risk reduction aspects.

Its aim is to bring transparency and accountability in all spheres of disaster management through Community Based Disaster Management (CBDM) such as involving local bodies, civil society, Panchayati Raj Institutions (PRI's).

4.8.6 National Disaster Management Plan

The NDMP was prepared by NDMA after considering the Sendai Framework for Disaster Risk Reduction (SFDRR) along with consultations with various stakeholders. It was released in June, 2016 which is available on the NDMA website. Thereafter, in 2019, the Plan was revised based on a Consultative Workshop of all the stakeholders after including the components from the three global agreements the Sendai Framework for Disaster Risk Reduction (UNISDR 2015a), Sustainable Development Goals (UN 2015) and COP21 Paris Agreement on Climate Change (UNFCCC, 2015) and PM's 10 Point Agenda on Disaster Management. The salient features of NDMP are mentioned below: -

- Conforming to the national legal mandates- The DM Act 2005 and the NDMP 2009
- Participating proactively to achieve the global goals as per agreements such as Sendai Framework for DRR, Sustainable Development Goals (SDGs) and Conferences of Parties (COP21) Paris Agreement on Climate Change
- Prime Ministers Ten Point Agenda for DRR articulating Contemporary national's priorities
- Social inclusion as a ubiquitous and cross cutting principle
- Mainstreaming DRR as an integral feature

4.8.7 Prime Minister's Agenda-10 on Disaster Risk Management

During the Asian Ministerial Conference on DRR (AMCDRR), 2016, the then Prime Minister of India presented a 10-point Agenda on Disaster Management. Its 10 Point agenda are mentioned below: -

- All development sectors must assimilate the principles of disaster risk management
- Risk coverage must include all, starting from poor households to SMEs to multi-national corporations to nation states

- Women's leadership and involvement should be central to disaster risk management
- Invest in risk mapping to improve global understanding of Nature and disaster risks
- Leverage technology to enhance the efficiency of disaster risk management efforts
- Develop a network of universities to work on disaster related issues
- Utilize the opportunities provided by social media for disaster risk reduction
- Build on local capacity and initiative to enhance disaster risk reduction.
- Make use of every opportunity to learn from disasters and, to achieve that, there must be studies on the lessons after every disaster.
- Bring about greater cohesion in international response to disasters.

4.9 DISASTER RISK REDUCTION PROGRAM IN INDIA

An effective disaster risk Prevention and Mitigation strategy involves reducing the loss of lives and damage to property. If natural hazards cannot be prevented, steps can be taken to reduce the vulnerability by taking Disaster Risk Reduction (DRR)measures. It underscores the importance of reducing the risk of the event to occur by reducing the vulnerability. Thus, the Government of India has acknowledged mitigation and prevention as essential components in development strategy. Moreover, the Central Government has constituted a fund known as National Disaster Mitigation Fund (NDMF) for the purpose of mitigation under the Disaster Management Act 2005. Various programs for disaster risk reduction in India taken by NDMA, GOI, other agencies are described below:

4.9.1 Earthquake

India has been divided into four seismic zones as per the expected intensity of earthquakes. Urbanization in India is increasing at a rapid pace and Metropolitan cities like New Delhi are located in high-risk seismic zones. In these areas, the majority of buildings are not earthquake resistant and do not follow the building-by laws. Therefore, if an earthquake strikes in these cities like this, the hazard might turn into a major disaster. Few of the measures which have been taken for the mitigation of earthquakes are mentioned below: -

4.9.1.1 National Earthquake Risk Mitigation Project

NDMA has formulated the National Earthquake Risk Mitigation Project (NERMP) to reduce the impact of earthquakes on life and property. This aims at increasing the capacities of the stakeholders, thereby reducing the vulnerability. This will also enable national and state entities to be able to effectively plan and respond to earthquakes. Key objectives of the NERMP Project are as under:

- Minimizing the vulnerability of the community to earthquakes.
- Earthquake Resistant Structures
- Ensuring the Safety of the community
- Improving the Techno-legal regime
- Ensuring improvement in the built environment
- Reducing the economic losses
- Capacity Development to mitigate and respond to disasters efficiently.

4.9.1.2 Geotechnical Investigation for Seismic Micro zonation of Indian Land Mass

The project involves making a technical document by considering all the details about Geotechnical/Geophysical Investigations for doing Seismic Microzonation. The document is significant for conducting micro-zonation of the urban centers in the entire country. This gives a rational design of structures, thus leading to building of safe and resilient habitat. The results thus produced would help planners and policy makers to incorporate seismic risk reduction measures for identifying appropriate land use planning.

4.9.1.3 Development of Probabilistic Seismic Hazard Map of India

NDMA has undertaken a study on Development of "Probabilistic Seismic Hazard Map of India" (PSHA) for Seismic Hazard Analysis.

4.9.1.4 Seismic Vulnerability Assessment of Buildings Types in India

This involves Preparation of catalogue of different types of buildings in India and developing vulnerability functions for these buildings through IIT Bombay and other IITs. The document is useful for assessment of buildings in each area and decides on retrofitting requirements.

4.9.1.5 Preparation of Upgraded Earthquake Hazard Maps and Atlases

NDMA through Building Materials and Technology Promotion Council (BMTPC) has developed and upgraded Earthquake Hazard Maps and Atlases for the entire country. These maps and atlases are available on the NDMA website.

4.9.2 Cyclones

The Indian subcontinent is among one of the most cyclone affected regions in the world. Thus, NDMA had initiated measures to handle the situation of cyclone and to mitigate its impacts. The details of the measures taken are given below: -

4.9.2.1 National Cyclone Risk Mitigation Project (Phase I)

NCRMP Phase I is a Centrally Sponsored Scheme of the Govt. of India (GOI) funded by the World Bank in 2011. National Disaster Management Authority (NDMA) which is the nodal agency for coordinating this project. In Phase-I, Odisha and Andhra Pradesh were the participating States. The objectives of the project include construction of Multi-Purpose Cyclone Shelters (MPCSs), upgrading the cyclone Early Warning Dissemination Systems (EWDS), building Roads, Bridges and Saline Embankments.

Under the Phase-I, 535 Multipurpose Cyclone Shelters, 32 Bridges and 88.12 Kms Saline Embankment, 1086 Kms of Roads, have been completed. Moreover, 275 Nos. Alert sirens, 476 Nos. Digital Mobile Radio and 34 Nos has been provided. The Project ended in 2018 (Annual Report NDMA, 2019-20). Some of Photographs of this project are shown in Fig.4.8-4.9.

Fig. 4.8: Photographs of Assets created in Odisha under NCRMP Phase-I

Fig. 4.9: Photographs of Assets created in Andhra Pradesh under NCRMP Phase-I

4.9.2.2 National Cyclone Risk Mitigation Project (Phase-II)

The GOI also approved Phase-II of NCRMP in 2015 for five years up to March, 2020. The project involved covering the States of Gujarat, Kerala, Goa, Maharashtra, Karnataka, and West Bengal. Some of the Photographs of this project are shown in Figs. 4.10-4.11.

Fig. 4.10: Photographs of Assets created in Gujarat under NCRMP Phase-II

Fig. 4.11: Photographs of Assets created in West Bengal under NCRMP Phase-II

4.9.3 Landslides

In view of destruction caused by landslides, NDMA launched the Landslide Risk Mitigation Scheme (LRMS) in July 2019. LRMS was adopted to provide technical and financial support to those states which are prone to Landslides for the purpose of mitigation. The LRMS scheme is a pilot scheme which seeks to demonstrate the benefits of monitoring, training and capacity building, awareness generation and mitigation of landslides. Its aim is to strengthen the structural and non-structural mitigation efforts, reduce the landslide risk and vulnerability by mitigation of site-specific landslides and minimize the risks arising out of it.

4.9.4 Droughts

The Drought Manual for Management of Droughts released in 2009 suggests famine codes for tackling the situations of hunger and destitution. It draws plans to address the impact of droughts taking into account all the capabilities of the state. Thus, it focuses on measures to mitigate the droughts, discovering newer technologies, enabling adoption of new legal framework and including area development and improvement programmes in drought mitigation.

Guidelines for managing the various disasters have been released by NDMA. Some of the significant guidelines are given Below:

- Management of Earthquake-2007
- Preparation of State Disaster Management Plans-2007
- Management of Floods-2008
- Management of Cyclones-2008
- Management of Landslides and Snow Avalanches-2009
- Management of Tsunami-2010
- Management of Drought-2010
- Preparation of Action Plan- Prevention and Management of Thunderstorm & Lightning/ Squall/ Dust/ Hailstorm and Strong Wind-2019

UNIT SUMMARY

- Disaster Management aims to reduce or prevent the potential losses due to the impact of hazards. Disaster Management integrates all the measures, activities and programs which are performed before, during and after the occurrence of a disaster.
- The disaster management cycle covers all aspects of disaster management, i.e., prevention, mitigation, preparedness, response, recovery, and building back better.
- The aim of Disaster prevention is to completely eliminate the risk of disaster, whereas Disaster mitigation aims to minimize the losses or damages due to hazards in advance.
- The aim of Disaster response is to provide prompt assistance to the people affected by disasters, whereas, the aim of Disaster recovery is to return the community to normal situation.
- EWS is a set of capacities that enable generation and dissemination of warning information about extreme events such as cyclones, floods, drought, etc., timely.
- Structural measures are defined as any physical construction, i.e., natural or artificial to decrease or eliminate the losses due to disasters.
- Non-structural measures are measures which include policies, laws, training and education, warning system, financial measures, and good management practices etc., so as to minimize the risk and impact from the hazards.
- Vulnerability and capacity assessment are to identify the causes of vulnerability and measure the capacities to cope in the existing situation. It enables assessing the preparedness and mitigation measures
- Components of disaster relief include the immediate needs of the communities affected by disasters such as food, water, health, shelter and waste management, sanitation, etc.,
- The Disaster Management Act, 2005 provides the core legal and institutional framework at the national, state and district levels for the effective management of disasters.
- National Disaster Management Authority (NDMA) is the apex body for Disaster Management in India.
- State Disaster Management Authority (SDMA) is the body responsible for Disaster Management in each state.
- District Disaster Management Authority (DDMA) is the body responsible for Disaster Management in each district.
- National Policy on Disaster Management (NPDM) covers every aspect of Disaster Management including legal and institutional arrangements, techno-legal regime, financial arrangements, research and development, Disaster risk reduction aspects.
- National Disaster Management Plan (NDMP) was prepared by NDMA taking into consideration the Sendai Framework for Disaster Risk Reduction (SFDRR) along with consultations with various stakeholders.
- Disaster Management is a comprehensive subject, which requires integration of various stakeholders to be able to efficiently manage disasters.

EXERCISES

Multiple Choice Questions

Q.1 In which city the National Institute of Disaster Management is situated?

a. Chennai
b. Hyderabad
c. New Delhi
d. Mumbai

Q.2 The state disaster management authority (SDMA) in Delhi is headed by

a. Chief Minister
b. Home Minister
c. Lieutenant Governor
d. Chief Secretary

Q.3 The Disaster Management Act was enacted in

a. 2006
b. 2003
c. 2009
d. 2005

Q.4 Which organization is the apex authority of managing disasters in India?

a. NDMA
b. NEC
c. NDRF
d. NIDM

Q.5 The first National Disaster Management Plan of India was released by

a. Manmohan Singh
b. Atal Bihari Vajpayee
c. Amit Shah
d. Narendra Modi

Q.6 The National Disaster Management Authority comes under which of the following ministry?

a. Ministry of Environment
b. Ministry of Home Affairs
c. Ministry of Pollution
d. Ministry of Foreign Affairs

Q.7 All activities related to Disaster management can be divided into

a. 3 phases
b. 4 phases
c. 5 phases
d. None of the above

Q.8 Which of the following is not a structural measure of Disaster Management?

a. Hazard mapping
b. Retrofitting of existing buildings
c. Construction of shelter
d. Building roads and bridges.
e. None of these

Q.9 Which of the following is the nodal agency for early warning of Tsunami?

a. IMD
b. INCOIS
c. CWC
d. GSI

Q.10 Mitigation means

a. To completely prevent the adverse effect of hazard
b. To minimize the adverse impact of hazard
c. To return the community to normal situation
d. Both a) and c)
e. None of these

Q.11 Recovery include(s): -

a. Rehabilitation
b. Reconstruction
c. Reconstruction and Rehabilitation
d. None of these

Q.12 The tools for Vulnerability assessment is/are: -

a. Transect Walk
b. Problem Tree
c. Livelihood Analysis
d. Focus Group Discussion

All of these

Q.13 which of the following is the first responder during a disaster?

a. Government
b. Media
c. Community
d. International agencies

Q.14 The tools for capacity assessment is/are:

a. Chapati diagram
b. Resource mapping
c. Resource matrix
d. All of these

Q.15 National Disaster Management Plan (NDMP), 2019 includes the components from: -

a. Sendai Framework for Disaster Risk Reduction (UNISDR 2015)
b. Sustainable Development Goals (UN 2015)
c. COP21 Paris Agreement on Climate Change (UNFCCC 2015)
d. PM's 10 Point Agenda on Disaster Management.
e. All of these

Answers of Multiple-Choice Questions

Answers of Multiple-choice questions				
4.1 **c**	4.2 **c**	4.3 **d**	4.4 **a**	4.5 **d**
4.6 **b**	4.7 **a**	4.8 **a**	4. 9 **b**	4.10 **b**
4.11 **c**	4.12 **e**	4.13 **c**	4.14 **d**	4.15 **e**

Short and Long Answer Type Questions

Category I

1. Describe the various phases of disaster management?
2. What is Disaster Management Act 2005? Explain in brief?
3. Explain Prevention. How is it different from Mitigation?
4. What is recovery?
5. What is the role of Early warning systems in Disaster Management?
6. Mention different structural Mitigation measures for Landslides.
7. What do you mean by Structural Mitigation measures?
8. What is the mandate of NDMA?
9. What are the salient features of NDMP 2019?
10. What is the role of Local Self Government in Disaster Management?

Category II

1. Describe disaster management cycles with a neat sketch, explaining the different phases.
2. What is an early warning system? What are the elements of the Early Warning System? Explain in detail?

3. What is the difference between structural and non-structural measures? Explain the structural and non-structural measures for cyclones?
4. What is vulnerability and capacity assessment and explain the various tools used for the vulnerability and capacity assessment?
5. What are different components of Disaster Relief? Explain in detail?
6. Explain policies and legislations for disaster management in India?
7. Elaborate the Disaster Risk Reduction (DRR) Program in India?

REFERENCES AND SUGGESTED READINGS

1. Chandol, T., Gupta, A. K., Amin, F., Bindal, M. K., (2021): Training Manual on Climate Change and Extreme Events Risk Reduction, NIDM, New Delhi
2. GIDM (2020): Training module on flood risk mitigation & management https://gidm.gujarat.gov.in/sites/default/files/educate_your_self_document/Training%20Module%20on%20Flood%20Risk%20Mitigation%20and%20Management.pdf
3. Guleria S. (2022): Training Module on Preparation of State Disaster Management Plans (SDMP), NIDM, New Delhi.
4. https://nidm.gov.in/PDF/Modules/NIDMSDMP_22.pdf
5. NDMA (2008): National Disaster Management Guidelines: Management of Floods. Ministry of Home affairs, GOI.
6. https://nidm.gov.in/PDF/pubs/NDMA/3.pdf
7. NDMA (2008): National Disaster Management Guidelines: Management of Cyclones. Ministry of Home affairs, GOI .
8. https://ndma.gov.in/sites/default/files/PDF/cyclone/cyclones.pdf
9. NDMA (2019): National Disaster Management Plan, Ministry of Home affairs, GOI.
10. NITI Aayog (2021): Report of the committee Constituted for formulation of strategy for flood management works in entire country and River Management activities and works related to border areas (2021-26).https://niti.gov.in/sites/default/files/2021-03/Flood-Report.pdf
11. World Meteorological Organization. 2019. The Role of Young Professionals in Driving the Integration of Early Warning Systems. Education and Training.
12. https://public.wmo.int/en/resources/bulletin/role-ofyoung-professionals-driving-integration-of-early-warning-sys
13. https://ndma.gov.in/
14. https://www.nidm.gov.in/PDF/Disaster_hymet.pdf

05 DISASTERS, ENVIRONMENT AND DEVELOPMENT

UNIT SPECIFICS

The salient objectives of this unit are to familiarize the students with the following:

- *To explain the various causes which influence vulnerability.*
- *To elucidate the relationship between disasters and development.*
- *To elucidate the relationship between disasters and the environment.*
- *To describe the impact of dams on disasters.*
- *To explain the different causes of environmental modifications.*
- *To throw light on sustainable recovery and reconstruction.*
- *To describe the importance of Sustainable Development Goals (SDG's) in Disaster Risk Reduction (DRR) efforts.*

In this unit, the different causes which influence vulnerability are discussed. It further explains the relationship between disasters, development and environment. An overview of different causes of environmental modification is presented and the impacts of dams on the disasters are elaborated in detail. The concept of Recovery and Reconstruction and their approaches are discussed. Furthermore, the significance of Sustainable Development Goals (SDG's) with special emphasis on integrating Disaster Risk Reduction (DRR) into development planning is highlighted.

A number of multiple-choice questions are given as well as questions of short and long answer types are marked in two categories following lower and higher order of Bloom's taxonomy. A list of references and suggested readings are given in the unit so that one can go through them for practice. It is important to note that for getting more information on various topics of interest some QR codes have been provided in different sections which can be scanned for relevant supportive knowledge.

RATIONALE

This unit helps students to gain insights about factors of vulnerability such as economic, social, political and physical. It describes the interlinkages between disasters, environment and development. This helps students to understand how the disasters affect the environment and development, how the development impacts the disasters and the environment and most importantly how the environment influences and is influenced by disasters and development. An overview of various causes of environmental modifications and impact of dams are presented so as to equip the students with means of reducing disaster risks. Moreover, the chapter further discusses the recovery and reconstruction process so as to give the reader an insight into the concept of Disaster Risk Management. Thereafter, the concepts of Sustainable development which incorporates Disaster Risk Reduction is underscored. This will also help readers evolve sustainable practices in their daily lives so as to truly achieve the aim of a safer world.

PRE-REQUISITES

NIL

UNIT OUTCOMES

List of outcomes of this unit is as follows:

U5-O1: Understand the different factors which affect vulnerability.

U5-O2: Understand the linkage between disasters, environment and development.

U5-O3: Comprehend environmental modifications and their impacts

U5-O4: Assess various aspects of Recovery and Reconstruction.

U5-O5: Understand the significance of Sustainable Development Goals.

Unit-5 Outcomes	EXPECTED MAPPING WITH COURSE OUTCOMES (1-WeakCorrelation;2-Mediumcorrelation;3-StrongCorrelation)					
	CO-1	CO-2	CO-3	CO-4	CO-5	CO-6
U5-01	-	1	1	2	2	3
U5-02	2	3	2	2	2	2
U5-03	-	-	1	1	1	-
U5-04	2	2	1	1	2	1
U5-05	1	-	-	1	2	3

5.1 INTRODUCTION

Disasters do not occur randomly or by accident. They are a combination of hazards and vulnerable conditions. Disasters, whether drought, tropical cyclones, storms, earthquakes, floods, wildfires, or volcanic eruptions result in huge losses of lives and livelihoods. Moreover, they do not just result from the underlying vulnerabilities such as environmental, political, economic, social, etc., but also worsens them. Therefore, these disasters create serious challenges including destruction of economic and social infrastructure, damage to the environment and damage to development.

There is a close association between disasters, development and the environment. It is because disasters damage the environment and the gains achieved due to development while the development may strengthen or weaken the environment and disasters. Moreover, the environment which is a significant factor in causing disasters can also act as a buffer in reducing the damages due to disasters. This indicates that vulnerability can lead to adverse impacts due to a disaster which means that the vulnerability determines to a large extent the severity of hazard.

Moreover, unsustainable development practices and the degradation of the environment are significantly increasing the disaster risk. Unplanned development has resulted in the construction of unsafe buildings in hazard prone areas reducing the capacity of the community to resist and recover from disasters. It has also increased the costs due to disasters.

In the past few decades, the frequency and severity of disasters especially as a result of population growth and urbanization, has increased. It is because there has been a focus on growth without consideration to development. Growth which focuses on development is sustainable and reduces the impacts of disasters. It means that sustainable development can increase society's capacity to resist disasters. Sustainable development is a combination of three distinct components viz. development, environment, and society.

Sustainable development should focus on socioeconomic development along with the environment. Therefore, efforts should be taken to mainstream climate change adaptation (CCA), environment, and DRR into development planning. It has also been observed that vulnerable groups are more susceptible to damage than others. They find it hard to recover and reconstruct as they are more vulnerable and also suffer more losses. Developmental planning should also incorporate their needs and concerns.

Measures such as Environmental management and Risk reduction play a significant role in formulating policies that contribute to sustainable development. Developmental projects such as the construction of dams therefore should consider the disaster adaptation and mitigation component as it helps in reducing risks. Furthermore, realizing the close linkages between Disaster Risk Reduction (DRR), Environment and Development has resulted in various global agreements which have a shared vision of building resilience. It can help realize the goal of Sustainable Development i.e., Development that considers the needs of the present generation without compromising the ability of future generations to meet their needs.

5.2 FACTORS AFFECTING VULNERABILITY

Vulnerability is a significant component of disaster risk. It is a complex phenomenon. Several factors such as physical, economic, social and environment enhances the vulnerability of an individual or a community towards a specific risk or hazard. In addition to the above factors it also is affected by usage of natural resources, influences from historical, cultural, institutional as well as political aspects (IPCC, 2012). Following factors influences the vulnerability to a disaster:

- Physical factors
- Social factors
- Economic factors
- Environmental factors

Physical factors which increase the vulnerability towards a disaster include unplanned land use, lack of building standards, poor housing design, use of poor construction materials in buildings, lack of access to services during an emergency among others. Other aspects such as population density, site location, its design and the materials used in construction for housing and other infrastructure also impact physical vulnerability.

Social factor which is mainly responsible for vulnerability is poverty. Poor persons as well as communities generally lack adequate access to basic resources and facilities like clean drinking water, healthcare and sanitation. Poverty also restricts access to education as well as employment furthering the circle of vulnerability. The absence of education, proper training, and awareness of the measures to safeguard from hazards, along with the lack of safety and security increases the vulnerability for risk. In addition, the lack of human rights and discrimination based on gender, social status, age, and disability also enhances susceptibility to hazards. Communities which reside in areas that are disaster prone are more vulnerable to the effects of such events.

Economic factors are concerned with susceptible livelihoods, emphasis on single means of income or industry, huge informal sector that is uninsured and predominantly global nature of businesses as well as supply chains. Combination of these factors results in declining of livelihoods of the already poor and vulnerable population, enhancing their dependence on single industries further pushing them to marginalization and poverty. In addition, since poor individuals and communities lack the resources to construct sturdy structures, they remain highly vulnerable to the harmful impacts of disasters.

Environmental factors include indiscriminate natural resource consumption, decline of ecosystem related services, adverse impacts of climate change and poor environmental management. Further environmental degradation caused by pollution or deforestation increases the vulnerability to natural disasters.

Developmental projects and environmental modifications are two factors that can adversely impact on vulnerability. Developmental projects are often aimed at improving the economic well-being of a region or country, but they can also have unintended severe consequences. One of the most harmful impacts of developmental projects is their effect on the environment. For example, the construction of dams or other such infrastructures can lead to the displacement of local communities and the destruction of ecosystems. It can lead to a loss of livelihoods for local people, as well as increased vulnerability to natural disasters like landslides, floods and cyclones.

5.3 DISASTERS AND DEVELOPMENT

Development is a double-edged sword. While on the one hand it raises the standard of living and well-being of the people, on the other it negatively impacts the environment thereby causing disasters which leads to deterioration in the quality of life. There is therefore a close association between Disasters and Development. They both are related in having beneficial as well as adverse impacts on each other as disasters destroy developmental gains and also result in opportunities for development. Developmental projects or schemes may also enhance or reduce vulnerability to natural disasters. Therefore, it is important to focus on proper developmental planning and making 'rational choices' that are based on the evaluation of hazards as well as risk assessment which will reduce the impact of disasters on development.

Development should focus on improving the social, economic and environmental dimensions of a nation through the management of a region's natural as well as human resources. However, unplanned development leads to newer disaster risks and results in death, disability, damage to property as well as infrastructure and the loss of ecosystem services. Vulnerable individuals and communities such as those belonging to poor strata, women and children, disabled and elderly are susceptible to disasters. The relation between disasters and development is shown in Fig. 5.1.

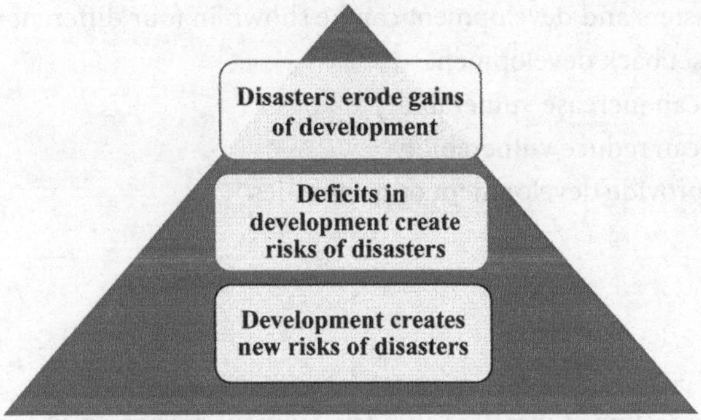

Fig. 5.1: Disaster and Development

Source: UNESCAP

For elucidating the association between disasters and development, it is necessary to understand the social and economic elements of development. The social and economic aspects of development may lead to a decrease or increase in disaster risk. The relation between social and economic development and disasters is shown in Table 5.1.

Table 5.1: Disaster and Development

	Economic Development	Social Development
Disaster limits development	Destruction of fixed assets. Loss of production capacity, market access or material inputs. Damage to transport, communications or energy infrastructure. Erosion of livelihoods, savings and physical capital.	Destruction of health or education infrastructure and personnel. Death, disablement or migration of key social actors leading to an erosion of social capital.
Development causes disaster risk	Unsustainable development practices that create wealth for some at the expense of unsafe working or living conditions for others or degrade the environment.	Development paths generating cultural norms that promote social isolation or political exclusion.
Development reduces disaster risk	Access to adequate drinking water, food, waste management and a secure dwelling increases people's resiliency. Trade and technology can reduce poverty. Investing in financial mechanisms and social security can cushion against vulnerability.	Building community cohesion, recognizing excluded individuals or social groups (such as women), and providing opportunities for greater involvement in decision-making, enhanced educational and health capacity increases resiliency.

Source: UNDP,2004

The linkage between disasters and development can be shown in four different ways as given below: -

- Disasters can set back development
- Development can increase vulnerability
- Development can reduce vulnerability
- Disasters can provide development opportunities

Development

The positive and Negative realms of disasters and development are shown in Fig.5.2.

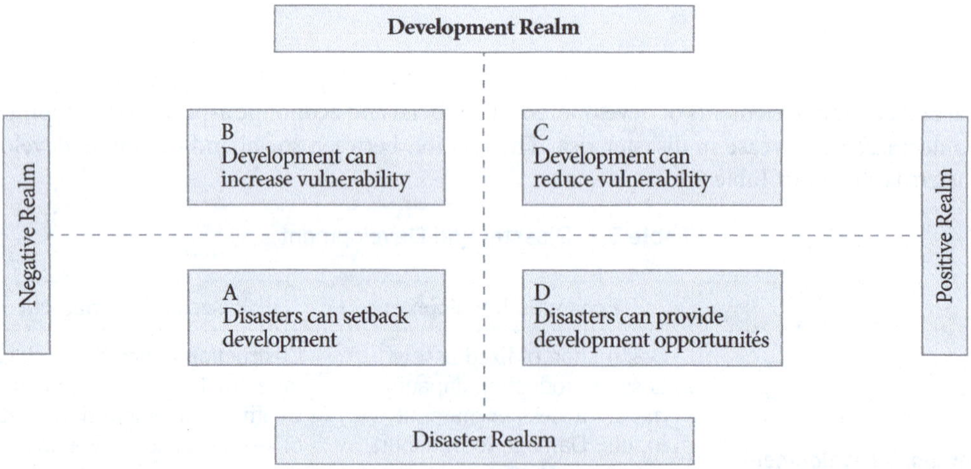

Fig. 5.2: Positive and Negative realms of disasters and development

Source: ADPC, 2014

These positive and negative realms are described below: -

Disasters can set back development

Disasters can retard social and economic development achieved from years of investments in a fraction of time. Disasters also divert resources for rescue, relief, reconstruction and recovery efforts. Additionally, they disrupt normal life through disturbances in existing services and infrastructure, creating a setback for positive development. Furthermore, they may lead to political instability or even riots.

Development can increase vulnerability

Social and economic development can aggravate the factors of vulnerability and expose the community to hazards. Such a development is usually unsustainable, as this increases disaster risks. This can be because of many reasons, such as development without following the building codes, without conducting a proper Environmental Impact Assessment (EIA), without studying the seismicity and ground stability and, etc.,. Additionally, this can also result from unplanned urbanization, which is a cause of worry.

Development can reduce vulnerability

Development can increase the vulnerability of any community to hazards. However, it can also reduce the vulnerability of the community if the development is done in a sustainable manner. Such a development is usually accompanied by proper prevention, preparedness, and mitigation measures. These measures are structural, like hazard-resistant buildings, and non-structural measures like disaster management plans, contingency planning, and capacity building. Additionally, it is also focused on strengthening critical facilities such as schools, hospitals, communication facilities, early warning systems, roads, etc.

Disasters can provide development opportunities

Disaster events can act as opportunities for development in the aftermath of a disaster. They can give a spur to development as they provide evidence of lessons learned. This can help make the best choices by using the best materials and technologies that suit the needs of the local communities. Such a development is usually disaster resistant and environment friendly such as construction following the building codes and bylaw, relocation to safer locations, etc... Thus, it can help Build Back Better (BBB) when accompanied by disaster- resilient structures and practices.

5.4 ENVIRONMENT AND DISASTERS

Environment refers to everything that surrounds us. It can be physical or natural. A good environment like clean air can enhance our experience of living and keep us healthier. On the other hand, if the environment constitutes poor quality air, it can create an uncomfortable situation. The environment can therefore exacerbate hazards or reduce their risk. There is a close association between Environment and Disasters. The Environment helps in regulating and mitigating natural hazards such as droughts, floods, landslides, etc,. It also provides ecosystem services such as food, medicines, air quality, fresh water, mental and physical health, well-being, livelihood, etc., They are related in having beneficial as well as adverse impacts on each other. These goods and services play a key role in enhancing the adaptive capacities of the community toward disaster risk. These act as environmental safeguards which play a significant role in the management of disaster risks. Functional and Healthy ecosystems act as a buffer for natural hazards which can reduce the exposure to hazards and risks of disasters. They mitigate the disaster and climate risks, thereby decreasing socioeconomic vulnerability and strengthening the resilience of communities.

However, when disasters strike, they lead to environmental degradation and the available ecosystem services adversely. This can impact the communities dependent upon them and disrupt their lives and livelihood. Furthermore, the loss of environmental safeguards exposes the community and exacerbates the impacts of disasters. Moreover, post-disaster emergency operations also impact the environment as the environment does not usually get the attention that is required to prevent further damage from occurring. This can be due to poor management of waste, carcasses, disaster debris, mismanagement, etc., This results in further degradation and depletion of natural resources. Environmental degradation is a key determinant of climate and disaster risk. It alters the ecosystem and its services which increases disaster vulnerability in multiple ways. The degradation undermines the resilience to future disasters and increases the frequency and intensity of these hazards. Some of the direct impacts caused by disasters on the environment are loss of biodiversity, damaged ecosystems, depletion in natural capital, etc., Further, this also undermines the recovery efforts and leaves the community more vulnerable and exposed. The environmental drivers which influence the disaster risks are shown in Fig. 5.3.

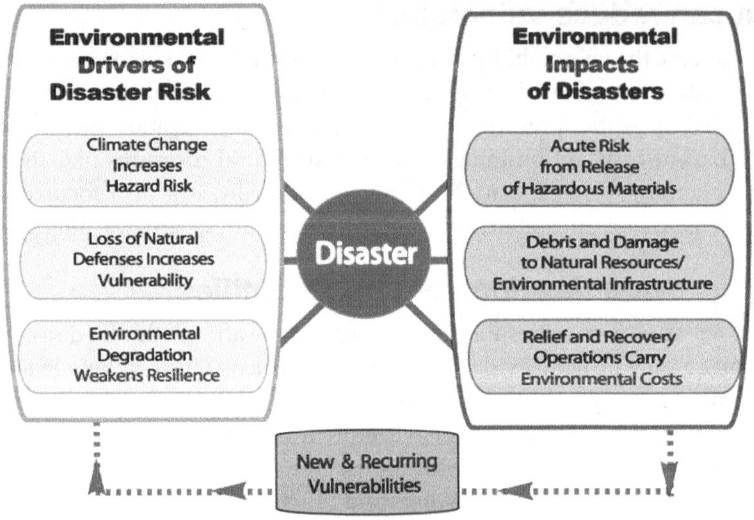

Fig. 5.3: Environment and Disaster Risk

Source: **UNEP: Environment and disaster risk)**

It is necessary to understand the adverse impacts of disasters on the environment and vice-versa. This is because the degradation of the environment affects the sustainability of the ecosystem which can be a hurdle to achieve sustainable development. Henceforth, in order to achieve sustainable development, it is important to understand and manage the vulnerabilities which contributed to disaster risks.

5.5 IMPACT OF DAMS

Dams are reservoir structures that are built for storing water and providing it when needed. However, these structures have a few limitations which can lead to disaster occurrence. The impacts of dams on disasters can be summarized under three different heads mentioned below: -

- Dam failure – induced Seismic Activity
- Dam failure – induced Floods

These are described below: -

Dams & Earthquake

5.5.1 Dam failure – induced Seismic Activity:

It has been observed that the seismic forces can be triggered by dams. Since dams are considered as Mega – Structures, their construction requires heavy machinery and operations for blasting. It can produce waves under the ground leading to man-made earthquakes.

Secondly, the generation of seismic loads is also dependent on the extra pressure created by the water inside the fissures and micro-cracks under the ground and near the reservoir. This results in greater unsteadiness under the ground surface. When the pressure of water inside the rocks surges, it acts as a lubricating agent to the faults present under the ground surface thus causing tectonic strain and resulting in the slipping action causing earthquakes. This movement becomes more critical when the level of the water in the dam changes at a speedy rate. As the level of the stored water increases, the magnitude of the pressure generated by the water on the ground increases, and when the level of the water stored decreases, the pressure also drops. This fluctuation in the magnitude of the pressure intensity generates the stress between the tectonic plates, and thus, generates a possibility of earthquakes. This phenomenon of the earthquake caused by a reservoir is commonly known as *"Reservoir Induced Seismicity"*.

There is evidence that five of the nine earthquakes that occurred on the Indian peninsula during the 1980s were strong enough to inflict damage that may have been caused by reservoirs. An example of Reservoir Induced Seismicity in India is the Koyna Earthquake (1967), Maharashtra, which caused an earthquake of magnitude 6.5 recorded on Richter Scale; resulting in death of nearly 200 people in the nearby area.

5.5.2 Dam failure – induced Floods

Dams are built to regulate the flow of water, provide irrigation, electricity generation and several other needs of the community. However, if dams are not properly maintained extreme meteorological conditions can cause floods. This is because these dams are unable to hold adequate water, and there is an uncontrolled release of water from a reservoir. The dam failure can be minor or even catastrophic, harming life and property. The following are typical causes of dam failures:

- Water level rises higher than the dam's storage capacity.
- Problems with the dam's supporting foundation.
- The Structure is prone to leakage or seepage of water.
- Inadequate maintenance and supervision.
- Inadequate engineering design.
- Landslides.
- The extensive melting of snow.
- Violence or sabotage.
- Failure brought on by earthquakes, volcanic eruptions, and hurricanes, among other natural catastrophes.

A dam failure downstream might have catastrophic effects on all life and property in its path. Landslides at the reservoir's edge, bank erosion, and damage to downstream habitats are further potential dangers from dam failure. Depending on what caused the dam to break, there may not be enough time to alert people. For instance, if the failure is brought on by heavy rain or a large amount of snowmelt, there may be adequate time to organize and carry out evacuations. However, it is unlikely that there would be any warning time available if the structural collapse was brought on by an earthquake.

When there is a failure in the structural configuration of a dam, it leads to a huge-scale release of water downstream of the river, which causes floods. This source of flood majorly generates losses related to infrastructure, livelihood, environment, and economy.

Environmental Modifications due to Dam failure is discussed in the next section.

5.6 ENVIRONMENTAL MODIFICATIONS AND THEIR IMPACT

Environmental modifications, such as deforestation, land use changes and urbanization, can have a significant impact on vulnerability by exacerbating social and economic inequalities. These modifications can lead to loss of biodiversity and ecosystem services, such as food, medicines, air quality, water filtration and soil fertility, which can increase the risk of environmental disasters such as droughts, floods, and wildfires. They can also result in the displacement, loss of traditional knowledge and practices, which can leave people more vulnerable to environmental hazards. Occurrence of Environmental modifications due to key developmental aspects are given below :-

- Land use changes.
- Urbanization.
- Climate Change
- Dams

5.6.1 Land Use Changes

Land Use Change (LUC) refers to a process that transforms the natural landscape as a result of anthropogenic activities such as economic uses, settlements, forestry and impacts the environment. The land is a significant natural resource and a key determinant of the socioeconomic and ecological health of a region. The natural land not only provides the material resources such as food, water etc., but also helps in regulating water resources, climate, and natural disasters. However, the resources are not available in abundance and are always scarce. Additionally, Land is a critical component of biodiversity; overuse of land for several different purposes has urged the need for its reversal. Thus, it is important to sustainably manage them to be able to become disaster resilient.

The land use of a region is primarily influenced by the nature of its economic activities. A large amount of land, which constituted forests, grasslands, wetlands has been converted into cities and farmland. Changes in land use patterns affect the balance of various systems and impact the soil environment, atmospheric environment and water environment etc.,. These changes have increased the intensity and frequency of natural disasters.

Hence, Land use changes, such as deforestation, urbanization and agricultural expansion, can also increase the risk of natural disasters. Activities such as converting forest land and lake beds to make housing complexes negatively impact the ecosystem services. These changes particularly affect the poor, who are largely reliant on ecosystems for their livelihoods.

Deforestation can increase the risk of natural disasters such as floods, landslides, wildfires, etc. It can lead to soil erosion, which can increase the risk of landslides and floods. In addition, deforestation can increase the frequency and severity of wildfires, which can destroy ecosystems and communities.

Urbanization can lead to increased runoff and the risk of flooding, as well as the degradation of the environment and loss of biodiversity. Agricultural expansion can lead to soil degradation, which can increase the risk of landslides and soil erosion. Both urbanization and agricultural expansion can also increase the risk of wildfires by altering landscape.

5.6.2 Urbanization

Urbanization is a process of a general rise in the population and industrialization. It is a process of moving to cities and changing to the urban way of life, which involves activities such as trade, industry, management, and services. In short, it can be described as a process of becoming urban. It is a process of expansion in the proportion of people living in urban areas. It thus indicates a shift from rural to urban. Urbanization impacts the social, economic, and environmental aspects of society in a significant way. The growth of cities and towns often leads to better economic opportunities for many. However, several others may face social inequality when they are denied access to resources. Urban expansion often occurs at the cost of loss of natural habitats, including wetlands, forests and increased pollution levels. This impacts biodiversity, water, and air quality, and causes climate change. Moreover, urbanization results in carbon emissions, and increase in energy consumption thereby leading to an increase in climate change.

Urbanization also impacts cultural identity and social cohesion. As people shift from rural to urban regions, they may experience a loss of link to their communities and cultural roots, thereby disrupting the traditional ways of life. Henceforth, Urbanization can transform their surrounding environment and contribute to generating new risks. A photograph of rapid urbanization is shown in Fig 5.4.

Fig. 5.4: Rapid Urbanization

Source: https://hdr.undp.org/content/rapid-urbanisation-opportunities-and-challenges-improve-well-being-societies

To address the impacts of urbanization, there is a need for sustainable development in urban areas. This includes the promotion of mixed-use urban areas that prioritizes cycling, using public transportation or even walking. It should also focus on protecting natural habitats and biodiversity and the promotion of sustainable energy and resource use. Additionally, Sustainable urban development also includes addressing social inequalities, thereby ensuring that all members of the community have access to basic services and opportunities. This includes the provision of education, healthcare, affordable housing, and employment opportunities.

5.6.3 Climate Change

Climate change refers to the changes in the weather patterns over an extended period of time. According to IPCC, this is due to the rise in global temperature primarily as a result of anthropogenic activities. Climate change leads to an increase in the temperature of air and sea surface, sea level rise, shifts in climate regimes, recession of glaciers, and an increase in extreme events. The emission of Greenhouse Gases (GHG) from land-use change and particularly due to the burning of fossil fuels, has impacted every region, country, and sector of the economy. Further, rise in GHG emissions will lead to warming of the earth system and consequential changes to our ecosystem, biodiversity, environment, and economy, which may be irreversible.

Climate Change is thus increasing the frequency and risk of the occurrence of extreme events due to climate variability. These extreme events manifest in the form of Cyclones, Floods, Hailstorms, Cold waves, LLOFs, GLOFs, Lightning, Land erosion, submergence, landslides, Droughts, Heat waves, Forest fires, Health hazards, etc.,. This may lead to adverse impacts on the ecosystem services, biochemical cycle, and ecological balance. Moreover, these extreme events are further aggravating the vulnerabilities and creating a threat to lives and livelihoods, and manifesting underlying economic, social, and environmental vulnerabilities. However, substantial emission reduction measures can help in reducing the risks of climate change.

Further, it is important to adopt such practices which help protect the ecosystem, i.e., they should be sustainable such as reforestation, conservation agriculture, sustainable land use practices, and green infrastructure in urban planning, which can reduce the risk of floods. Mitigating Climate. Additionally, policies which incorporate renewable energy mandates, and carbon pricing can help achieve sustainable development.

In conclusion, environmental modifications and developmental projects are factors that have a substantial impact on exposure to extreme events. These factors can increase the risk of environmental disasters and other hazards. To mitigate these, it is important to adopt a participatory and holistic approach to development, which gives priority to the protection and restoration of biodiversity, and ecosystems as well as the aspirations of local communities.

5.6.4 Dams

There are several negative environmental effects that large dams have, including direct effects on the chemical, biological and physical aspects of riverine and riparian habitats. They can cause habitat fragmentation, flooding, greenhouse gas emissions, silt build-up, downstream sediment erosion, detrimental effects on local fisheries, and the creation of methylmercury.

Dams that obstruct fish migration upstream and downstream along a river results in habitat fragmentation. The full separation of spawning grounds from places appropriate for rearing, particularly for particular species, can occur when fish migrations are impeded by dam walls. Dams also store sediments that are essential for preserving physical processes and habitats further downstream. Dams produce a reservoir upstream of the dam that has the potential to overflow into the surroundings, resulting in flooding and the obliteration of habitat. Numerous things, including people, plants, and animals, may perish or be displaced as a result of this.

The replacement of a once-free-flowing riverine ecology by a man-made slack-water reservoir habitat upstream of the dam has obvious and major ramifications. Reservoirs frequently have suboptimal circumstances that are incompatible with the aquatic species that have developed alongside a certain river system, such as changes in chemical composition, temperature, dissolved oxygen levels, and physical qualities. In reality, invasive and non-native species, such as algae, snails, and predatory fish, frequently thrive in reservoirs, endangering native plant and animal habitats along the river. The main and long-lasting effects of dams on the environment often result from changes in river flow and sediment transfer downstream. The biota that lives in and around a river can be dramatically impacted by the amount and timing of its flow. Even little changes in water flow can be as harmful to the creatures living in a river's sections as full drying of those sections. This can affect aquatic and riparian species and disrupt the biological interdependence of a river system.

Dams that flood neighboring environments cause nearby trees and other plant life to die and degrade, which releases carbon dioxide into the atmosphere. As a result of stagnation brought on by the loss of freely flowing water, the reservoir's oxygen level drops and methane, a potent greenhouse gas, is produced. Sediment accumulates behind dams, altering the distribution of plant and animal life. Downstream, sediment erosion is increased due to the reduced sediment flow. This results in a shortage of sediment load, and the riverbed gradually deepens and narrows, reducing support for wildlife.

Additionally, dams stop the natural sediment replenishment of ecosystems downstream, reducing the amount of silt in the river. As a result, the river seeks to make up for this by eroding the banks and riverbed further downstream, endangering infrastructure like bridges, buildings along the river, and vegetation. After a dam is closed, riverbeds may erode by several metres, resulting in damage that can be seen tens to hundreds of kilometers downstream. Furthermore, riverbed incision resulting from damming can lead to a drop in groundwater levels along the river, reducing the accessibility of water for plant roots and human settlements that depend on wells for their water supply. Alterations to the riverbed can also reduce habitat for invertebrates and fish that breed on the river bottom.

Dams can cause organic material to build up, which increases the need for oxygen as it breaks down and creates "dead zones" unsuitable for river life. Diverse water temperatures in dam reservoirs make it more difficult for marine life that has evolved to withstand temperature variations to live. Reservoirs may produce methylmercury as a result of the deterioration of organic matter from decomposing plants. Methylmercury accumulates in the body and can be dangerous for both people and animals who eat fish from reservoirs.

The construction of large dams has led to numerous irreversible ecological consequences, including the extirpation of a myriad of aquatic fauna, the disappearance of avifauna in floodplains, substantial agricultural, wetland, and forest losses, and the deterioration of coastal deltas. While dams serve to retain water, control floods, and provide economic benefits, they also have significant negative impacts on the environment. One of these impacts is the hindrance of fish and other aquatic species' migration through the dam. Failure to design the dam appropriately for this purpose can cause habitat loss and ecological disruption in the aquatic community.

5.7 SUSTAINABLE RECOVERY

Recovery is considered the most complex function of the disaster management process. It affects a large number of people and involves a variety of stakeholders thereby impacting a community's economic and social well-being.

A sustainable recovery integrates Disaster Risk Reduction measures into its efforts. These measures include reducing vulnerabilities, protecting the environment, engaging people in decision making, strengthening infrastructure, etc.,. Coordination among the stakeholders is needed to ensure a sustainable recovery. However, to ensure long-term sustainability and promote resilience, it is important to ensure that the recovery is environment friendly. This means reducing the environmental impacts of recovery, such as minimizing pollution, promoting sustainable land use, protecting the biodiversity and natural habitat, and reducing emission of GHG, and prioritizing sustainability during rebuilding and reconstructing.

Recovery is defined as "The restoring or improving livelihoods and health, as well as economic, physical, social, cultural and environmental assets, systems and activities, of a disaster-affected community or society, aligning with the principles of sustainable development and "build back better", to avoid or reduce future disaster risk." (UNISDR 2016).

Disasters such as cyclones, floods, and earthquakes leave a trail of damage and destruction to life, livelihoods and property. Recovering from disasters can be a challenging process. It takes years to recover from the damage and delivering improved resilience may take even longer. Recovery starts after the emergency phase of disaster response ends. However, it is important to plan for disaster recovery as soon as the disaster response starts as the recovery should be based on pre-existing policies and strategies that cater to the institutional responsibilities for effective action. The post disaster recovery aims to strengthen the coping capacities of the people, and the government to recover from the impacts of a disaster, and reduce the risk of future disasters. Henceforth, the focus should be on sustainable development which incorporates the principle of "Build Back Better". This principle considers disaster as an opportunity to mainstream disaster risk reduction measures into developmental plans which can help build disaster resilience.

Thus, the disaster recovery primarily has the following three components: -

- Physical Recovery
- Social Recovery
- Economic Recovery

Physical Recovery includes reconstruction of the built environment, and restoring the critical infrastructure, cultural heritage buildings and private houses. Secondly, social recovery includes the psychological and social aspects which aim at achieving the well-being of the individual as well as the community. Thirdly, economic recovery includes restoring and making resilient the market services, productive activities, and livelihoods.

Furthermore, recovering from a disaster broadly focuses upon: -

- Shifting focus towards restoring livelihoods
- Strengthening national capacities
- Empowering communities
- Mobilizing conditions for future development

Sustainable Recovery

Preventing the disaster from recurring

Shifting focus towards restoring livelihoods

As soon as the disaster occurs, the focus is on saving lives. However, after the end of the relief and rescue phase, there should be a focus on restoring livelihoods. Livelihoods bring life back to normalcy and are essential to reactivate the social, economic, and sustainable development of the affected groups. Restoring livelihoods requires the active involvement of the government and private sector.

Fig. 5.5: Restoring Livelihoods in Post-earthquake Nepal

Source: World Bank, 2018

Strengthening national capacities

Building national capacity is an ongoing process and a part of the development of the nation. This process involves equipping officials, stakeholders, and the people to be better prepared during disasters and also to reduce the risk of disasters. It includes human resource development which incorporates individual training as well as organizational development. The National Institute of Disaster Management (NIDM) is the capacity building arm at the national level.

Empowering communities

The community is at the forefront responding to any disaster occurrence. Community empowerment involves creating awareness among the community about the importance of disaster and disaster risk management. This can be done through devising local methods and tools to be able to respond to disasters and clearly devolving responsibilities by developing strategies. This also involves mobilizing resources and practicing before the actual occurrence of disaster among others.

Mobilizing conditions for future development

A disaster not only brings damage but exposes the pre-existing vulnerabilities of society. These vulnerabilities can act as an opportunity for bringing about transformation. For this, it is required to conduct hazard, Risk and Vulnerability analysis of the region and learn from the lessons of the disaster. Therefore, understanding the root causes and factors is crucial to addressing vulnerabilities. This can contribute towards building a sustainable solution to disaster recovery which encompasses future development.

Preventing the disaster from recurring

A disaster is an extreme event that brings a shock to society. An effective recovery plan should focus on achieving the highest standards of management. This means developing such strategies which in the first place prevents the disaster from recurring. This can be done through practices such as following the building codes, including all the communities, and educating the community. This can enable in many situations that the hazard does not translate into a disaster.

5.7.1 Process of Disaster Recovery

After a disaster occurs, a Post-Disaster Needs Assessment (PDNA) should be conducted. PDNA consists of 'Damage and Loss Assessment (DaLA), a 'Human Recovery Needs Assessment' (HRNA) and a 'Recovery and Reconstruction Framework. These assessments are a guide to developing recovery and reconstruction strategies. Thus, the PDNA is a platform for organizations including the international community to help in rebuilding the lives and livelihoods of the people as this also incorporates Disaster Risk Reduction (DRR) measures.

As mentioned in NDMP (2019), the disaster recovery process consists of the following activities as under: -

- Damage and needs assessments (PDNA, DALA, HRNA)
- Developing a recovery framework including institutional arrangements and financing plans.
- Measures to ensure socially inclusive recovery.
- Focus on sustainable development and climate change adaptation.
- Demolition of damaged structures, debris clearance, removal and its environmentally safe disposal.
- Restoration and even upgrading utilities including communication networks
- Re-establishment of major transport linkages.

- Temporary housing and detailed building inspections.
- Redevelopment planning.
- Environmental assessments.
- Reconstruction.
- Integrating DRR into various development initiatives.
- Financial management.
- Economic impact analyses

5.7.2 Components of Disaster Recovery Framework

According to NDMP (2019), following are the Components of Recovery Framework as mentioned below: -

- Institutional arrangements
- Coordination
- Public-Private Partnerships (PPP)
- Information and Communication Technology (ICT)
- Decision Support System (DSS)
- Pool of Expertise
- Community Participation
- Monitoring and Evaluation (M&E)

NDMP

Institutional arrangements: Making arrangements at the institutional levels can ensure that all the affected communities are provided with the resources that they require.

Coordination: An effective coordination between the government, private sector, non-governmental organizations and international agencies, etc., is crucial in realizing the objectives of recovery.

Public-Private Partnership (PPP): Leveraging private partnership can help in prompt achievement of recovery goals as the private sector is driven by outcome-based goals.

Information and Communication Technology: Information and Communication Technology (ICT) is an effective tool in facilitating the dissemination of information which is very useful in the recovery program.

Decision Support System: Decision Support System (DSS) which is useful in the disaster framework includes databases, Management Information System (MIS) and deployment of spatial data management technologies.

Pool of Expertise: A pool of experts from disaster management areas, and professionals in different areas can integrate their knowledge to arrive at the solutions to the complex problems that the recovery scenario presents.

Community Participation: Involvement of communities through outreach programs, empowerment measures, and through ensuring gender equity can enable the communities to be disaster resilient in the face of a disaster.

Monitoring and Evaluation (M&E): This component is useful in delineating timelines and targets along with measurable outcomes. This can enable in achieving the targets along with making improvements along the recovery process. Additionally, this can also help in maintaining transparency and realizing the possibilities in case of disaster recovery.

For ensuring a successful recovery, it is essential to ensure that there is proper coordination among individuals, organizations and communities. Additionally, disaster recovery should be carried out considering the environment. Nature acts as a buffer against disasters. Thus, deploying nature-based solutions for disaster recovery can ensure development which considers the needs of the future, thereby enabling sustainable development. Hence, the recovery process should be sustainable, and due consideration should be given to the environment.

5.8 RECONSTRUCTION

Reconstruction involves constructing the infrastructure that has been damaged as a result of the disaster. This includes the reconstruction of public infrastructure, adequate Housing, restoration the heritage buildings, and building of adequate temporary shelters.

As per UNDRR, Reconstruction is defined as "The medium- and long-term rebuilding and sustainable restoration of resilient critical infrastructures, services, housing, facilities and livelihoods required for the full functioning of a community or a society affected by a disaster, aligning with the principles of sustainable development and "build back better", to avoid or reduce future disaster risk."

The living conditions determine to a large extent the standard of living of the individuals. During the reconstruction phase, it is essential that the government and other agencies devolves sufficient time and resources in order to carry out the reconstruction process.

5.8.1 Infrastructure Reconstruction

The aim of the Reconstruction of the infrastructure is to restore the functioning of the existing structures or upgrade the existing ones in order to meet the needs of the community. A holistic and comprehensive strategy is required to implement the reconstruction programme to achieve the goal of "Build Back Better". Few of such strategies are mentioned below.

- Creating a framework for sustainable reconstruction.
- Mainstreaming reconstruction as an integral part of pre-disaster planning.
- Recognizing the leading role of governments.
- Prioritizing the need for enhanced protection of critical infrastructure.
- Ensuring climate change adaptation and enhancing environmental system recovery.
- Recognizing disasters as developmental opportunities.
- Exploring a fresh approach to funding and financing reconstruction and recovery.

5.8.2 Approaches to Reconstruction and Recovery

Reconstruction programs are a complex set of activities involving interactions amongst key players such as government agencies, local authorities and communities. Therefore, it is essential to delineate approaches to reconstruction and recovery. This can enable effective reconstruction which can be useful for all the concerned stakeholders. These approaches are mentioned in NDMP-2019 and also in NPDM-2009. Some of its salient provisions are given below:

- The approach to the reconstruction process has to be comprehensive so as to convert adversity into opportunity. Incorporating disaster resilient features to 'build back better' will be the guiding principle. The appropriate choice of technology and project impact assessment needs to be carried out to establish that the projects contemplated do not create any side effects on the physical, socio-cultural or economic environment of the communities in the affected areas or in their neighborhood. Systems for providing psycho-social support and trauma counseling need to be developed for implementation during the reconstruction and recovery phase (Para 9.1.1 of the NPDM).

- Reconstruction plans and designing of houses need to be a participatory process involving the government, affected community, NGOs, and the corporate sector. After the planning process is over, while owner driven the construction is a preferred option, contribution of the NGOs and corporate sector will be encouraged. The reconstruction programme will be within the confines and qualitative specifications laid down by the Government (Para 9.2.1 of NPDM).
- Essential services, social infrastructure and intermediate shelters/camps will be established in the shortest possible time. For permanent reconstruction, ideally, the work including the construction of houses, must be completed within two to three years. Relevant Central Ministries/Departments and the State Governments should create dedicated project teams to speed up the reconstruction process (Para 9.3.1 of NPDM).
- Plans for reconstruction in highly disaster-prone areas need to be drawn out during the period of normalcy, which may include architectural and structural designs in consultation with the various stakeholders (Para 9.3.2 of NPDM).
- State governments should give the emphasis to restoration of the permanent livelihood of those affected by disasters and to pay special attention to the needs of women-headed households, artisans, farmers and people belonging to marginalized and vulnerable sections (Para 9.5.1 of NPDM).

5.8.3 Sustainability in Reconstruction

Reconstruction activities that are led by the goal of sustainability will be able to converge the needs of the present while preserving the biodiversity and natural resources for future generations. A sustainable reconstruction should incorporate the following:

- Institutional sustainability
- Technical sustainability
- Environmental sustainability
- Social sustainability
- Economic sustainability

Therefore, it is important to ensure that reconstruction plans should be accurate and aligned with the needs of the community, along with considering the protection of the environment. This can be done through collaboration with the local authorities so as to implement measures that are traditionally sustainable and can be accommodated with the local needs.

5.9 SUSTAINABLE DEVELOPMENT GOALS AND DISASTER RISK REDUCTION

The year 2015 became a landmark year for future global actions on DRR, climate change and sustainable development with the signing of the three important agreements. These three agreements were: -

- Sendai Framework for Disaster Risk Reduction (2015-2030)
- The Paris Agreement (COP-21)
- Sustainable Development Goals (SDG)

These three agreements commonly aim for adapting to climate change. It is also agreed that the widest possible cooperation is needed to adapt and mitigate the impacts of Climate Change. As per the Sendai Framework, "disasters, many of which are exacerbated by climate change and which are increasing in frequency and intensity, significantly impede progress towards sustainable development".

The interconnections between Sustainable Development Goals, Sendai Framework for Disaster Risk Reduction and Climate Change adaptation are shown in Fig. 5.6.

Thus, these three agreements have created new opportunities for mainstreaming Disaster Risk Reduction (DRR) within Development.

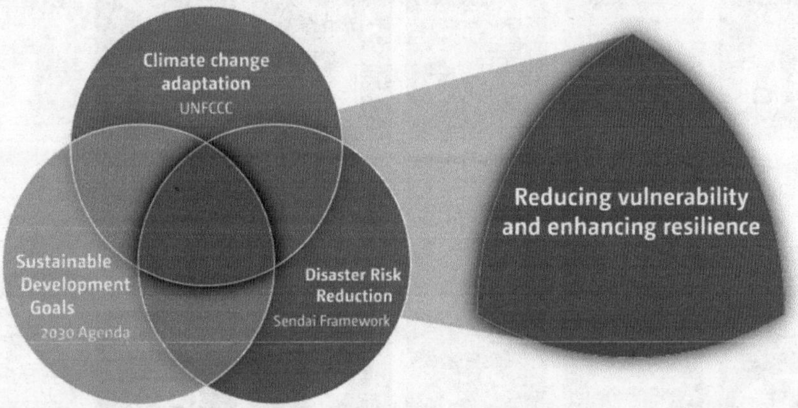

Fig. 5.6: Interconnections between Climate Change adaptation, Sendai Framework and Sustainable Development

Source: https://unfccc.int/sites/default/files/resource/techpaper_adaptation.pdf

The Agenda on Sustainable Development Goals aims to achieve its full implementation by 2030. The Sustainable Development Goals (SDGs), adopted by the UN General Assembly on 25 September 2015, consist of 17 Global Goals as shown in Fig. 5.7. These are a blueprint for achieving a sustainable future for all. Moreover, they address the global challenges which also focus on Disaster Risk Reduction including climate change, and environmental degradation, among others. These Sustainable Development Goals are: -

- Goal 1. No Poverty
- Goal 2. Zero Hunger
- Goal 3. Good Health and well-being
- Goal 4. Quality Education
- Goal 5. Gender Equality
- Goal 6. Clean Water and Sanitation
- Goal 7. Affordable and clean energy
- Goal 8. Decent work and economic growth
- Goal 9. Industry, Innovation and Infrastructure
- Goal 10. Reducing Inequality
- Goal 11. Sustainable cities and Communities
- Goal 12. Responsible Consumption and Production
- Goal 13. Climate Action

SDG

- Goal 14. Life Below water
- Goal 15. Life on Land
- Goal 16. Peace, Justice and strong institutions
- Goal 17. Partnerships for the Goal

Fig. 5.7: Sustainable Development Goals

Source: https://www.un.org/sustainabledevelopment/blog/2015/12/sustainable-development-goals-kick-off-with-start-of-new-year/

The concept of DRR and Sustainable Development are closely associated. A disaster event like a tsunami, an earthquake can erode development achieved over several years. Similarly, a stress incident such as sea level rise, salinity intrusion, and groundwater stocks can damage the socio-economic scenario of the region. Moreover, Climate change can aggravate the frequency and severity of extreme weather events.

SDG goals comprise climate action, environmental issues and development of resilient cities along with the developmental goals. 10 SDG goals and 25 targets are linked with disaster risk reduction establishing that DRR is a core component of the developmental strategy. These 10 goals, which focus on disaster risk management are mentioned below: -

- Goal 1. No Poverty
- Goal 2. Zero Hunger
- Goal 3. Good Health and well-being
- Goal 4. Quality Education
- Goal 6. Clean Water and Sanitation
- Goal 9. Industry, Innovation and Infrastructure
- Goal 11. Sustainable cities and Communities
- Goal 13. Climate Action

DRR

- Goal 14. Life Below water
- Goal 15. Life on Land

Achieving Sustainable Development Goals can significantly ensure a prosperous and safer world. Therefore, policies and activities aiming to achieve SDG's must integrate Disaster Risk Reduction into the developmental planning and environmental protection. Mainstreaming DRR can significantly reduce the risk posed by hazards and reduce vulnerabilities. Mainstreaming DRR is also mandated by the Disaster Management Act (2005).

UNIT SUMMARY

- Disasters are a combination of hazards and vulnerable conditions.
- Factors such as physical, economic, social and environmental enhances the vulnerability of the community towards a specific risk or hazard.
- There is therefore a close association between Disasters and Development. While on the one hand Development raises the standard of living of the people, on the other it creates vulnerabilities thereby causing disasters.
- Environment helps in regulating and mitigating the natural hazards. However, exposure of the community exacerbates the impacts of disasters.
- Degradation of the environment affects the sustainability of the ecosystem which can be a hurdle to achieve sustainable development.
- Environmental modifications, such as deforestation, land use changes and urbanization, can have a significant impact on vulnerability by exacerbating social and economic inequalities.
- Land use changes can also increase the risk of natural disasters.
- Urbanization impacts biodiversity, water and air quality, and causes climate change.
- Dams are built to regulate the flow of water, provide irrigation, electricity generation and several other needs. However, if dams are not properly maintained or if extreme meteorological events occur, they can lead to dam failure causing floods.
- Climate Change is thus increasing the frequency and risk of the occurrence of extreme events due to climate variability. These extreme events are manifesting in the form of Floods, Cyclones, Hailstorms, Cold waves, LLOFs, GLOFs, Lightning, Land erosion, submergence, landslides, Droughts, Heat waves, Forest fires, Health hazards, etc.
- Recovery is considered as the most complex function of the disaster management process. Recovering from disasters can be a challenging process. It takes years to recover from the damage and delivering improved resilience may take even longer.
- A sustainable recovery integrates Disaster Risk Reduction measures into its efforts.
- The aim of Reconstruction of the infrastructure is to restore the functioning of the existing structures or upgrade the existing ones in order to meet the needs of the community and achieve the goal of "Build Back Better".
- Sustainable Development Goals (SDG's) address the global challenges which focuses on Disaster Risk Reduction including climate change, environmental degradation, among others.
- Achieving Sustainable Development Goals can significantly ensure a prosperous and safer world.

EXERCISES

Multiple Choice Questions

Q.1 Physical factors which increase the vulnerability towards a disaster include

a. Unplanned land use, b. Lack of building standards

c. Poor housing design d. All of these

Q.2 Development can

a. Increase vulnerability b. Reduce vulnerability

c. Both (a) and (b) d. None of the above

Q.3 According to NDMP (2019), which of the following are **not** the Components of Recovery Framework: -

a. Institutional arrangements b. Decision Support System (DSS)

c. Redevelopment planning d. Monitoring and Evaluation (M&E)

Q.4 The linkage between disasters and development can be described as: -

a. Disasters can set back development.

b. Development can increase vulnerability.

c. Development can reduce vulnerability.

d. Disasters can provide development opportunities.

e. All the above

Q.5 Which of the following are a part of Sustainable Development Goals ?

i. To end poverty and hunger

ii. To Achieve better standards of healthcare and education, particularly with regard to water quality and better sanitation.

iii. To achieve gender equality

iv. To reach Sustainable economic growth along with promoting jobs and stronger economies Code:

a. I, II & III b. I, III & IV

c. I & III d. I, II, III & IV

Q.6 The UN General Assembly (UNGA) set up The United Nations Commission on Sustainable Development (CSD) in which of the following year: -

a. 1992 b. 1993

c. 1994 d. 1995

Q.7 Which one of the following is not a parameter of sustainable development?

a. Inter and Intra-generation equity b. Carrying capacity

c. Gender disparity and diversity d. None of the above

Q.8 How many Sustainable Development Goals are related to the Disaster Risk Reduction

a. 10 b. 11

c. 17 d. 20

Q.9 PDNA consists of

a. Damage and Loss Assessment (DaLA)

b. Human Recovery Needs Assessment (HRNA)

c. Recovery and reconstruction Framework
d. All the above

Q.10 A sustainable reconstruction should integrate which of the following:
a. Environmental sustainability
b. Institutional sustainability
c. Technical sustainability
d. All the above

Q.11 The disaster recovery primarily has which of the following components: -
a. Physical Recovery
b. Social Recovery
c. Economic Recovery
d. All the above

Q.12 The principle of "Build Back Better" can be applicable during which phase of disaster management?
a. Mitigation
b. Preparedness
c. Response
d. Reconstruction

Q.13 Disaster Management aims at:
a. Preparedness
b. Mitigation
c. Reconstruction
d. Rehabilitation
e. All of the above

Answers of Multiple-Choice Questions

Answers of Multiple-choice questions				
5.1 **d**	5.2 **c**	5.3 **c**	5.4 **e**	5.5 **d**
5.6 **a**	5.7 **d**	5.8 **a**	5. 9 **d**	5.10 **d**
5.11 **d**	5.12 **d**	5.13 **e**		

Short and Long Answer Type Questions

Category I

1. What are the factors which affect the vulnerability of a community?
2. Disasters and Development are interlinked. Comment.
3. Disasters and Environment are interlinked. Explain.
4. Elucidate the benefits of Sustainable Recovery
5. What are the impacts of dams on Flood Risk Management?
6. What is RIS?
7. Why is there a need for Sustainable Reconstruction?
8. What is the aim of Reconstruction of Infrastructure?
9. What are the activities as per NDMP (2019), in a disaster recovery process?
10. 10.What do you mean by Post Disaster Needs Assessment (PDNA).

Category II

1. What are the impacts of Disasters on Development and Environment? In what ways are they related? Explain in detail.
2. Development can be a boon or a bane for Disaster Risks. Elaborate.

3. Environmental modifications, such as deforestation, land use changes and urbanization, can have a significant impact on vulnerability. Elucidate.
4. What do you mean by SDG's? Are the SDG's same for all the countries? How can you as an individual contribute to the SDG's.?
5. What steps can be taken to mainstream Disaster Risk Reduction into Development Planning. What are the benefits of undertaking such measures?
6. Recovery is considered as the most complex function of the disaster management process. Explain how recovering from disasters is a challenging process and what efforts can be made to achieve sustainable recovery.
7. 7. NDMP-2019 and NPDM-2009 have mentioned some of the approaches to Disaster recovery and reconstruction. What are its salient provisions?

REFERENCES AND SUGGESTED READINGS

1. ADPC. (2014). Mainstreaming DRR & CCA into Developmental Process at local level. https://www.adpc.net/igo/category/ID791/doc/2015-r74Ypd-ADPC-publication_MainstreamingHandbookSindhWEB.pdf
2. Chandol, T., Gupta, A. K., Amin, F., Bindal, M. K., (2021). Training Manual on Climate Change and Extreme Events Risk Reduction, National Institute of Disaster Management, Delhi, India.
3. Guleria S. (2022): Training Module on Preparation of State Disaster Management Plans (SDMP), NIDM, New Delhi. https://nidm.gov.in/PDF/Modules/NIDMSDMP_22.pdf
4. DEWGA. (2008). Linking Disaster Risk Reduction, Environment Management and Development Practices and Practitioners in Asia Pacific Region: A review of opportunties for integration. Disasters Environment Working Group for Asia.
5. Gupta, A.K., Jafar, E., Bhardwaj, S., Tyagi, N., Mahajan, V., Sethia, R., Parveen, U. and Bindal, M.K. (2022). Climate Proofing Disaster Relief and Recovery. National Institute of Disaster Management, Delhi, India.
6. IPCC. (2012). Summary for Policymakers. In: Managing the Risks of Extreme Events and Disasters to Advance Climate Change Adaptation. Cambridge, UK, and New York, NY, USA: A Special Report of Working Groups I and II of the Intergovernmental Panel on Climate Change. Cambridge University Press.
7. NDMA (2019): National Disaster Management Plan, Ministry of Home affairs, GOI.
8. UNEP(2004):Environment and Disaster Risk, prepared on behalf of the UN ISDR Environment and Disaster Working Group.
9. UNDP (2004) : A report Reducing Disaster Risk:A challenges for Development, United Nations Development Programme,New York, NY.
10. UNESCAP. (n.d.). Mainstreaming DRR into National Development Planning and Financing in and Financing in Asia-Pacific https://www.unescap.org/sites/default/d8files/knowledge-products/Mainstreaming%20DRR%20in%20Development%20Planning%20and%20Finance%20by%20P.G%20Dhar%20Chakrabarti.pdf
11. UNISDR (2016) Report of the open-ended intergovernmental expert working group on indicators and terminology relating to disaster risk reduction.
12. https://archive.internationalrivers.org/earthquakes-triggered-by-dams

CO AND PO ATTAINMENT TABLE

Course outcomes (COs) for this course can be mapped with the programme outcomes (POs) after the completion of the course and a correlation can be made for the attainment of POs to analyze the gap. After proper analysis of the gap in the attainment of POs necessary measures can be taken to overcome the gaps.

Table for CO and PO attainment

Course Outcomes	Attainment of Programme Outcomes *(1- Weak Correlation; 2- Medium correlation; 3- Strong Correlation)*											
	PO-1	PO-2	PO-3	PO-4	PO-5	PO-6	PO-7	PO-8	PO-9	PO-10	PO-11	PO-12
CO-1												
CO-2												
CO-3												
CO-4												
CO-5												
CO-6												

Index

F

G

H

I

L

M

U

V

W